# Bloodborne

**TITAN®**
COMICS

# Bloodborne

## TITAN COMICS

EDITOR: JAKE DEVINE
ART DIRECTOR: OZ BROWNE

MANAGING EDITOR: Martin Eden
TITAN COMICS EDITORIAL: Jonathan Stevenson, Tolly Maggs
SENIOR PRODUCTION CONTROLLER: Jackie Flook
PRODUCTION ASSISTANT: Rhiannon Roy
PRODUCTION CONTROLLER: Peter James
ART DIRECTOR: Oz Browne
SALES & CIRCULATION MANAGER: Steve Tothill
SENIOR PUBLICIST: Will O'Mullane
PUBLICIST: Imogen Harris
COMMERCIAL MANAGER: Michelle Fairlamb
HEAD OF RIGHTS: Jenny Boyce
PUBLISHING DIRECTOR: Darryl Tothill
OPERATIONS DIRECTOR: Leigh Baulch
EXECUTIVE DIRECTOR: Vivan Cheung
PUBLISHER: Nick Landau

**WWW.TITAN-COMICS.COM**

BLOODBORNE: A SONG OF CROWS
9781787730144

Published by Titan Comics © 2019 All rights reserved.
Titan Comics is a registered trademark of Titan Publishing Group Ltd.
144 Southwark Street, London, SE1 0UP

*Bloodborne* © 2019 Sony Interactive Entertainment Inc.

A CIP catalogue record for this title is available from the British Library

10 9 8 7 6 5 4 3 2 1

Follow us on
Twitter @comicstitan

Become a fan on
Facebook.com/comicstitan

First Published August 2019
Printed in China

For rights information contact jenny.boyce@titanemail.com

# oodborne

## A SONG OF CROWS

**WRITTEN BY**
### ALEŠ KOT

**ARTWORK BY**
### PIOTR KOWALSKI

**COLORS BY**
### BRAD SIMPSON

**LETTERS BY**
### ADITYA BIDIKAR

ORIGINAL GAME
PUBLISHED BY
**SONY INTERACTIVE
ENTERTAINMENT**
DEVELOPED BY:
**FROMSOFTWARE, INC.**

Set in the world of Bloodborne

The city of Yharnam: an ancient, gothic metropolis
and home to the Healing Church.

Recent days have seen the city fall foul to a nightmarish
plague known as the Ashen Blood disease, the source of
which remains a mystery.

In a world of gods and monsters, sanity is merely
subjective, and fear and blood are sanctified.

Hunters now stalk the streets in search of beasts as the
moon hangs ominously low in Yharnam's sky.

But as uncertainty fills the air, and the thirst for blood
becomes insatiable, the hunters become the hunted…

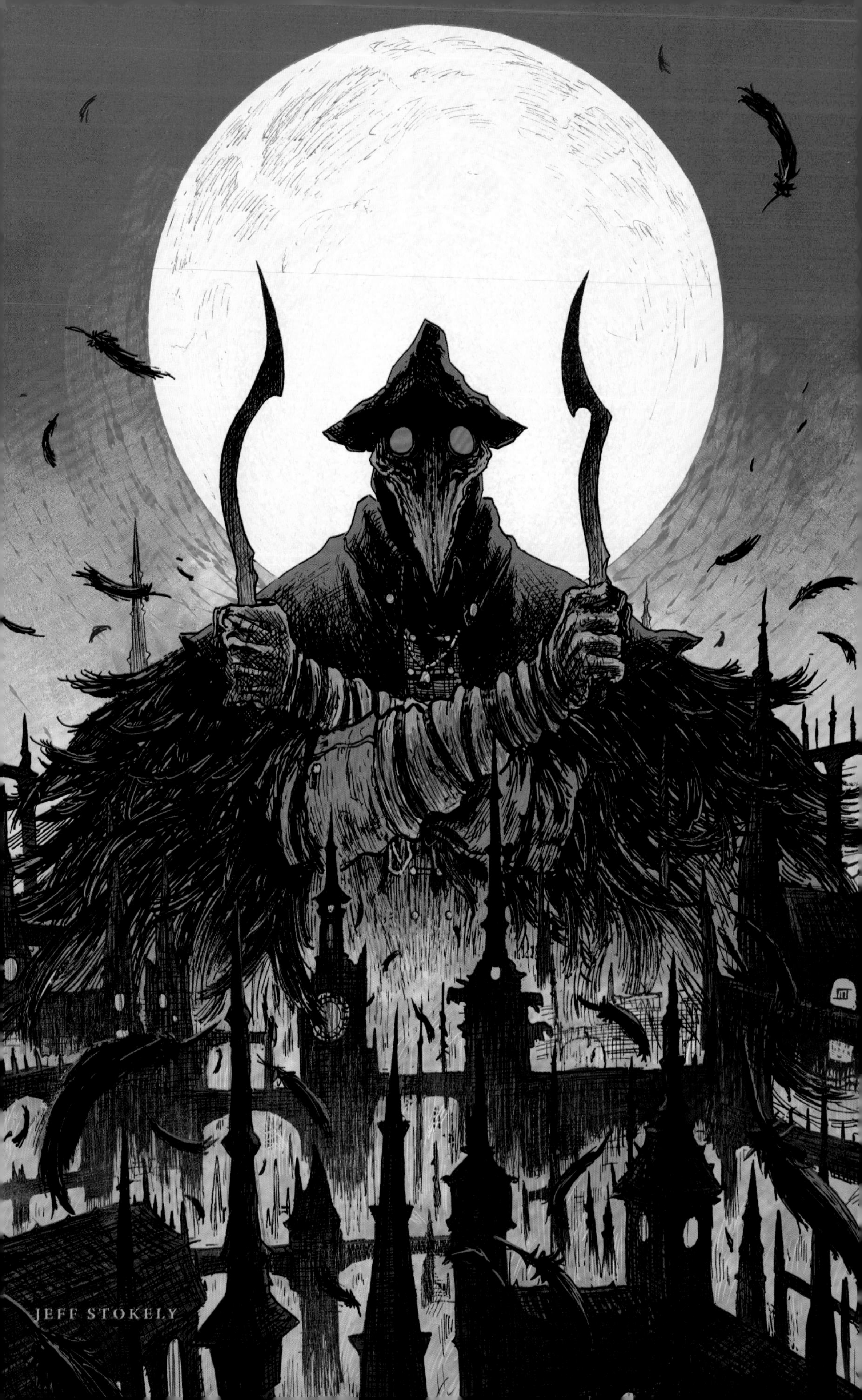
JEFF STOKELY

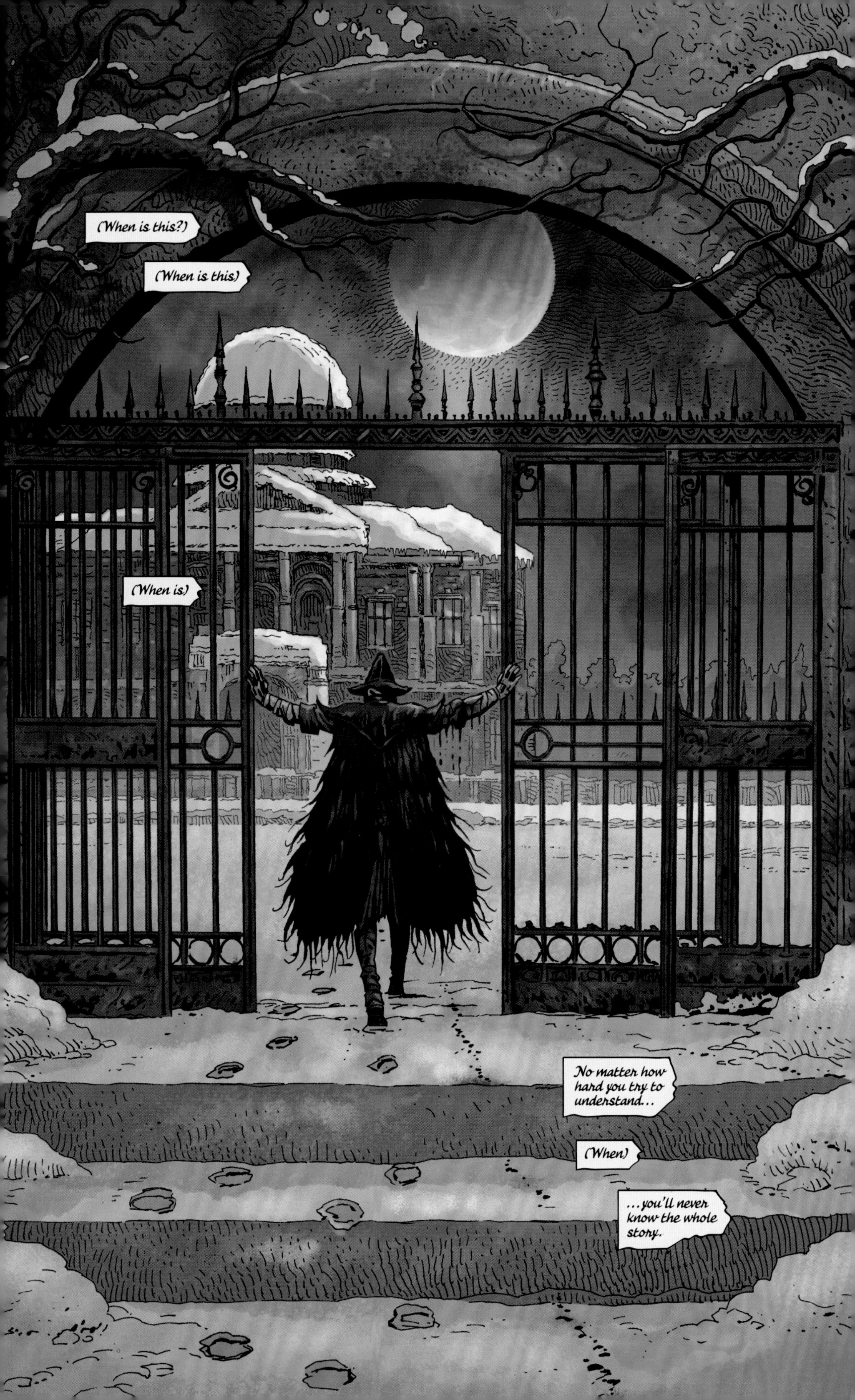
(When is this?)
(When is this)
(When is)
No matter how hard you try to understand...
(When)
...you'll never know the whole story.

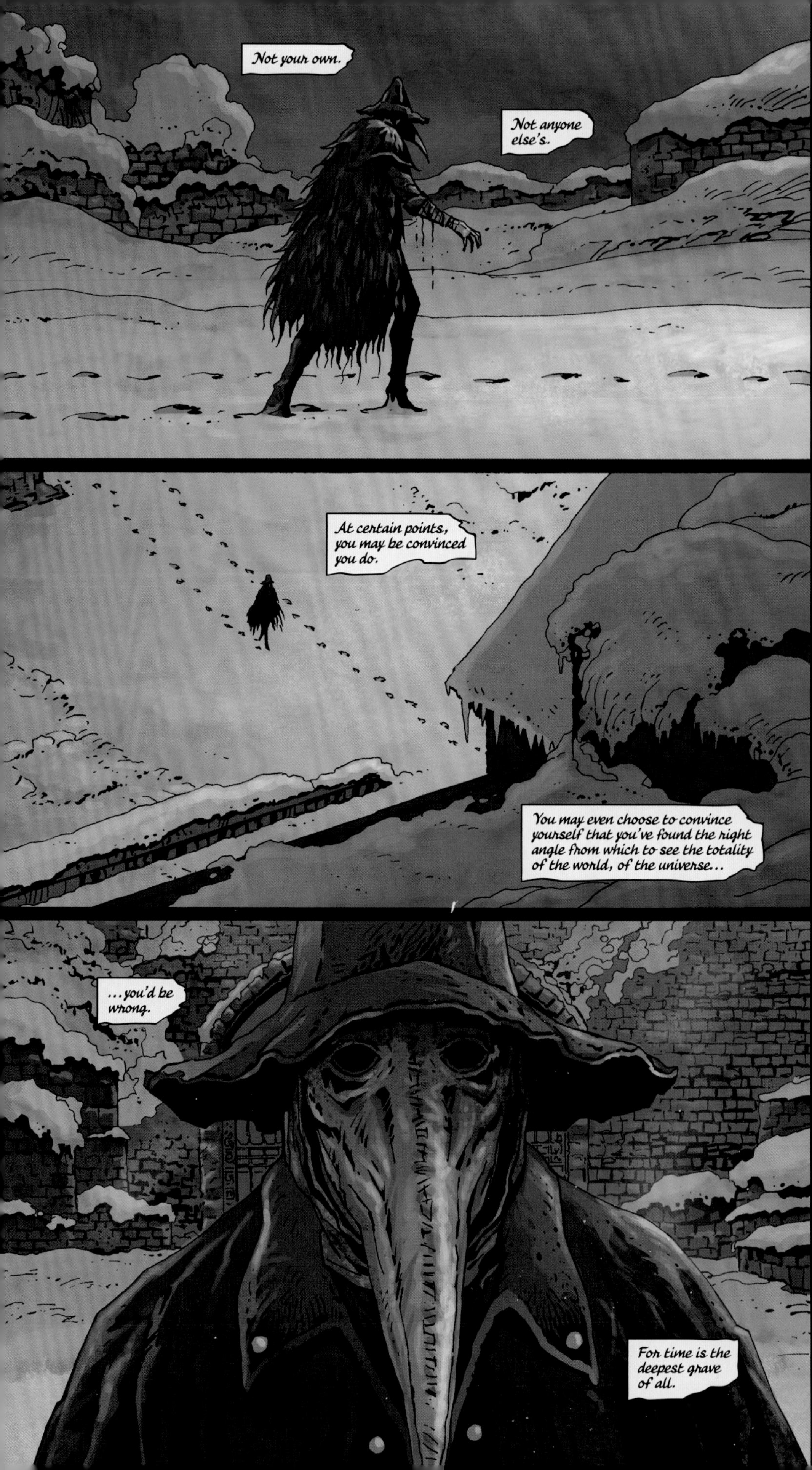
Not your own.
Not anyone else's.
At certain points, you may be convinced you do.
You may even choose to convince yourself that you've found the right angle from which to see the totality of the world, of the universe...
...you'd be wrong.
For time is the deepest grave of all.

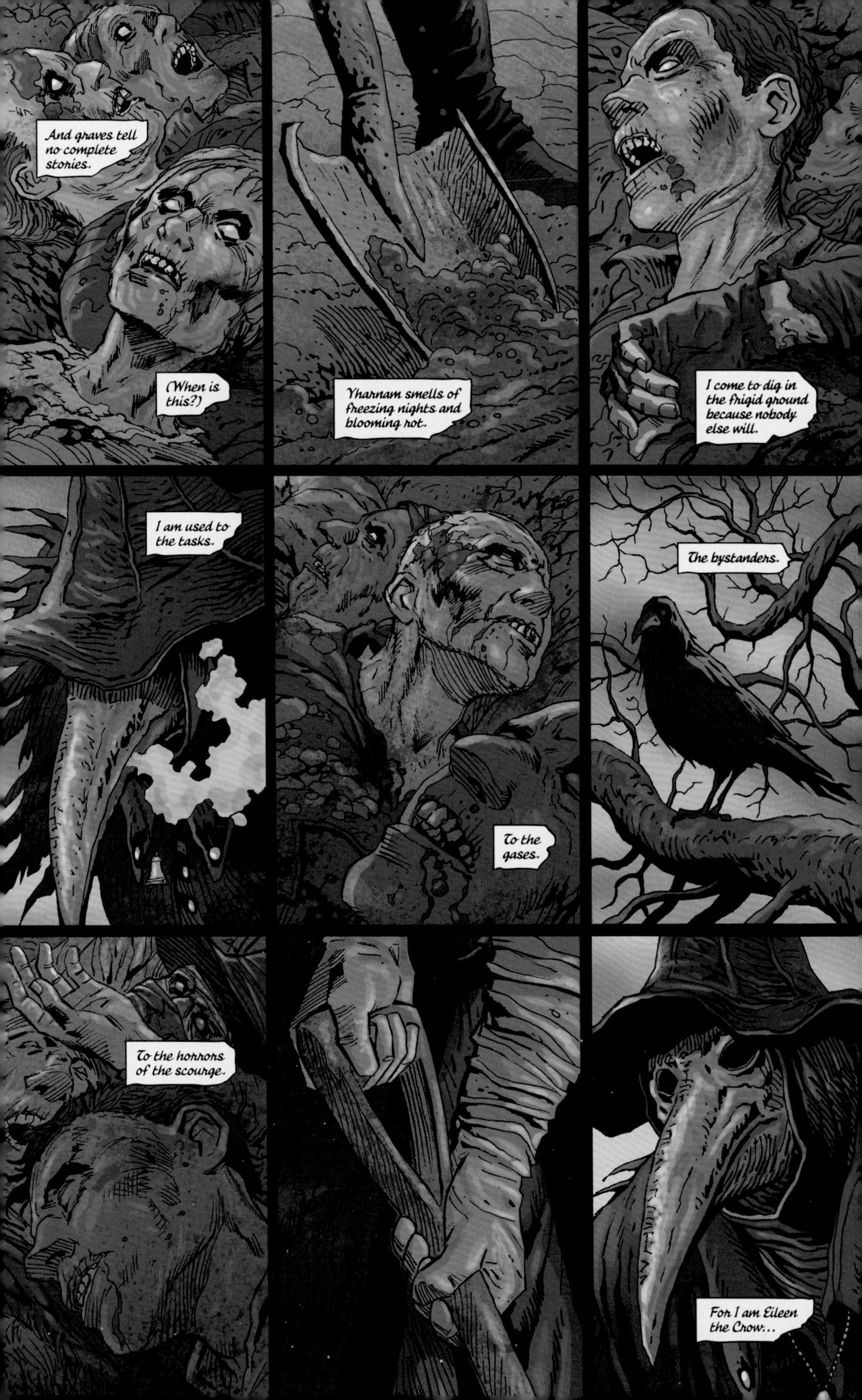
And graves tell no complete stories.
(When is this?)
Yharnam smells of freezing nights and blooming rot.
I come to dig in the frigid ground because nobody else will.
I am used to the tasks.
To the gases.
The bystanders.
To the horrors of the scourge.
For I am Eileen the Crow...

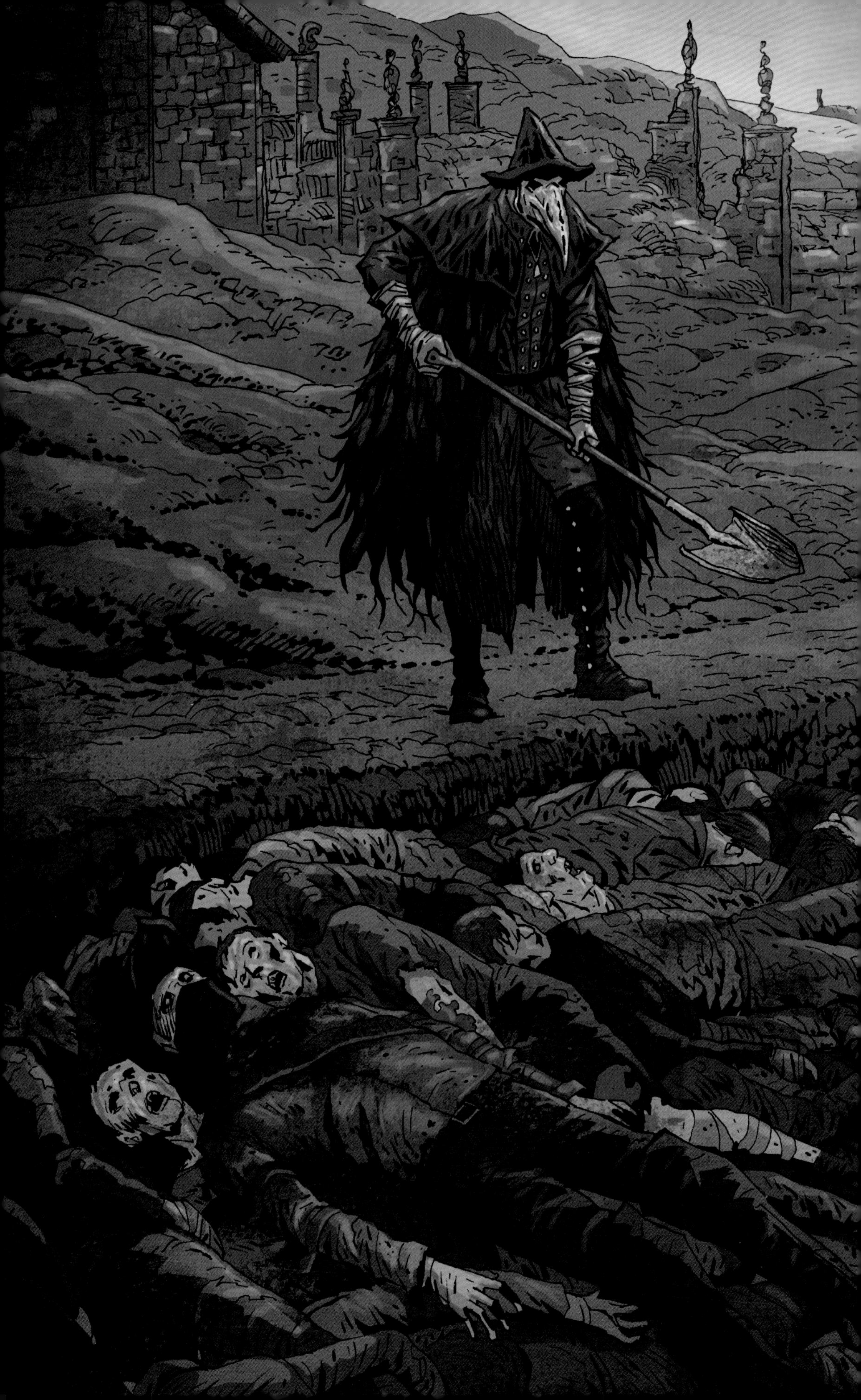

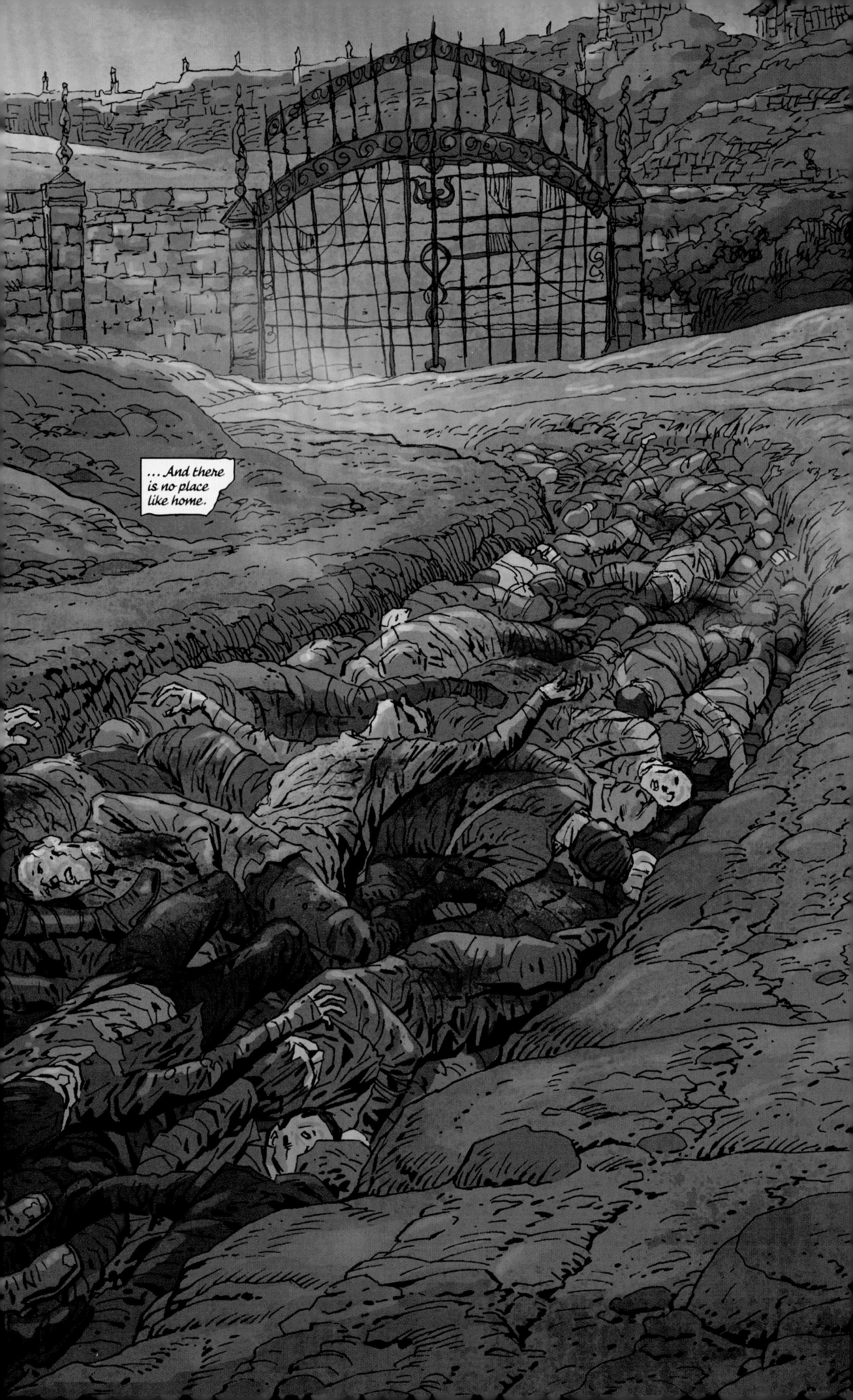
...And there is no place like home.

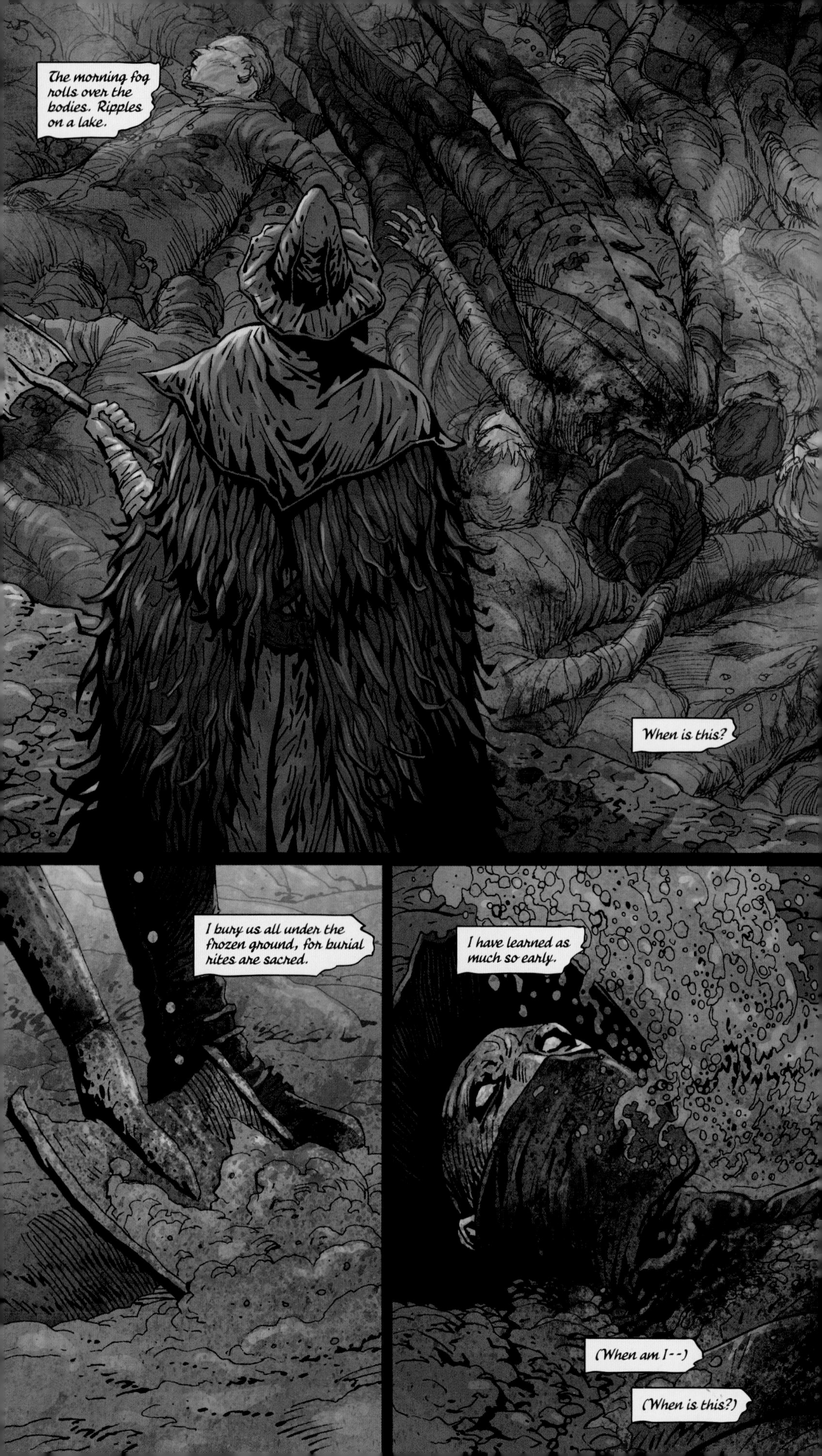
The morning fog rolls over the bodies. Ripples on a lake.
When is this?
I bury us all under the frozen ground, for burial rites are sacred.
I have learned as much so early.
(When am I--)
(When is this?)

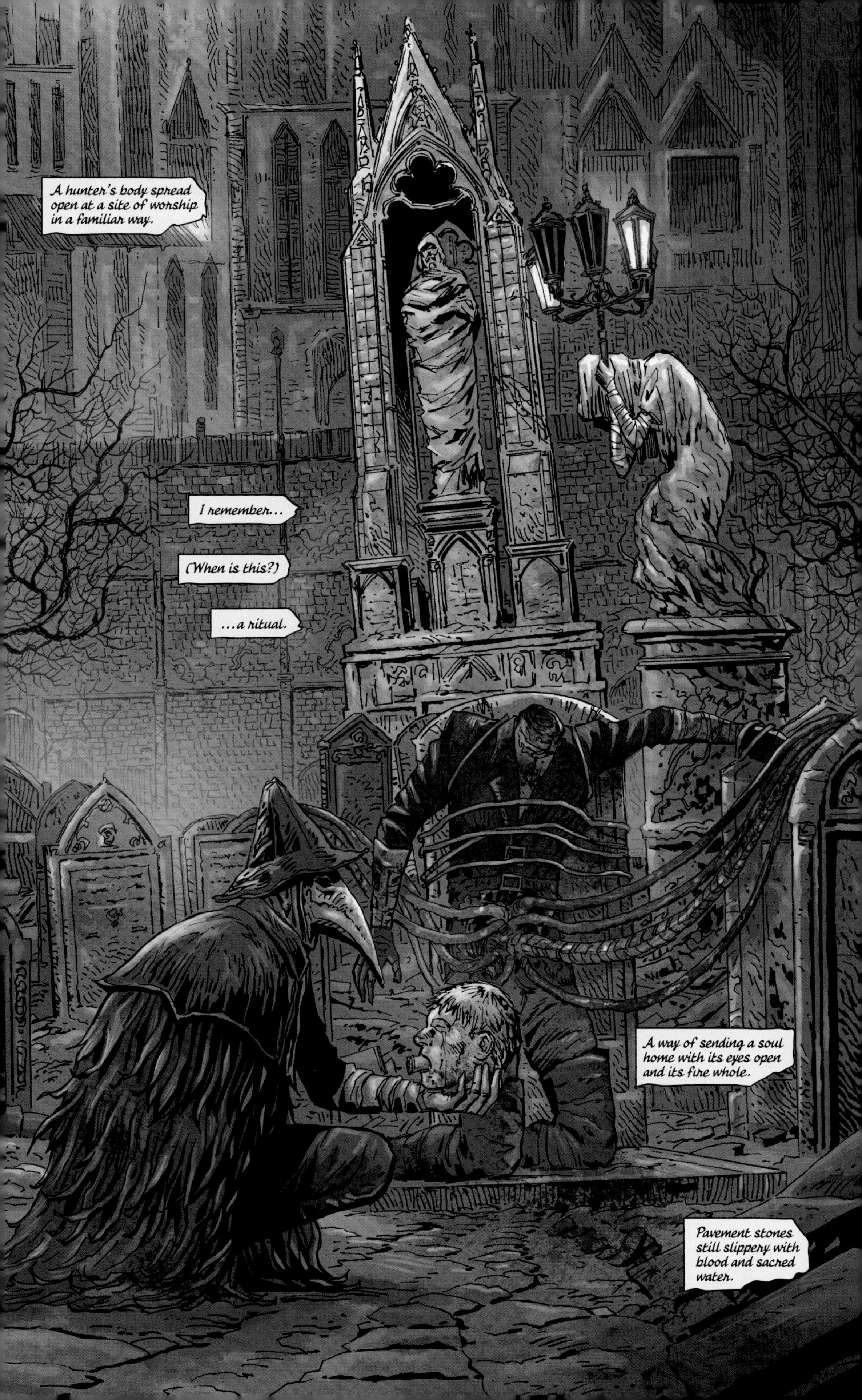
A hunter's body spread open at a site of worship in a familiar way.
I remember...
(When is this?)
...a ritual.
A way of sending a soul home with its eyes open and its fire whole.
Pavement stones still slippery with blood and sacred water.

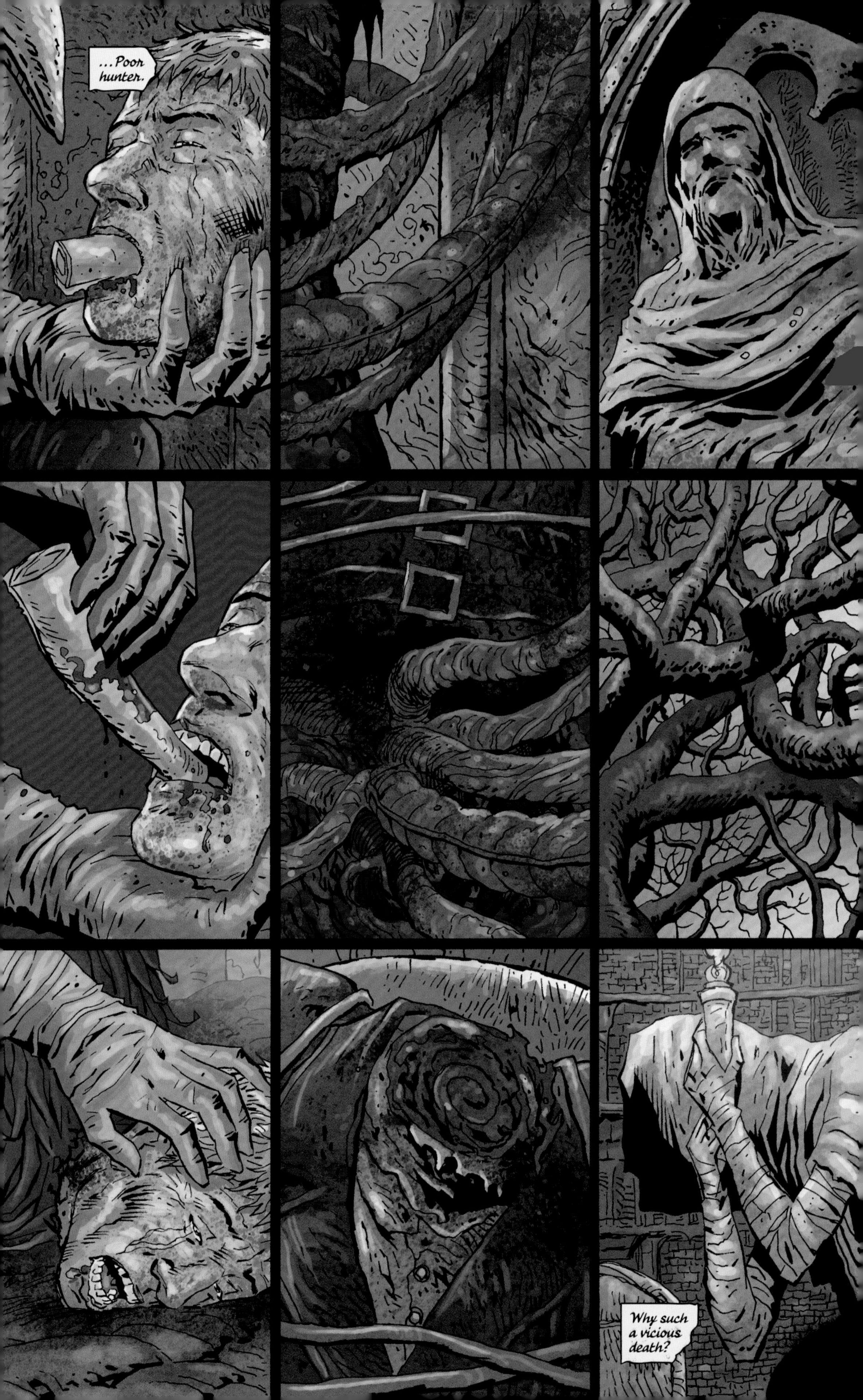
...Poor hunter.
Why such a vicious death?

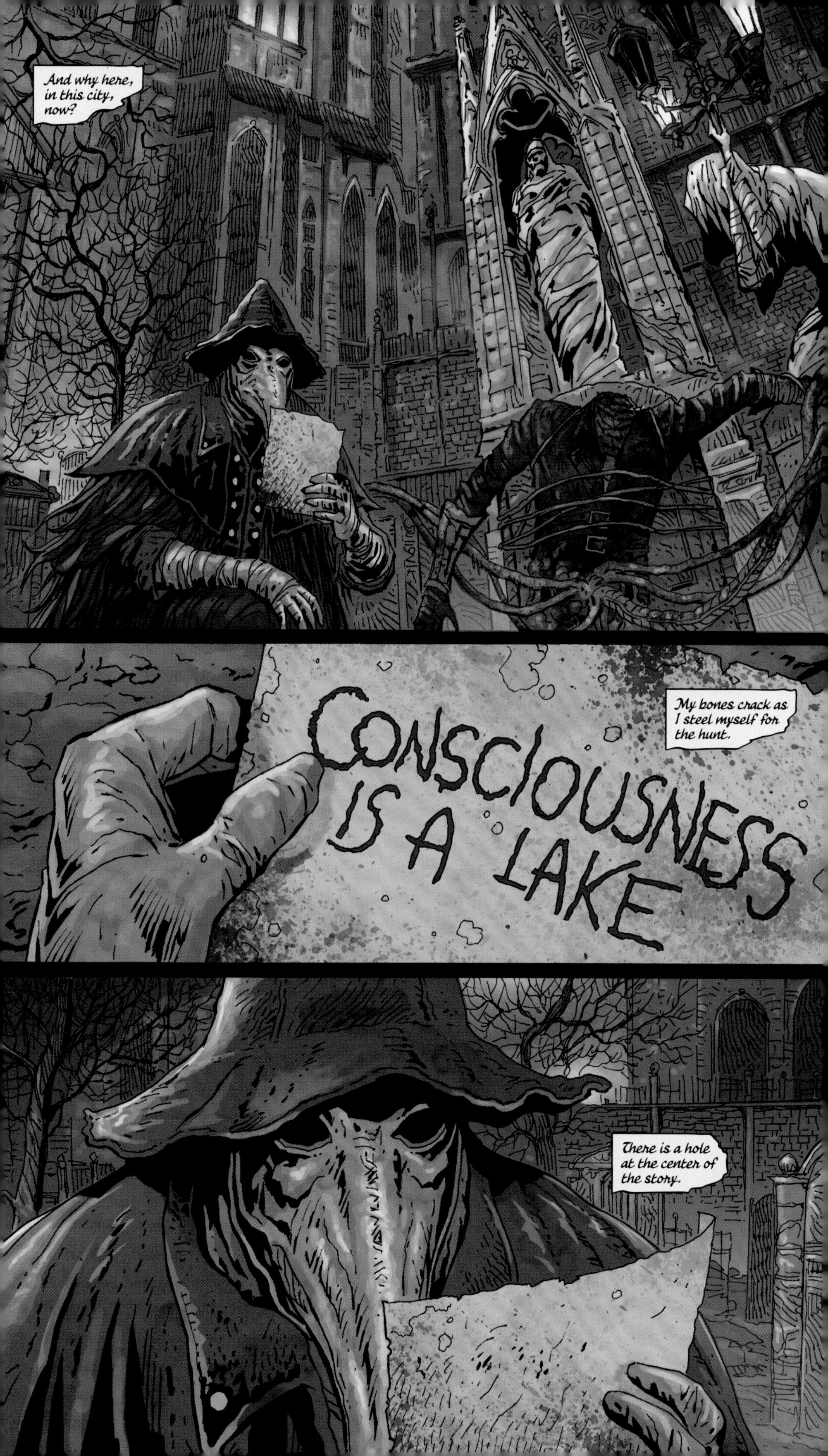
And why here, in this city, now?
CONSCIOUSNESS IS A LAKE
My bones crack as I steel myself for the hunt.
There is a hole at the center of the story.

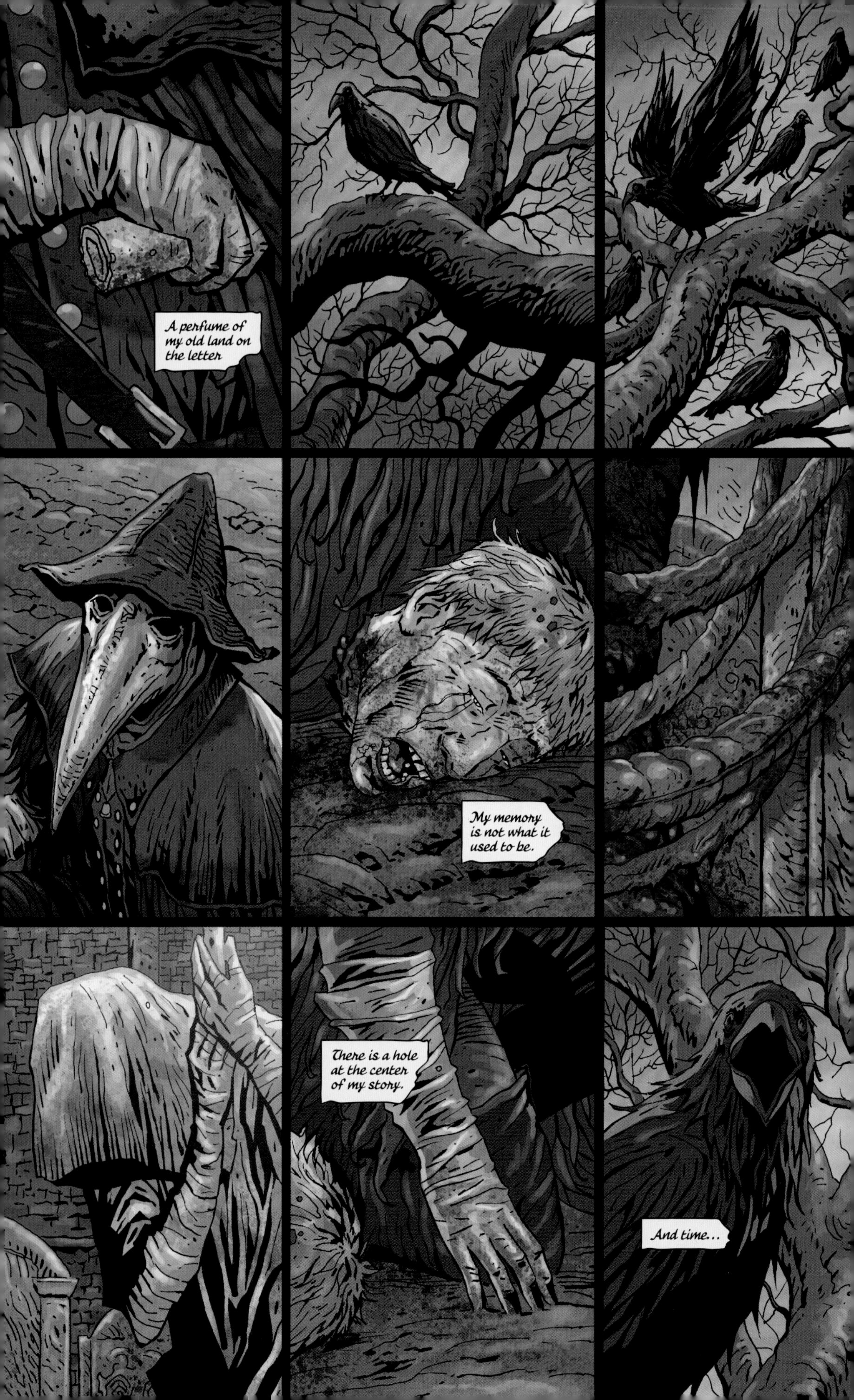
A perfume of my old land on the letter
My memory is not what it used to be.
There is a hole at the center of my story.
And time...

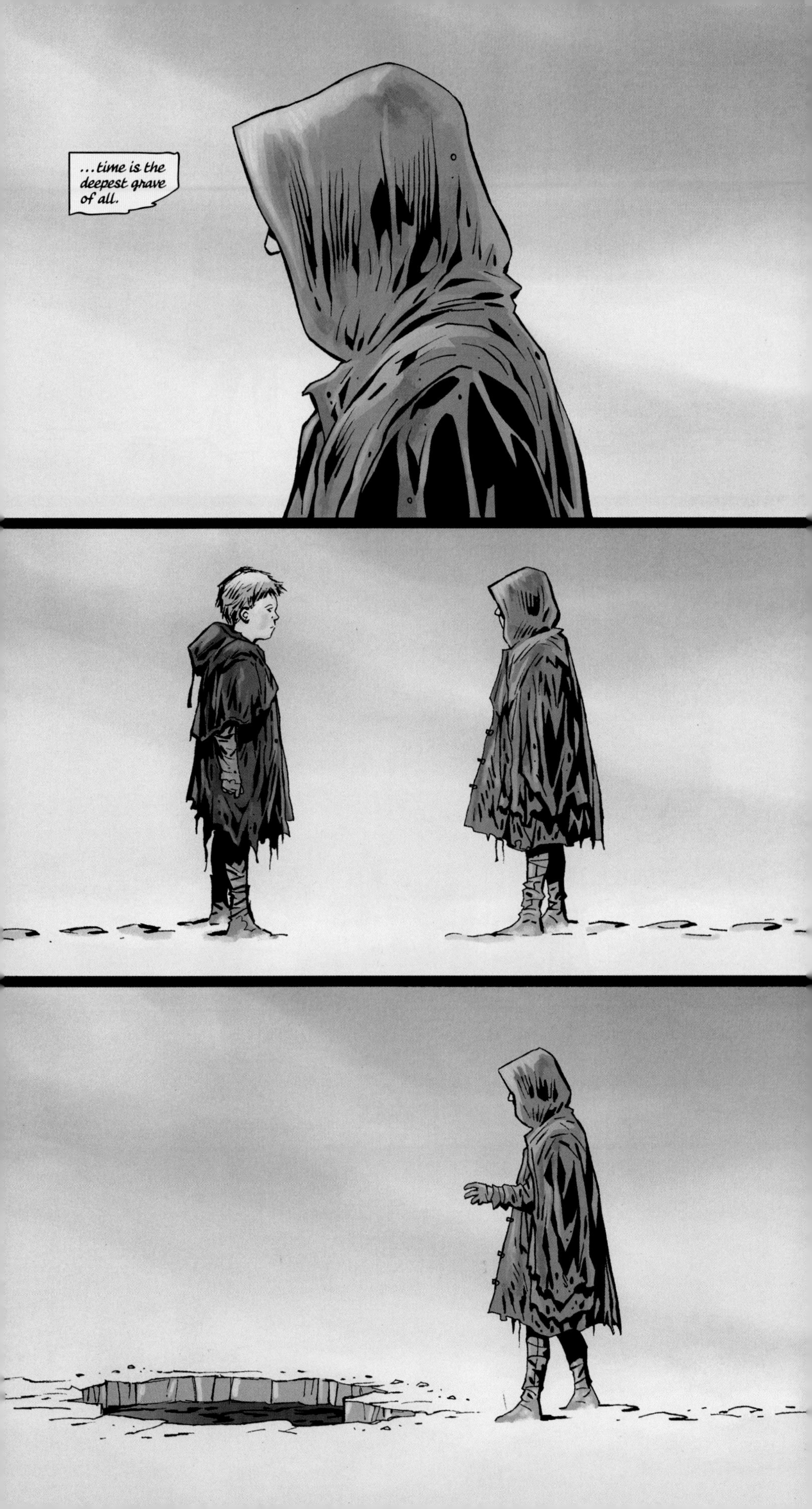
...time is the deepest grave of all.

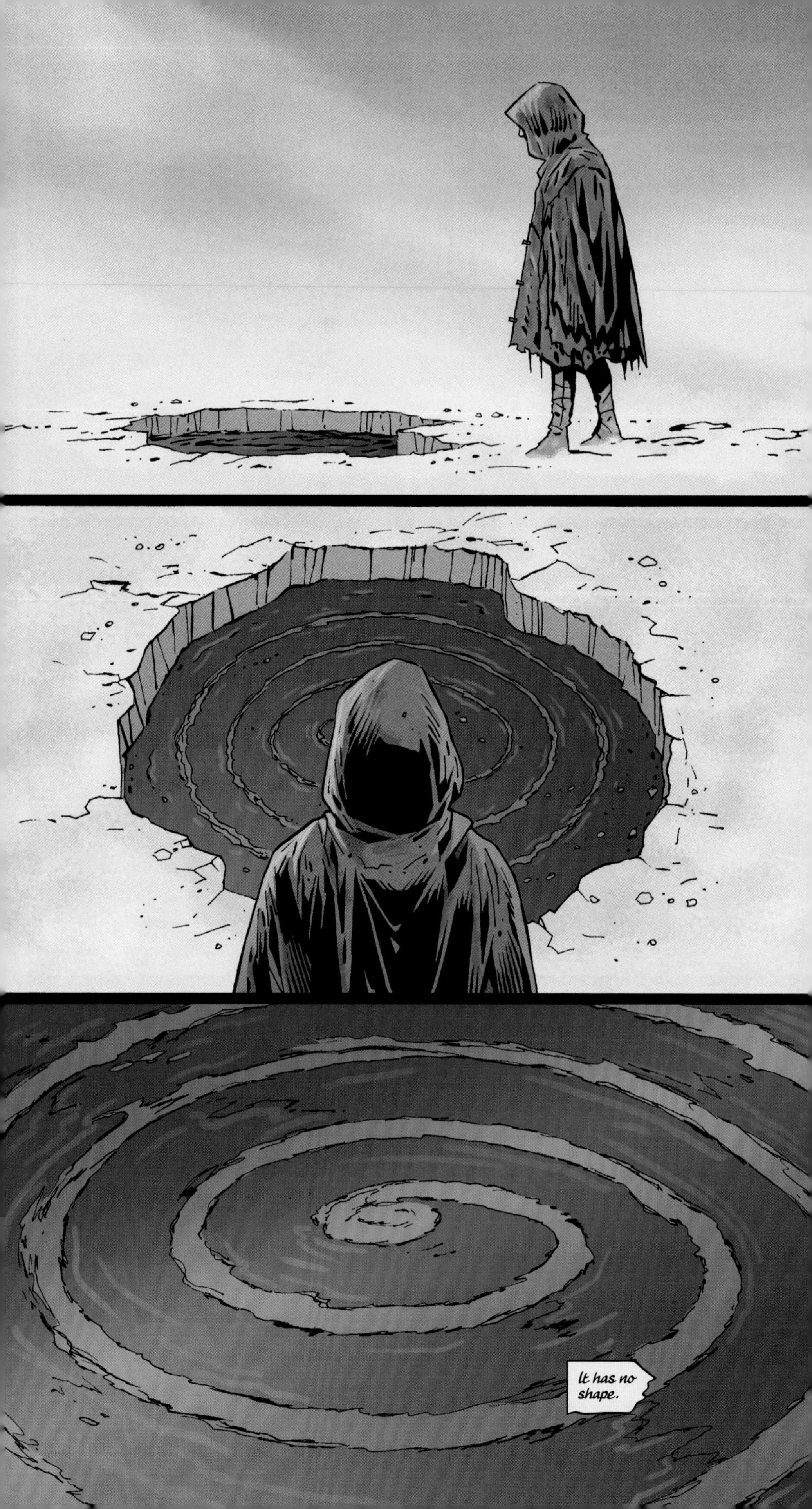
It has no shape.

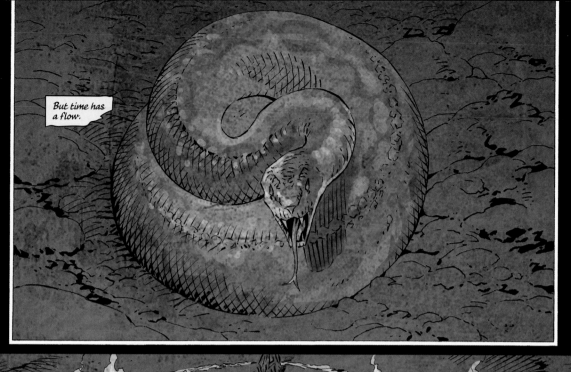

But time has a flow.

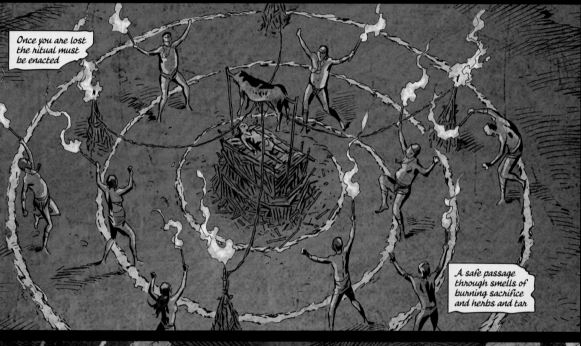

Once you are lost the ritual must be enacted

A safe passage through smells of burning sacrifice and herbs and tar

We dance with the guts to see clearly what we do will do

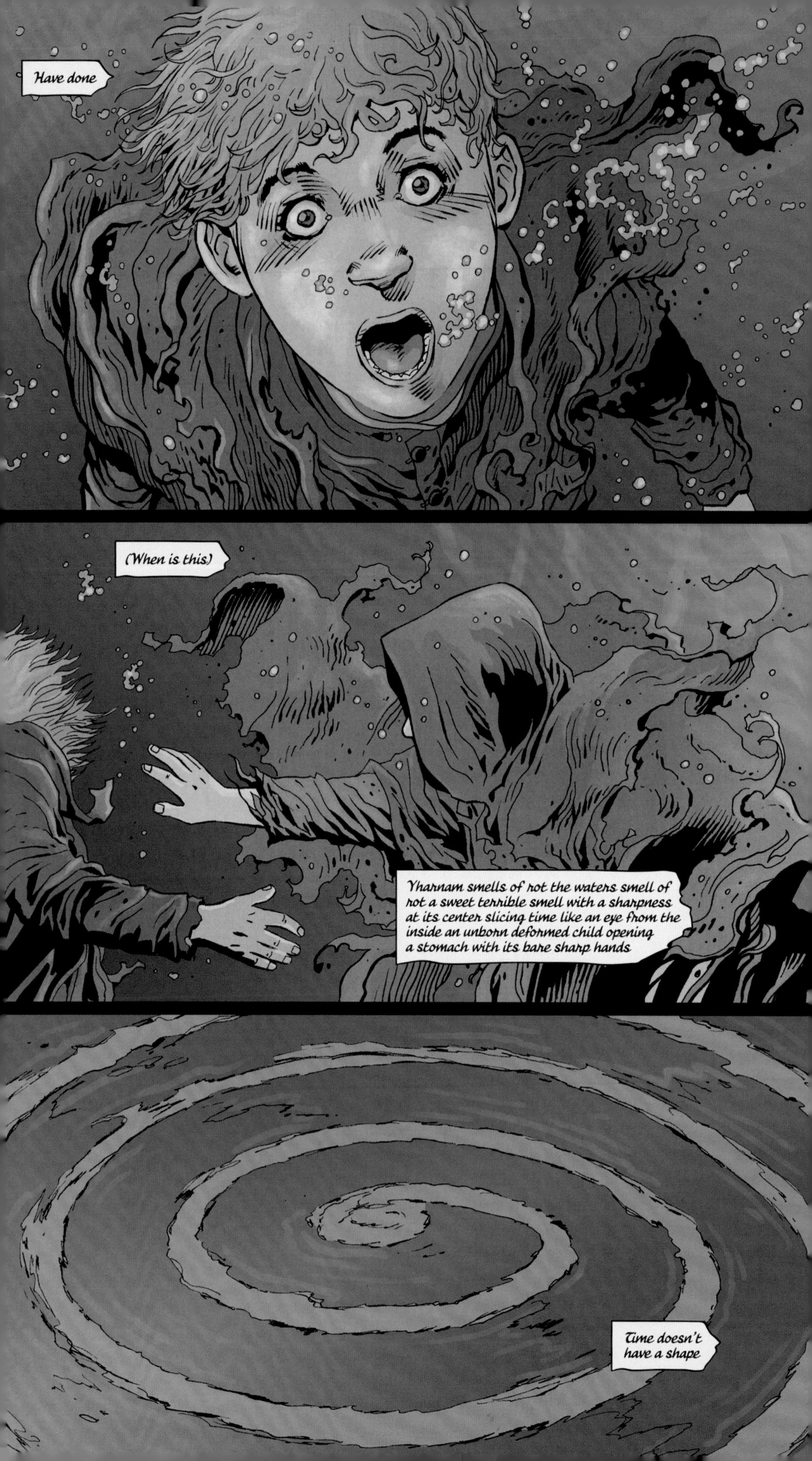
Have done
(When is this)
Yharnam smells of rot the waters smell of rot a sweet terrible smell with a sharpness at its center slicing time like an eye from the inside an unborn deformed child opening a stomach with its bare sharp hands
Time doesn't have a shape

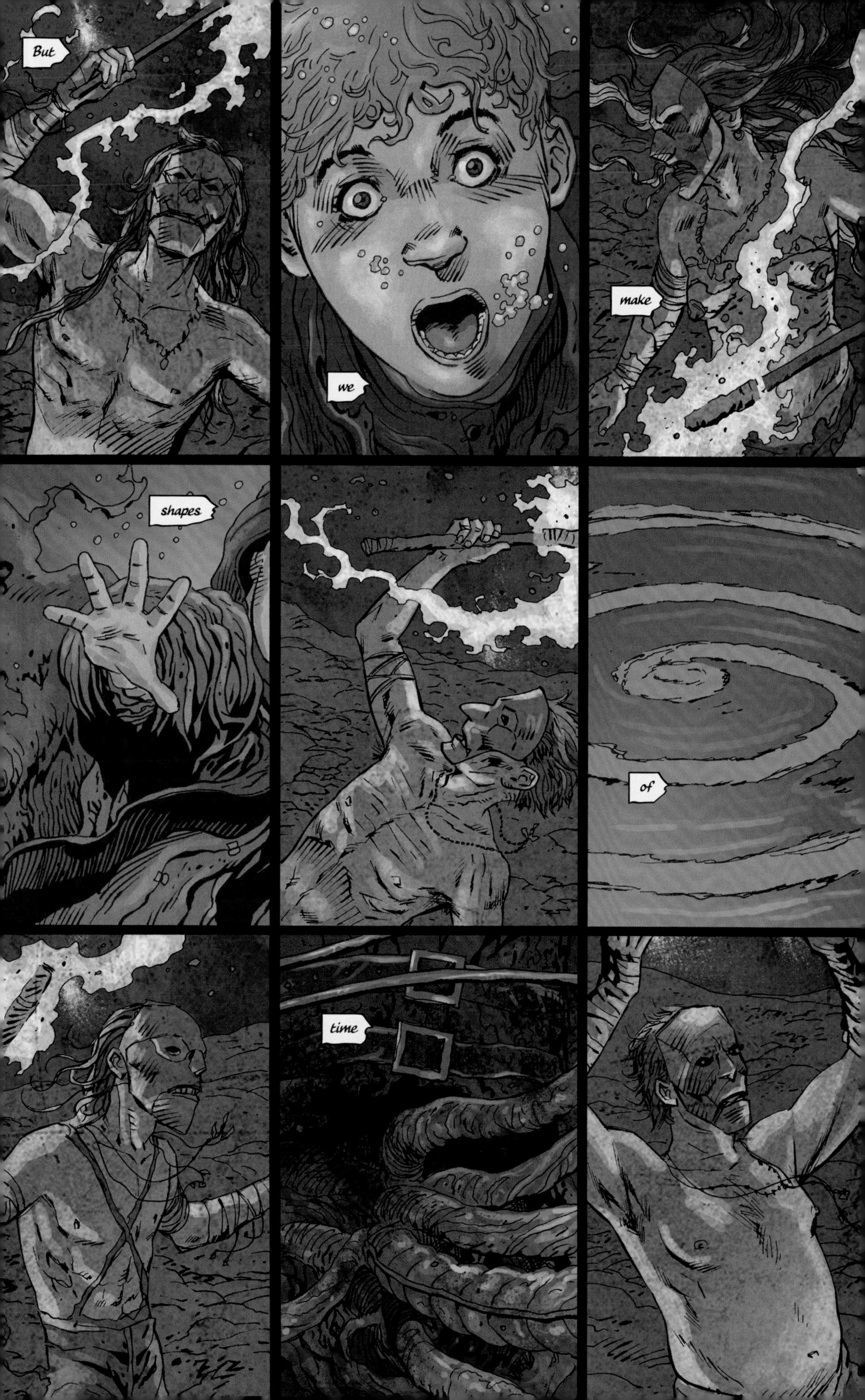
But
we
make
shapes
of
time

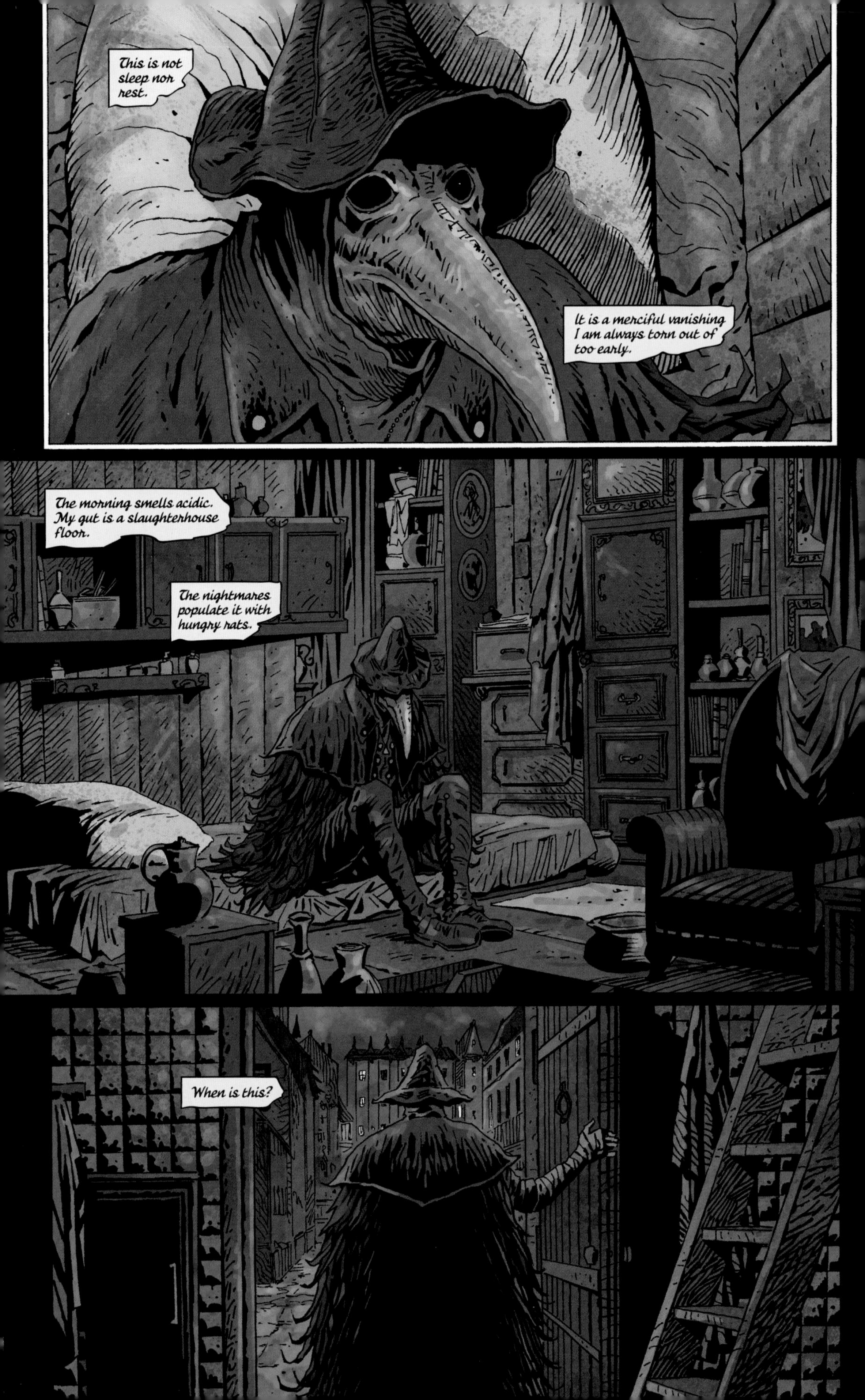
This is not sleep nor rest.
It is a merciful vanishing I am always torn out of too early.
The morning smells acidic. My gut is a slaughterhouse floor.
The nightmares populate it with hungry rats.
When is this?

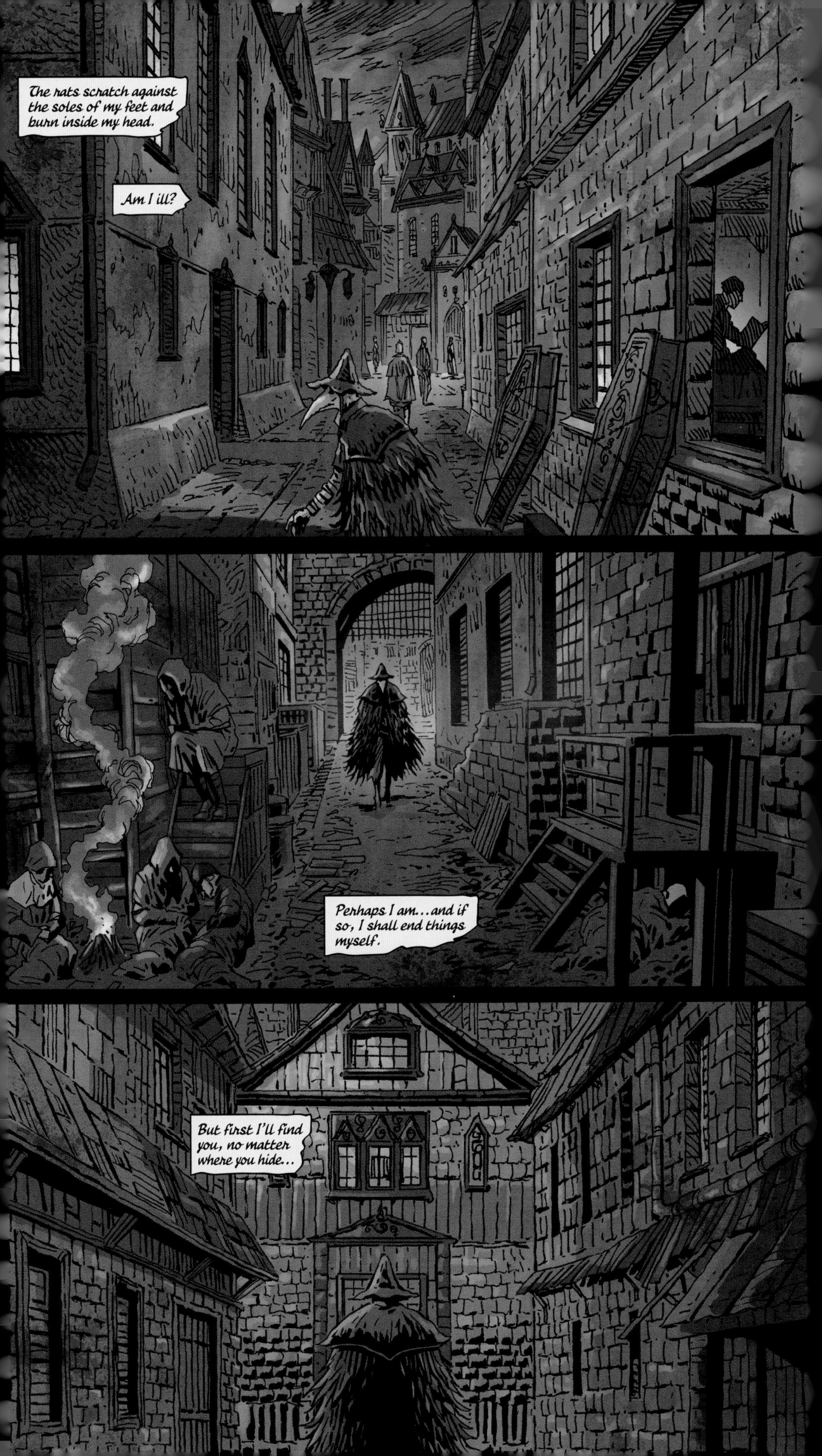
The rats scratch against the soles of my feet and burn inside my head.
Am I ill?
Perhaps I am...and if so, I shall end things myself.
But first I'll find you, no matter where you hide...

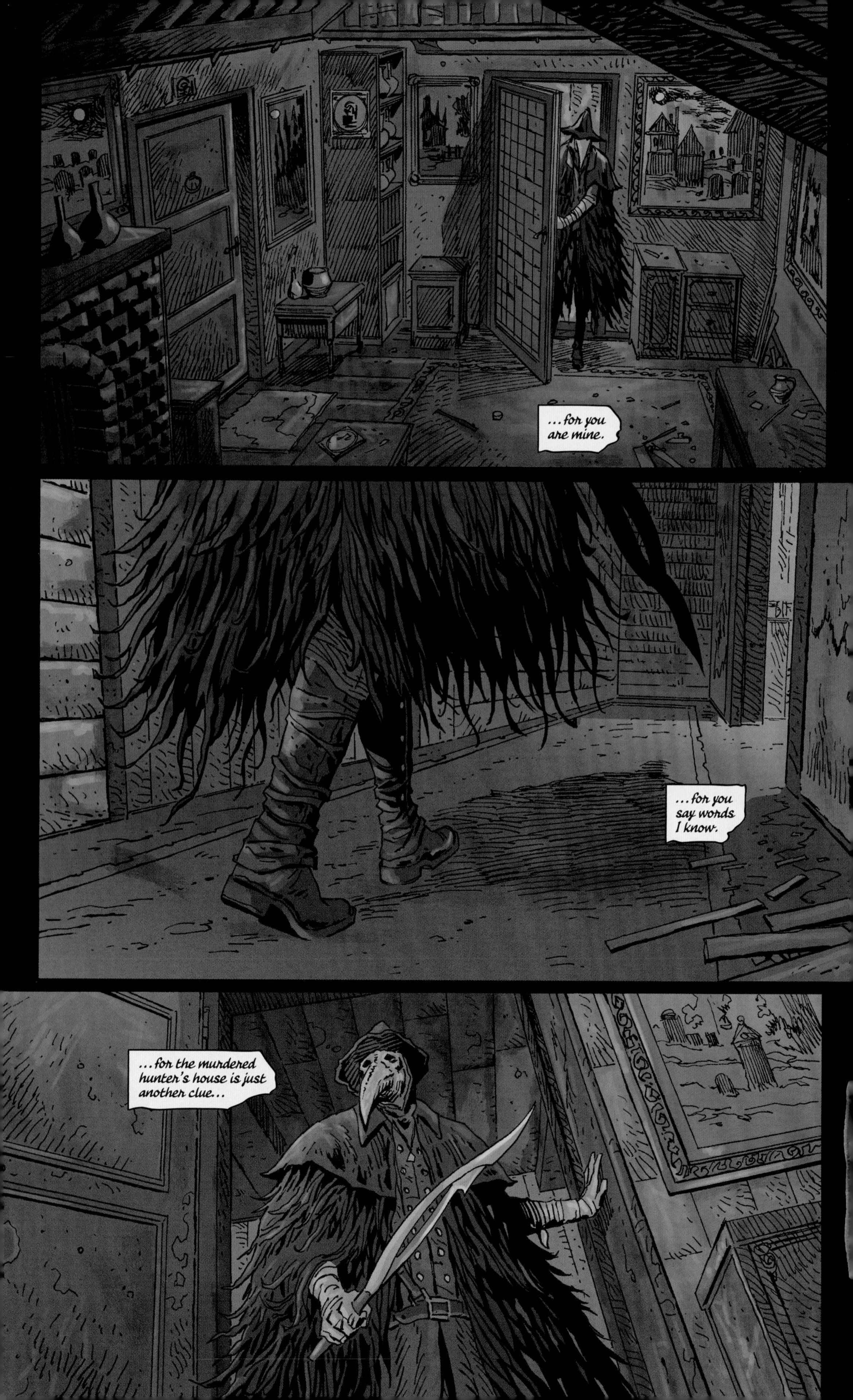
...for you
are mine.
...for you
say words
I know.
...for the murdered
hunter's house is just
another clue...

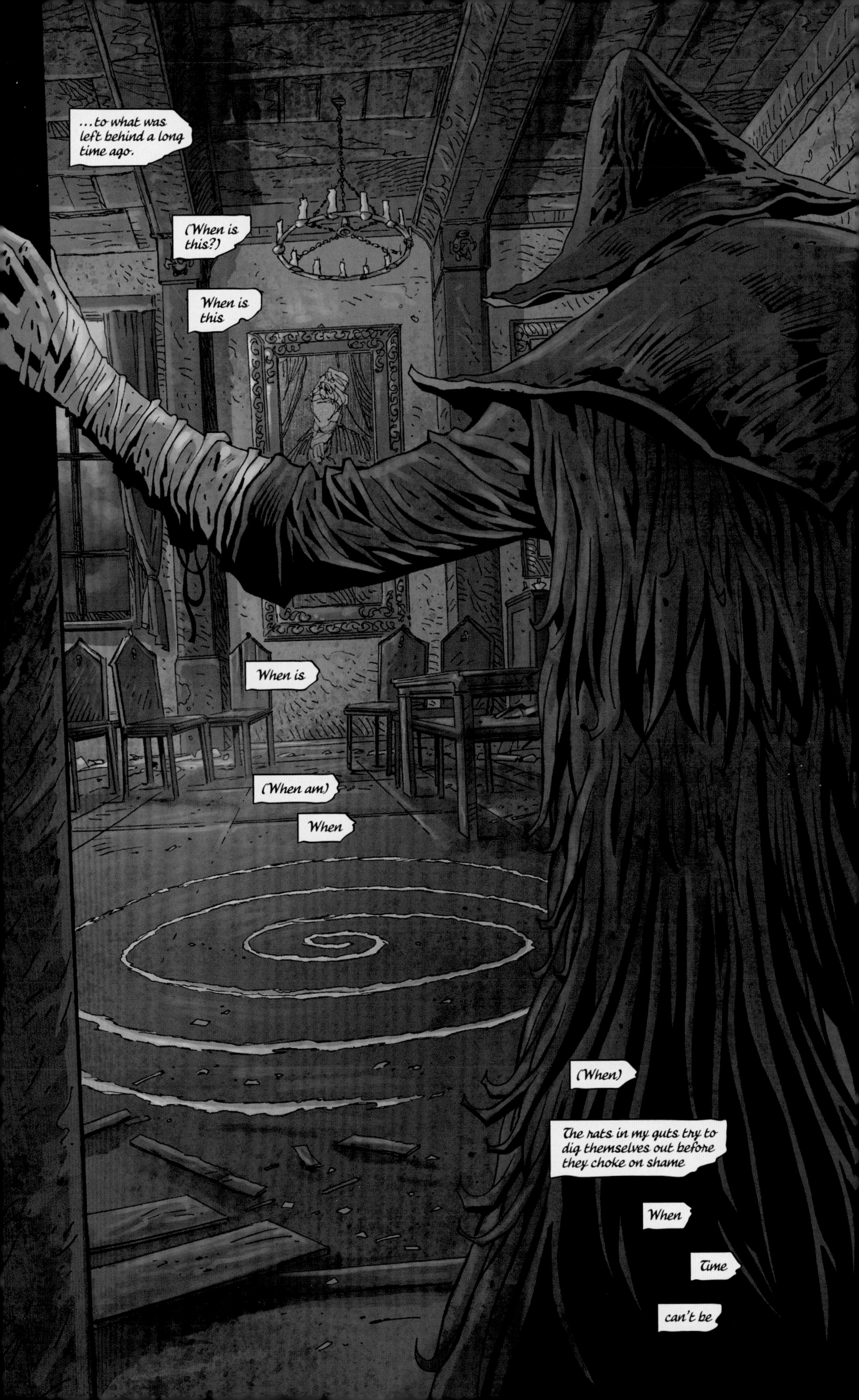
...to what was left behind a long time ago.
(When is this?)
When is this
When is
(When am)
When
(When)
The rats in my guts try to dig themselves out before they choke on shame
When
Time
can't be

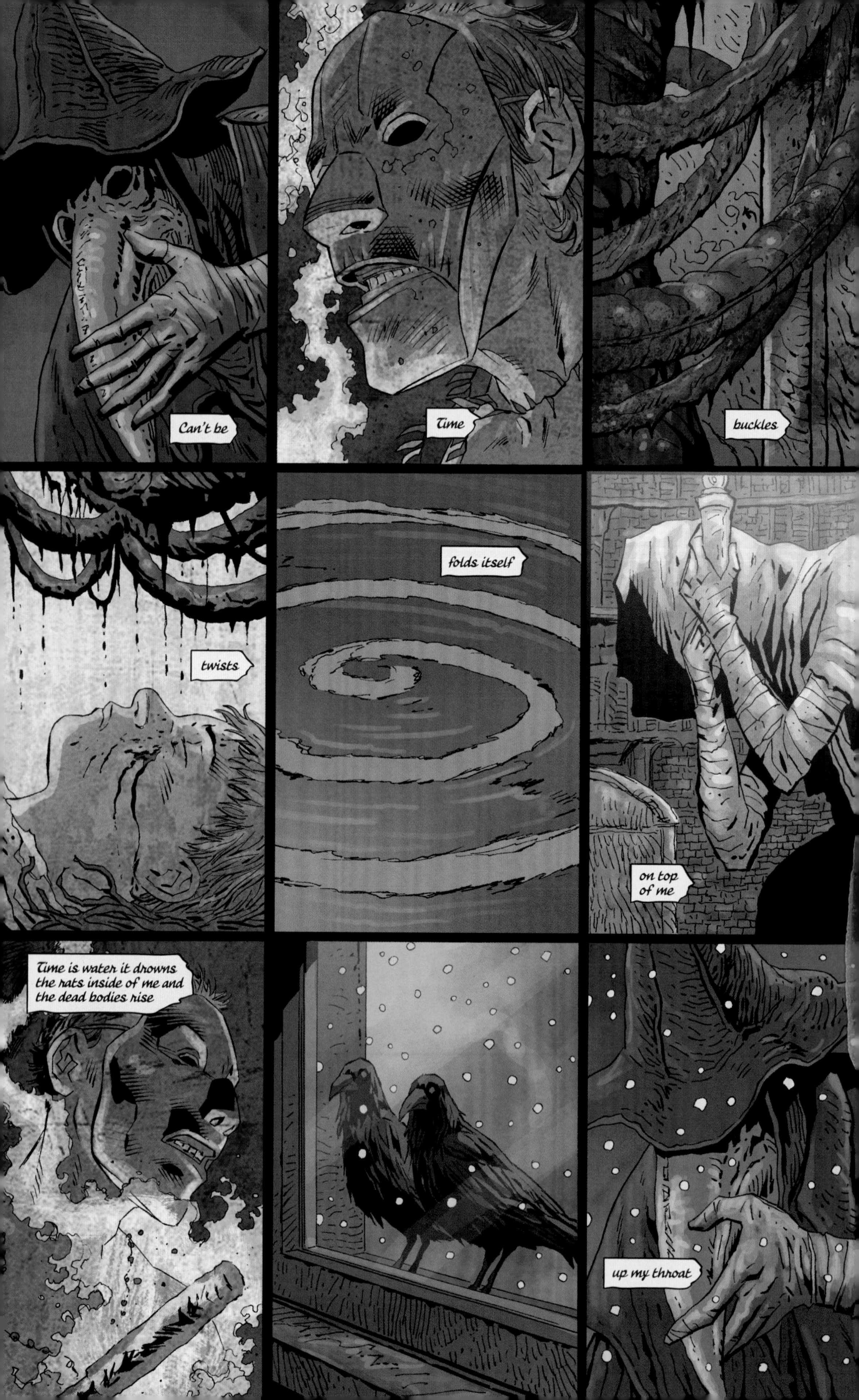
Can't be
Time
buckles
twists
folds itself
on top of me
Time is water it drowns the rats inside of me and the dead bodies rise
up my throat

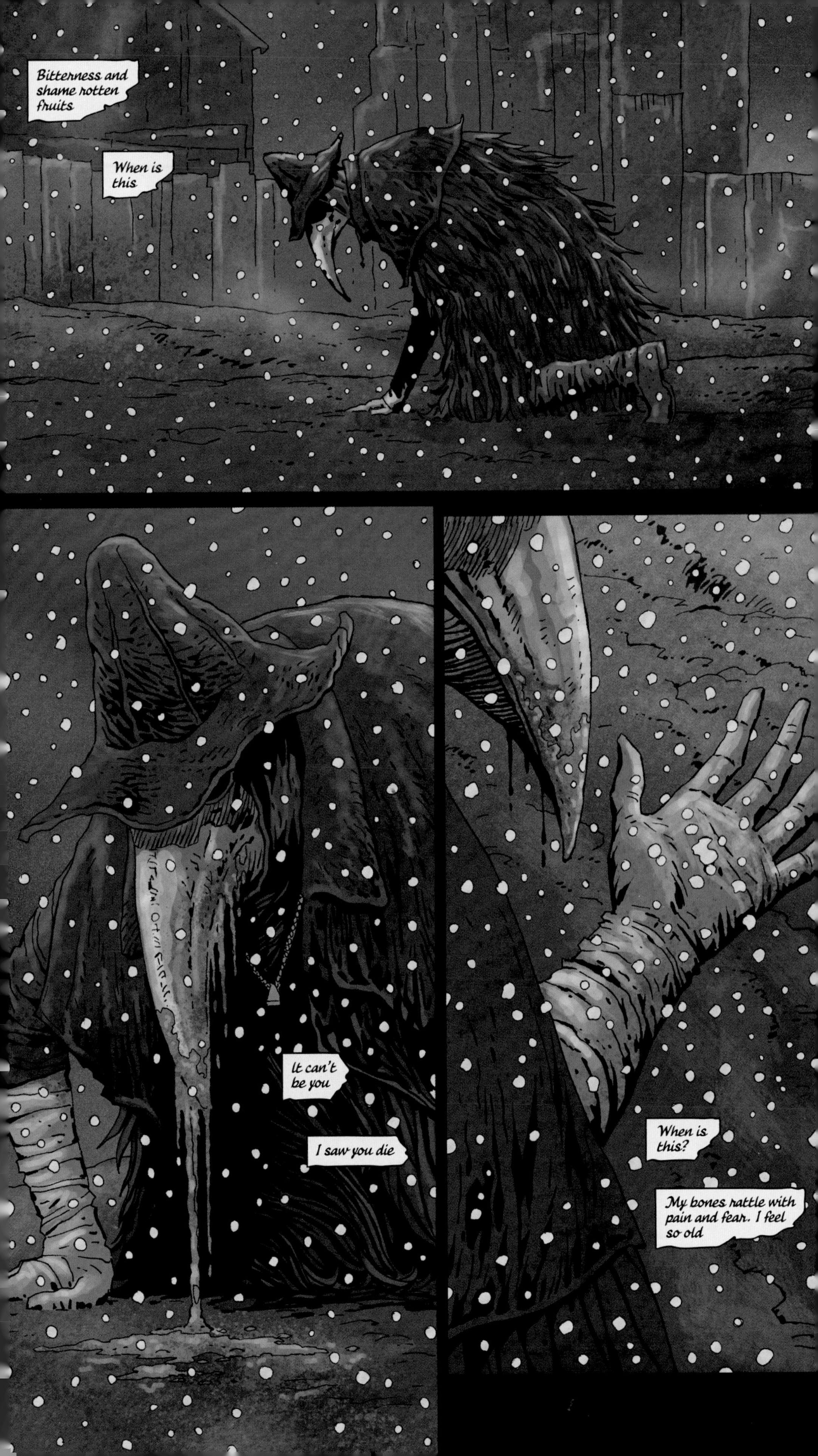
Bitterness and shame rotten fruits
When is this
It can't be you
I saw you die
When is this?
My bones rattle with pain and fear. I feel so old

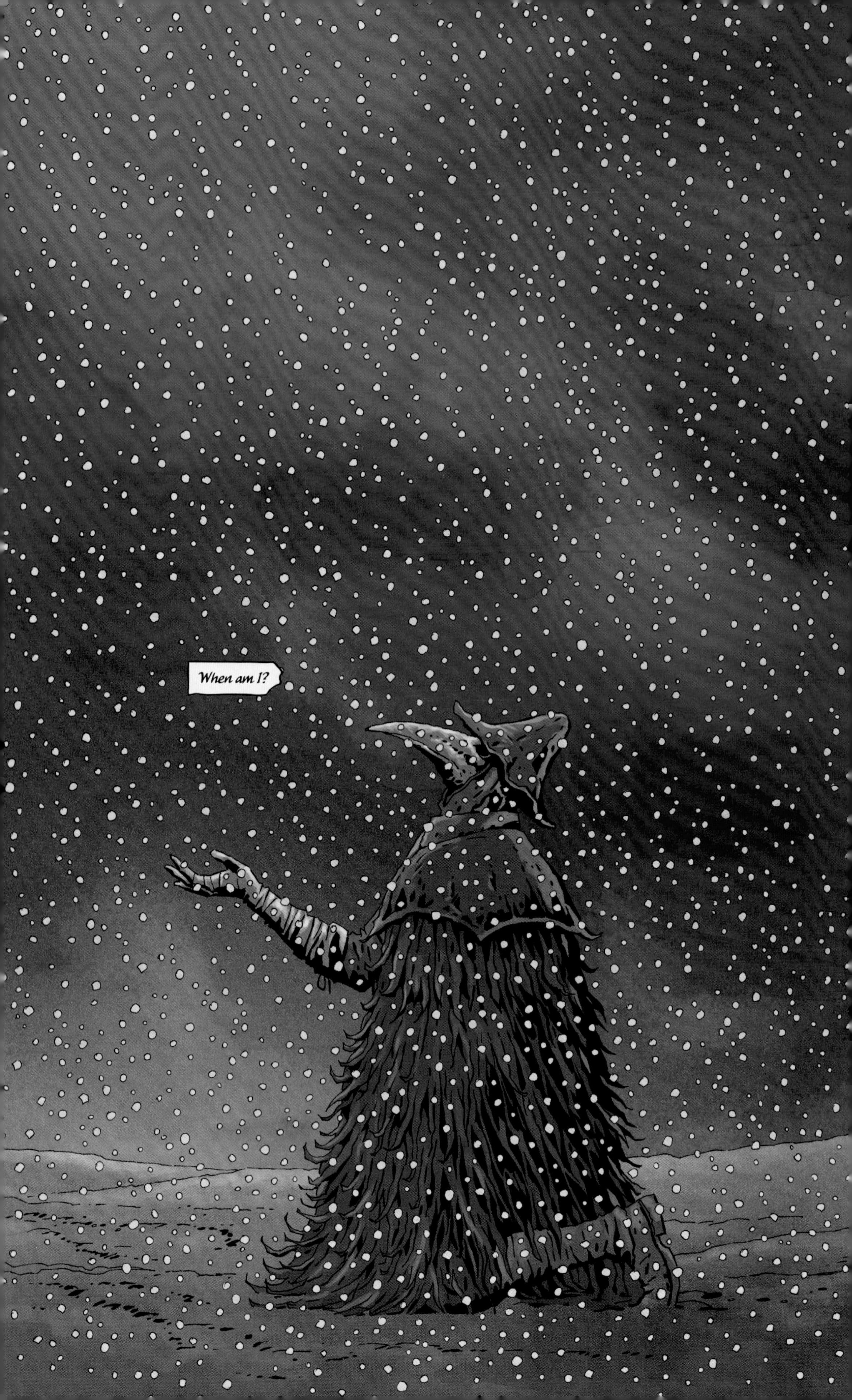
When am I?

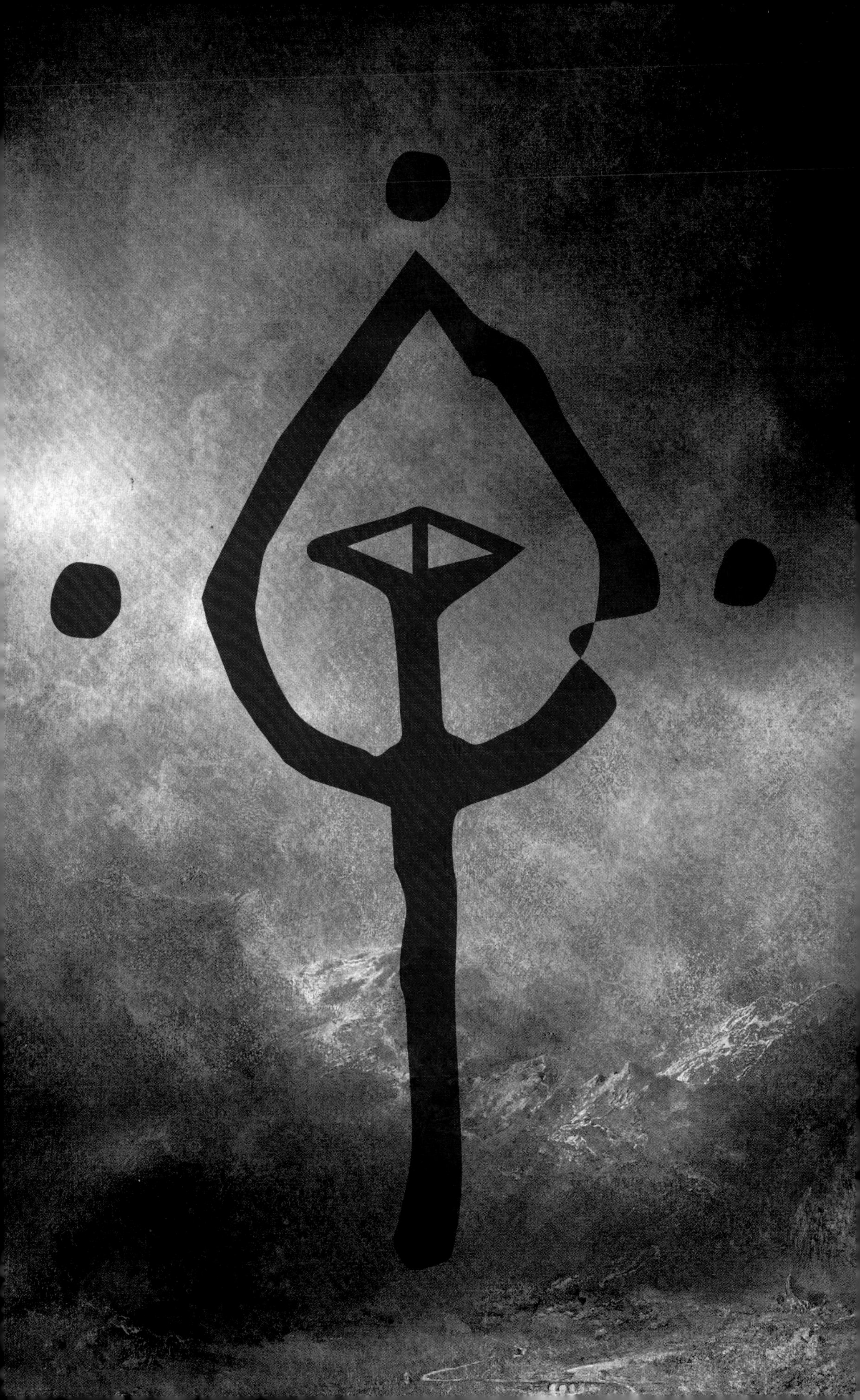

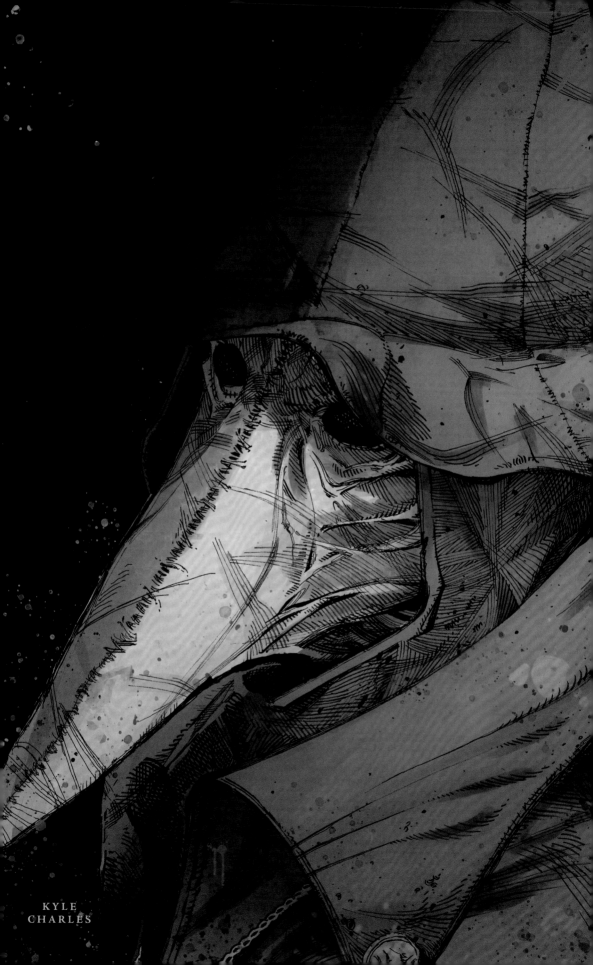

KYLE
CHARLES

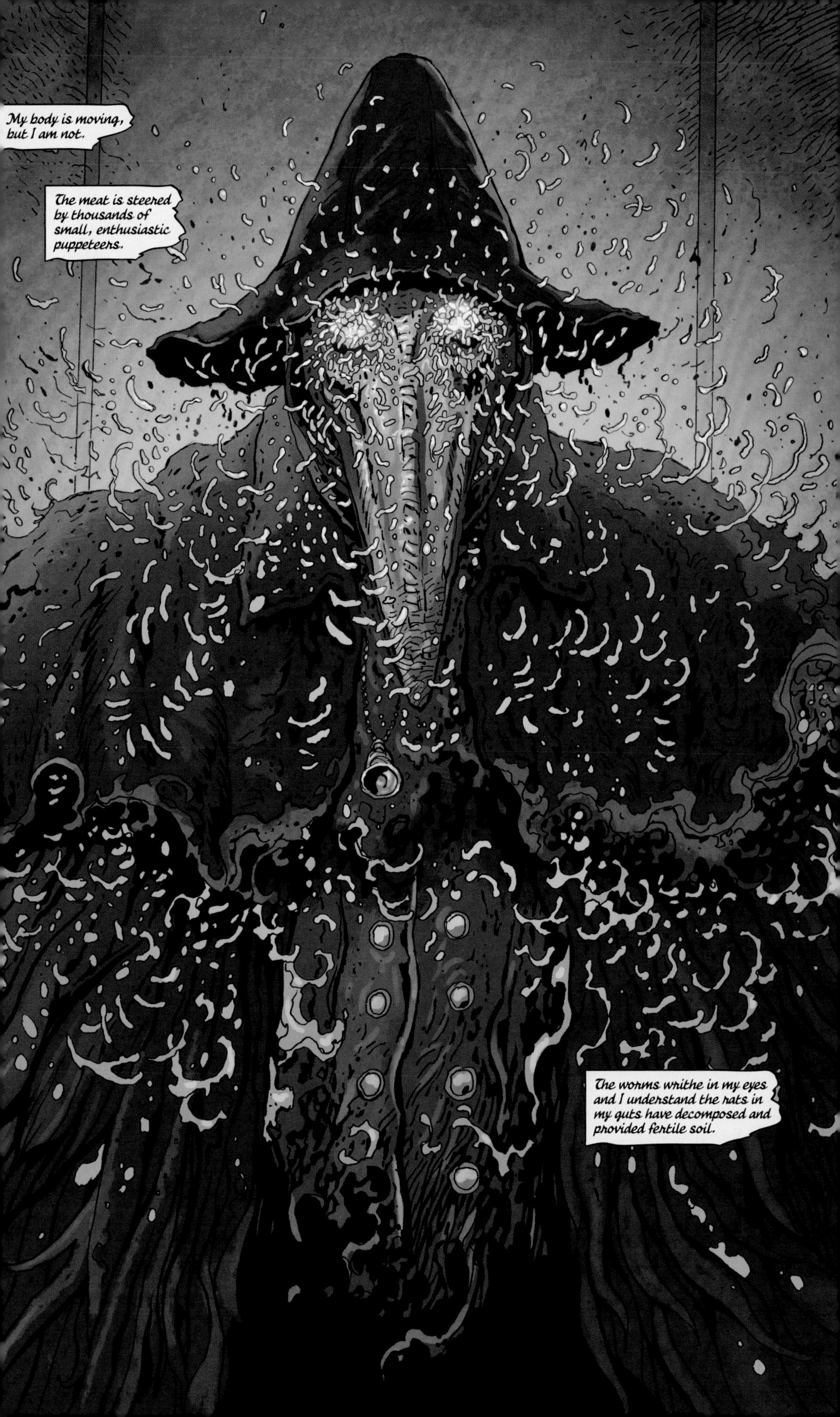
My body is moving, but I am not.
The meat is steered by thousands of small, enthusiastic puppeteers.
The worms writhe in my eyes and I understand the rats in my guts have decomposed and provided fertile soil.

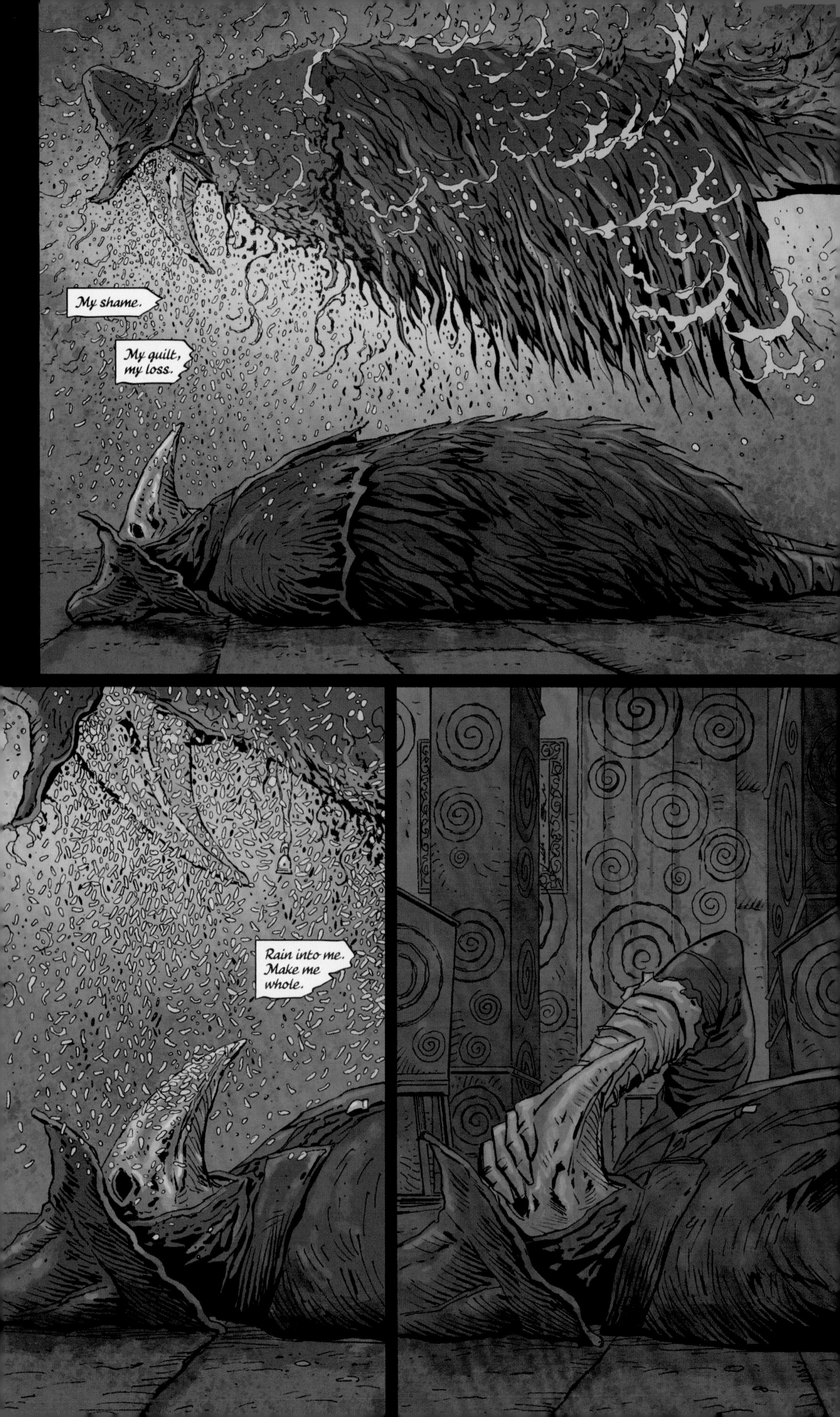
My shame.
My guilt, my loss.
Rain into me. Make me whole.

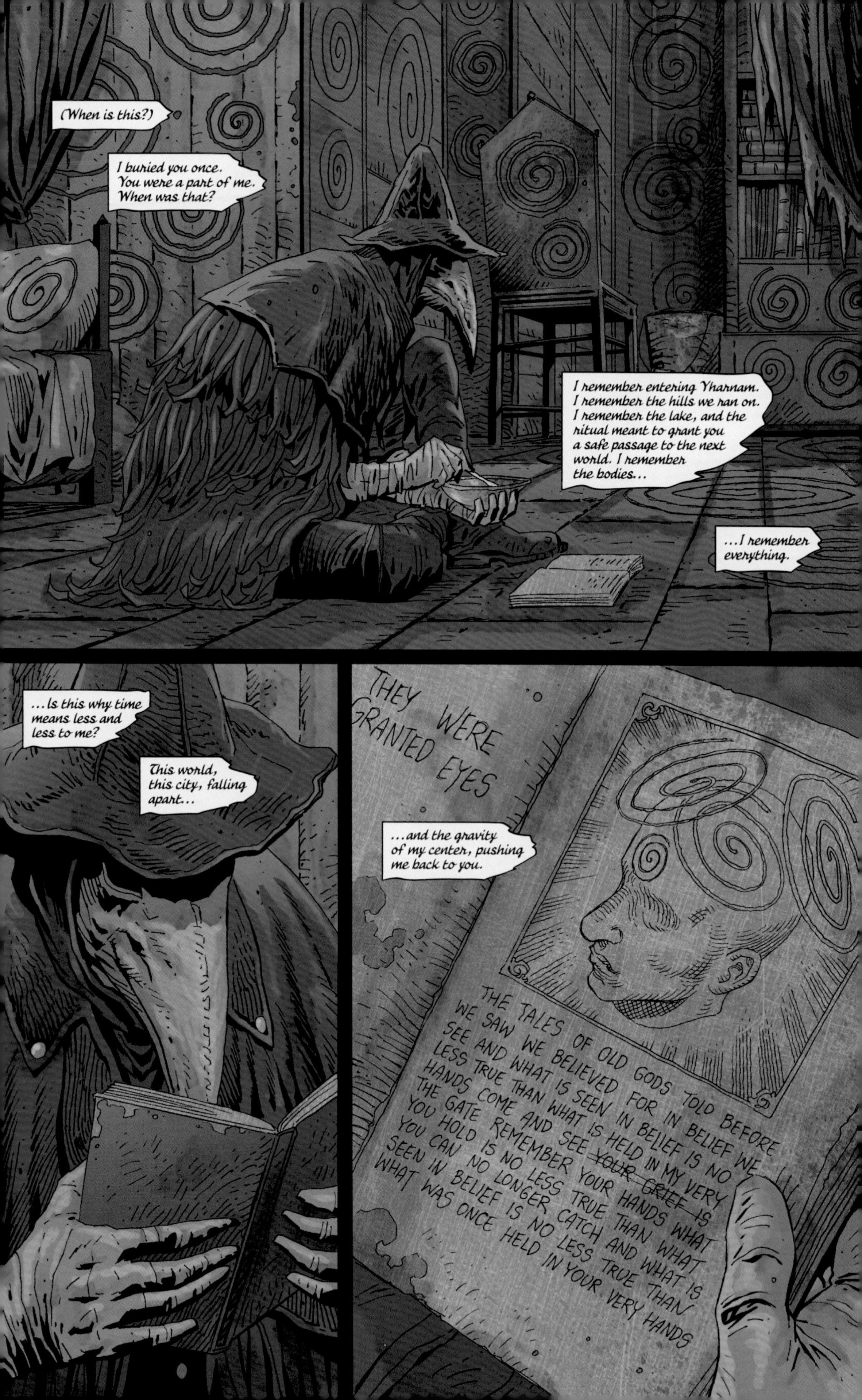
(When is this?)
I buried you once. You were a part of me. When was that?
I remember entering Yharnam. I remember the hills we ran on. I remember the lake, and the ritual meant to grant you a safe passage to the next world. I remember the bodies...
...I remember everything.
...Is this why time means less and less to me?
This world, this city, falling apart...
THEY WERE GRANTED EYES
...and the gravity of my center, pushing me back to you.
THE TALES OF OLD GODS TOLD BEFORE
WE SAW WE BELIEVED FOR IN BELIEF WE
SEE AND WHAT IS SEEN IN BELIEF IS NO
LESS TRUE THAN WHAT IS HELD IN MY VERY
HANDS COME AND SEE YOUR GRIEF IS
THE GATE REMEMBER YOUR HANDS WHAT
YOU HOLD IS NO LESS TRUE THAN WHAT
YOU CAN NO LONGER CATCH AND WHAT IS
SEEN IN BELIEF IS NO LESS TRUE THAN
WHAT WAS ONCE HELD IN YOUR VERY HANDS

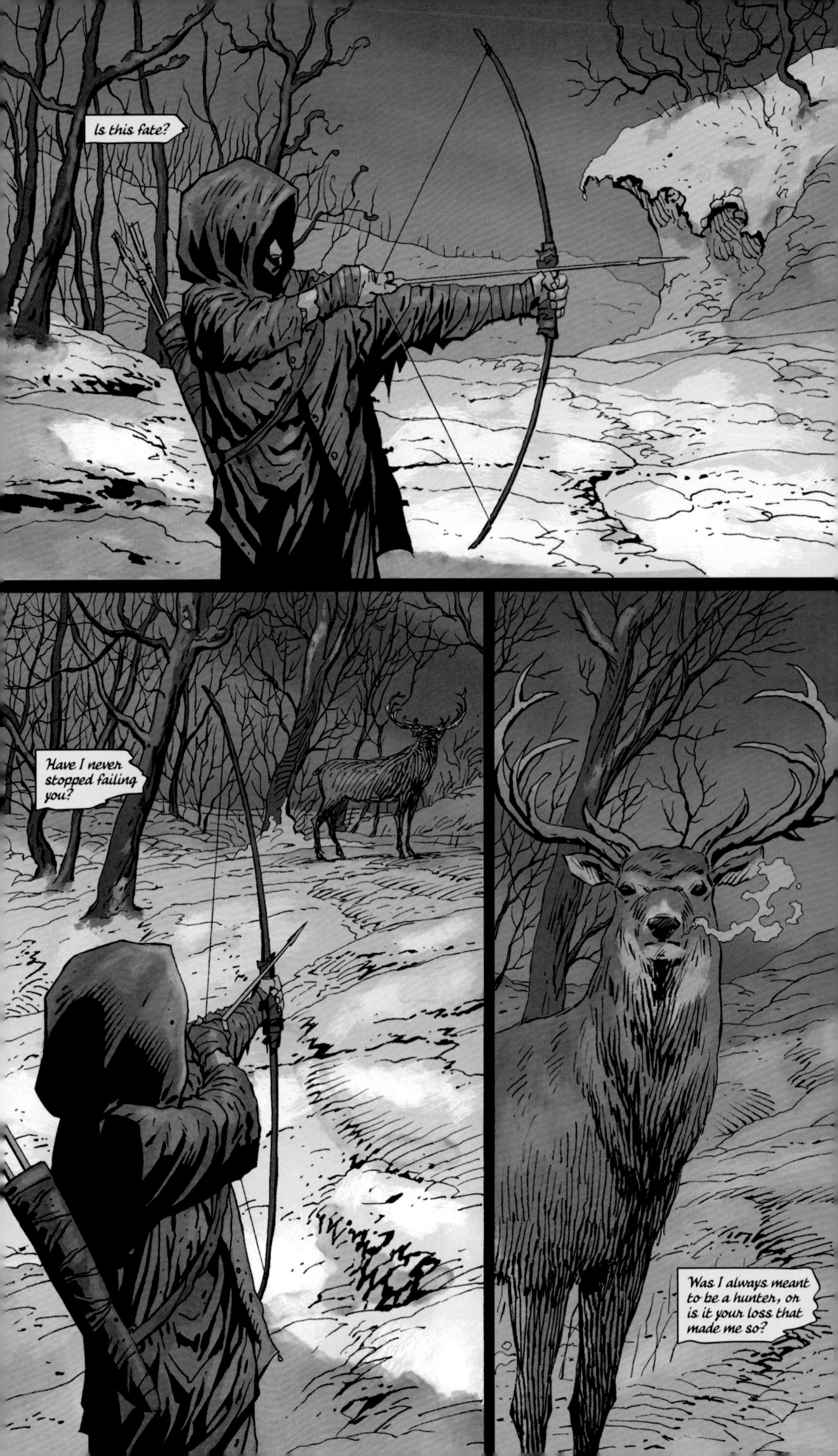

Is this fate?
Have I never stopped failing you?
Was I always meant to be a hunter, or is it your loss that made me so?

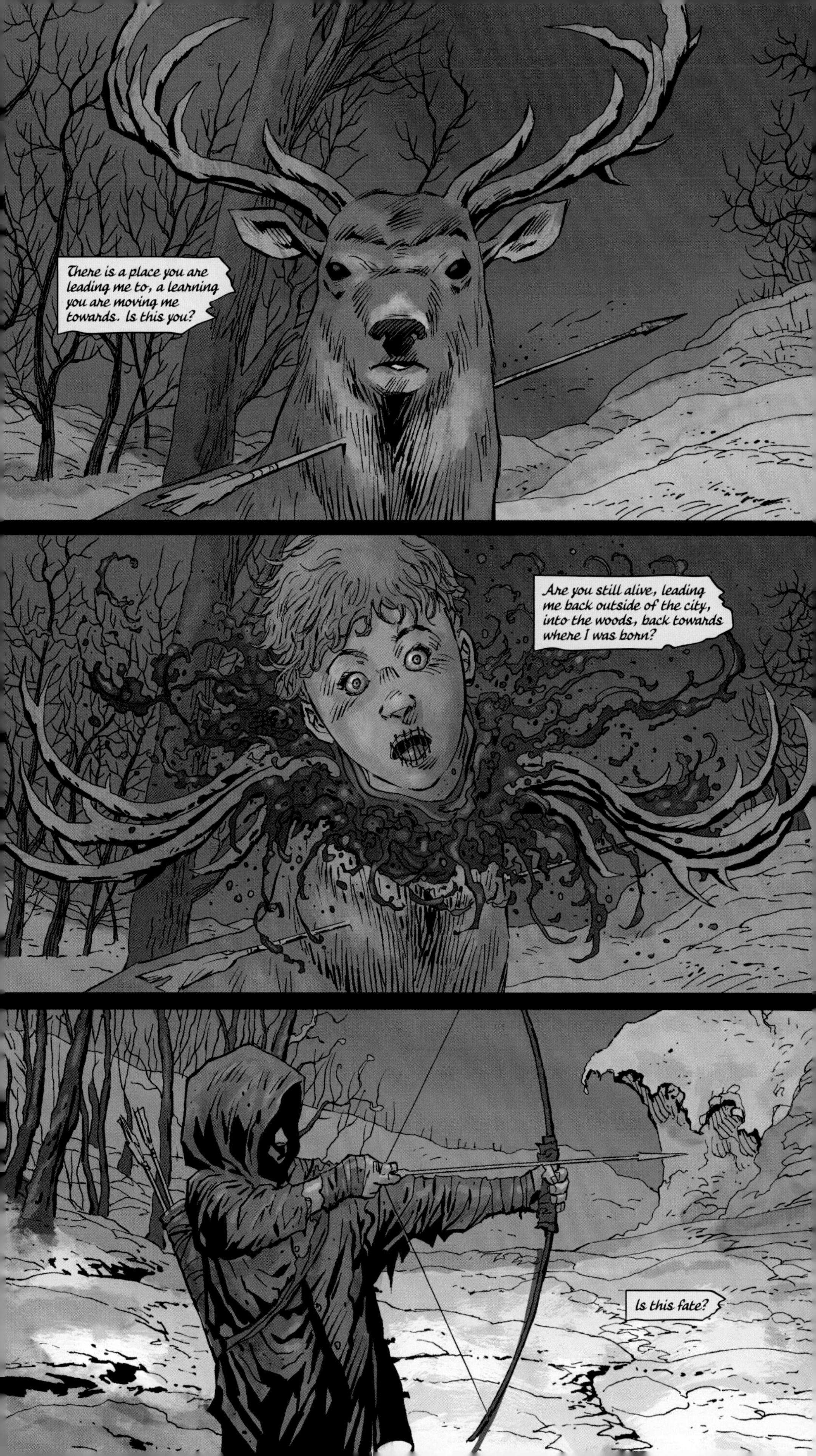
There is a place you are leading me to, a learning you are moving me towards. Is this you?
Are you still alive, leading me back outside of the city, into the woods, back towards where I was born?
Is this fate?

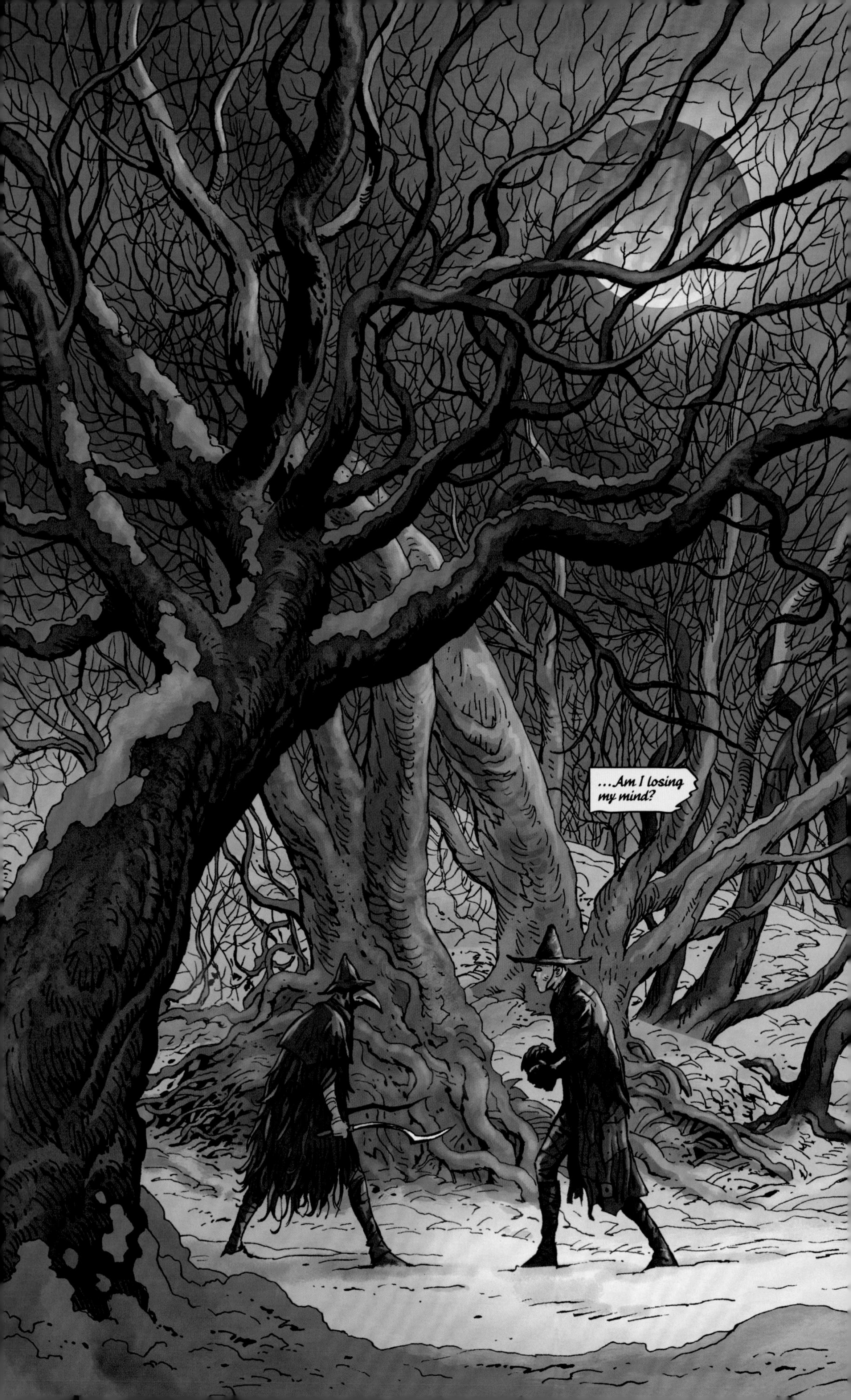
...Am I losing my mind?

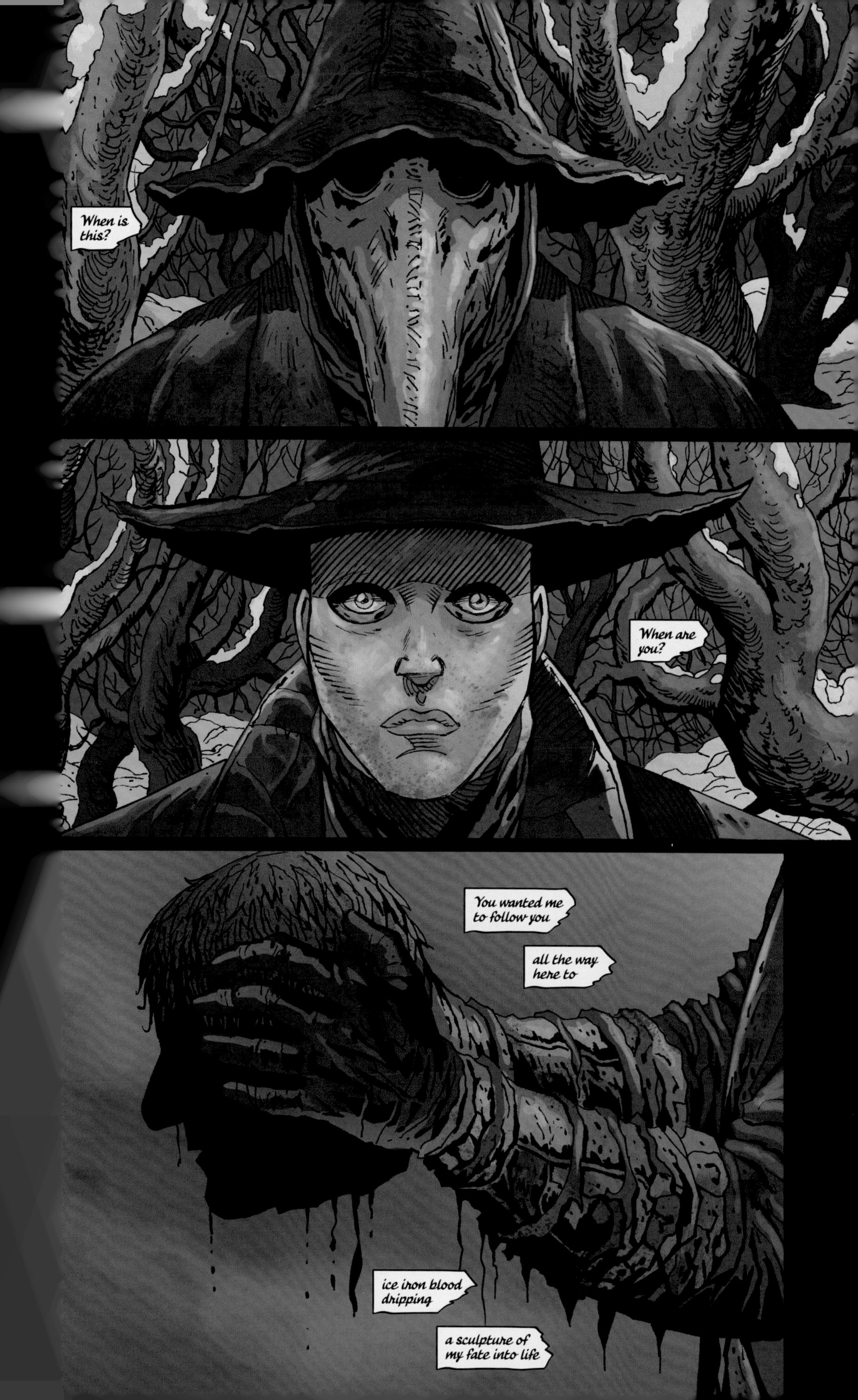
When is this?
When are you?
You wanted me to follow you
all the way here to
ice iron blood dripping
a sculpture of my fate into life

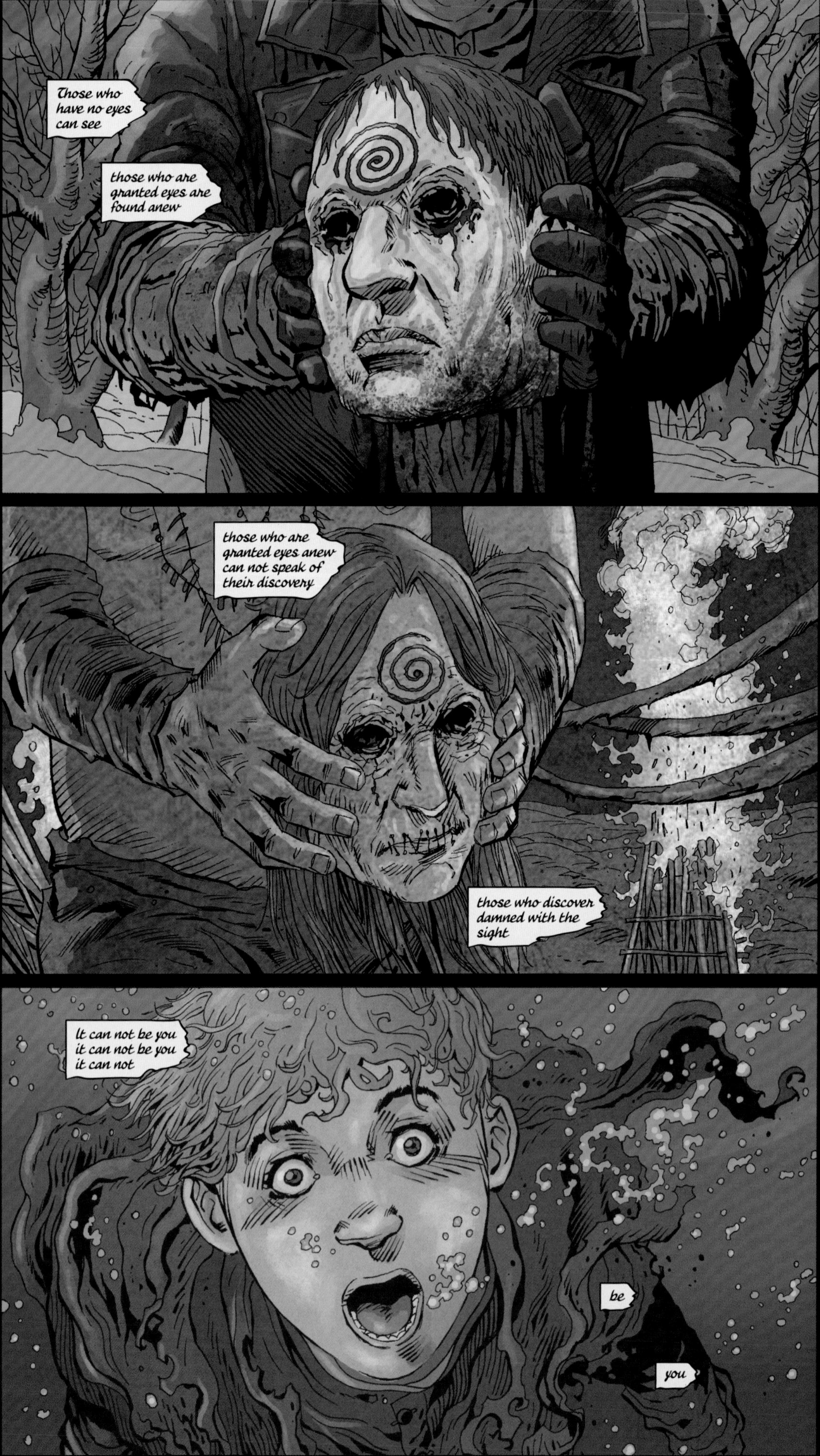
Those who have no eyes can see
those who are granted eyes are found anew
those who are granted eyes anew can not speak of their discovery
those who discover damned with the sight
It can not be you it can not be you it can not
be
you

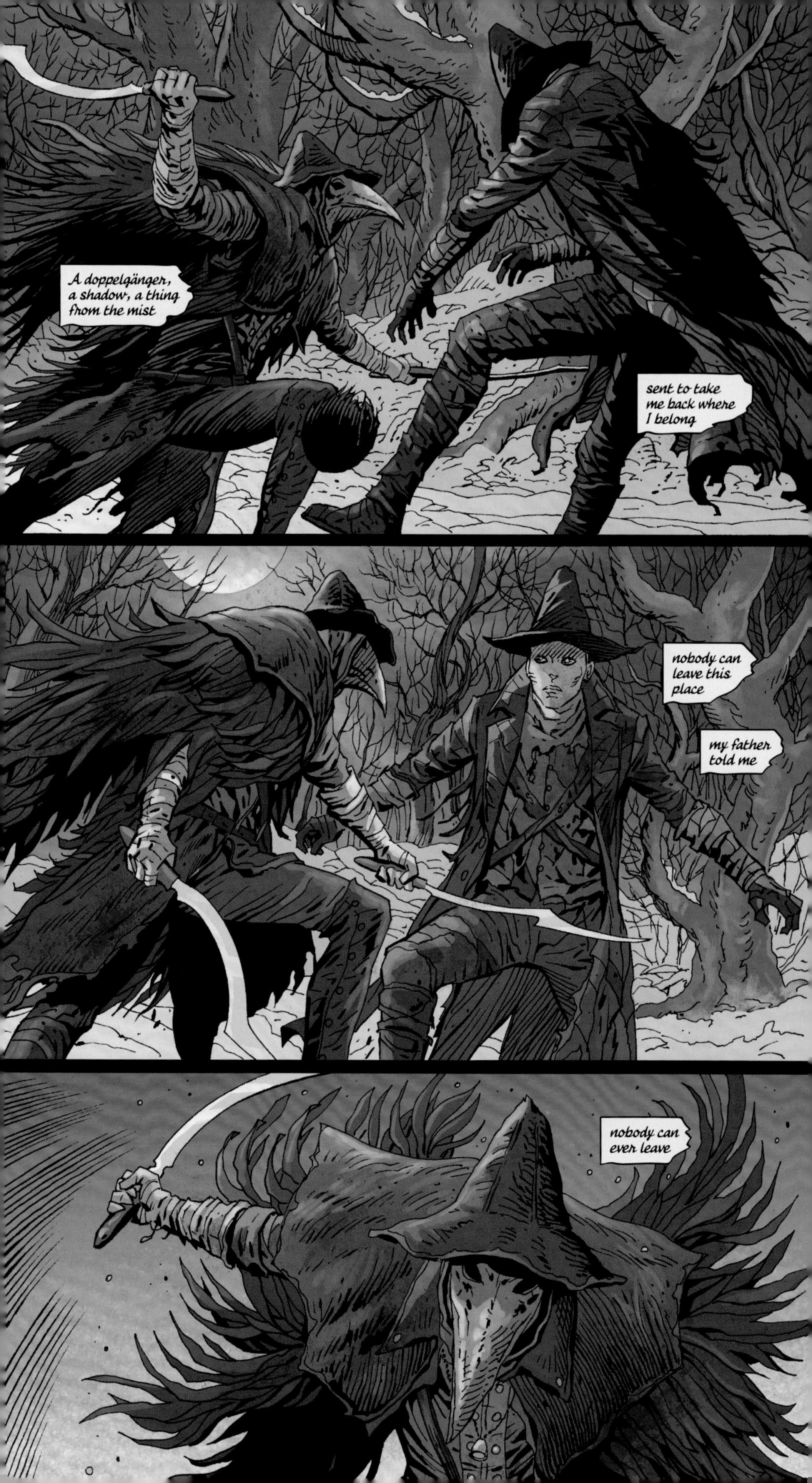
A doppelgänger, a shadow, a thing from the mist
sent to take me back where I belong
nobody can leave this place
my father told me
nobody can ever leave

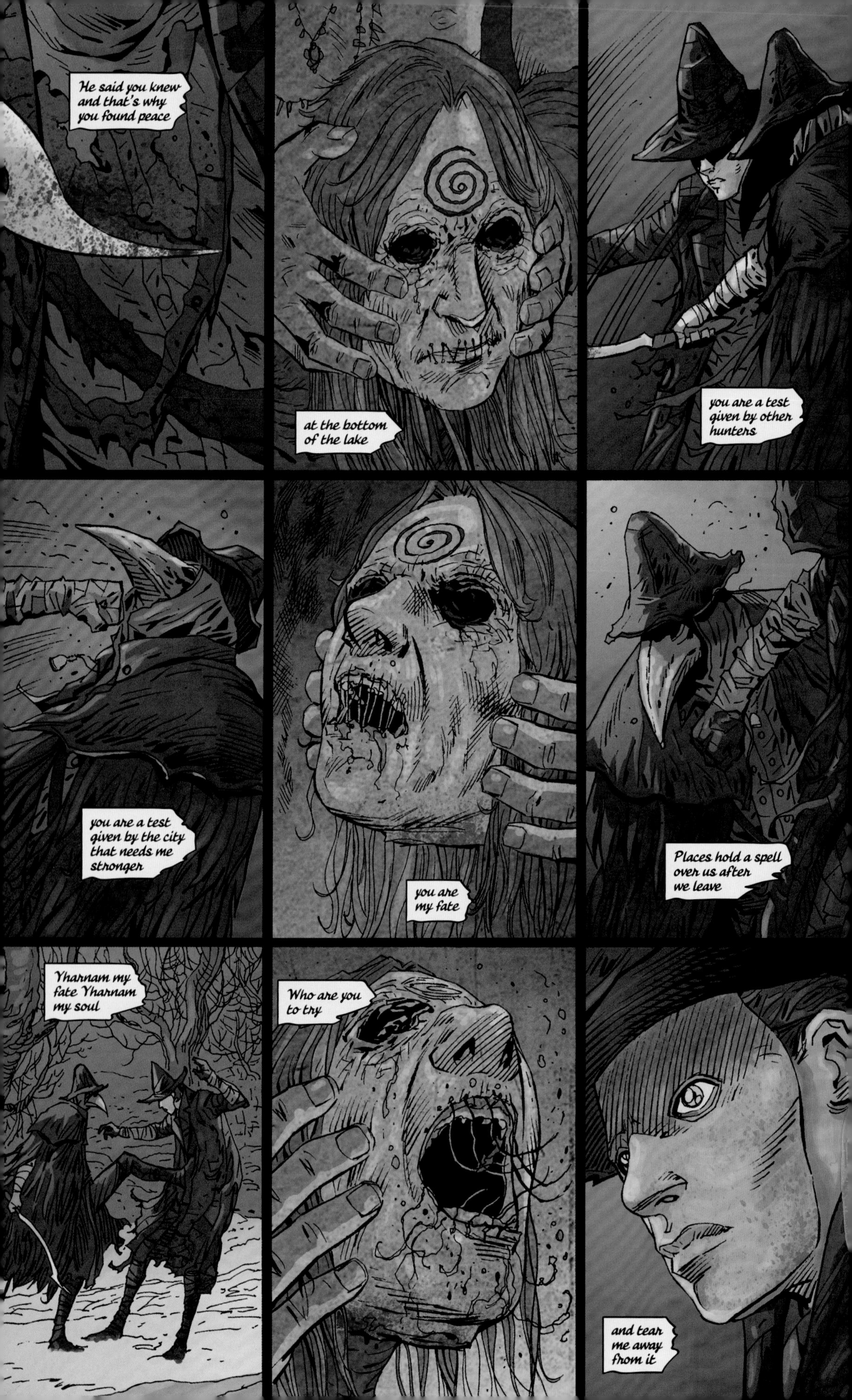
He said you knew and that's why you found peace
at the bottom of the lake
you are a test given by other hunters
you are a test given by the city that needs me stronger
you are my fate
Places hold a spell over us after we leave
Yharnam my fate Yharnam my soul
Who are you to try
and tear me away from it

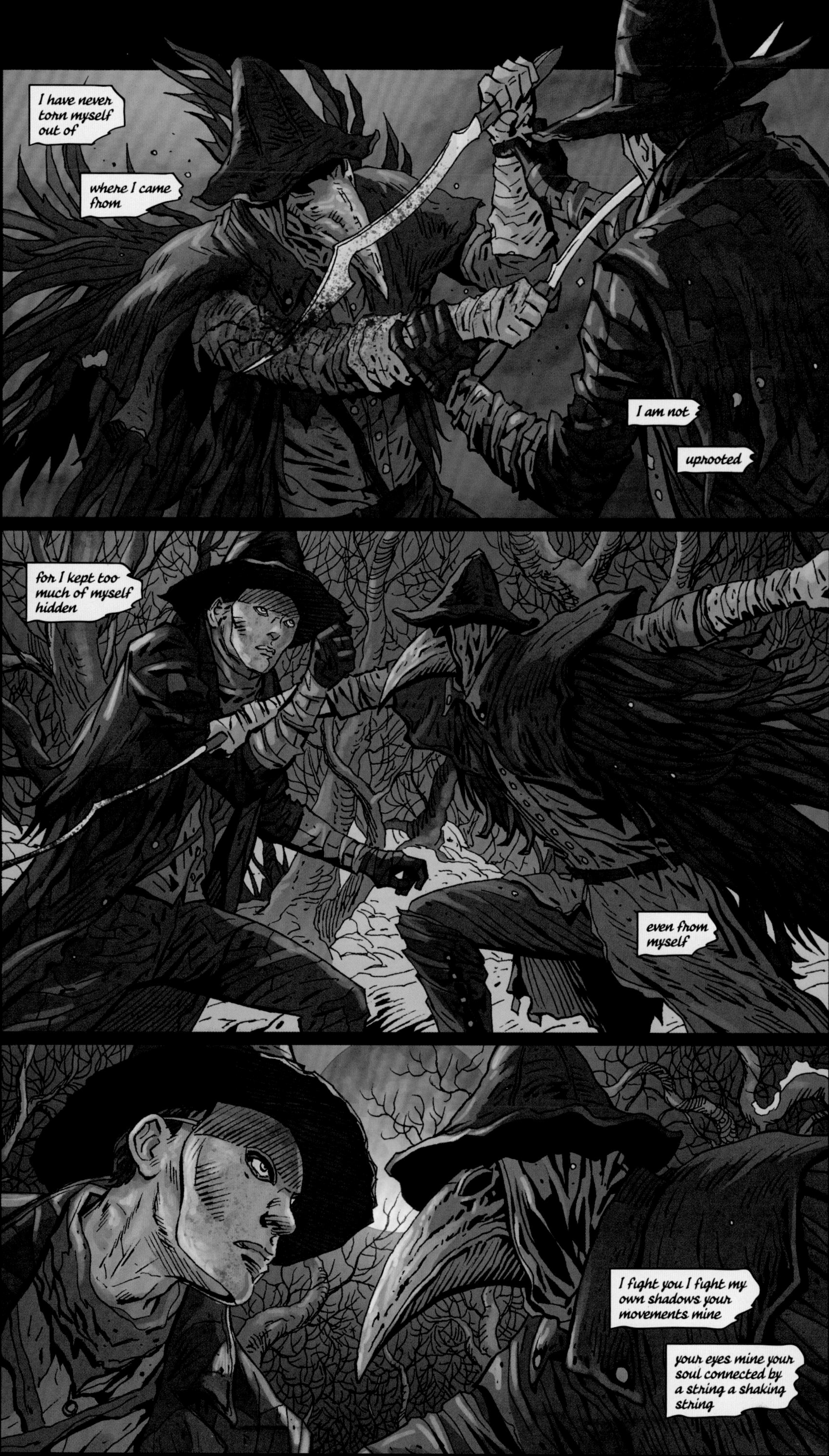

I have never torn myself out of
where I came from
I am not
uprooted
for I kept too much of myself hidden
even from myself
I fight you I fight my own shadows your movements mine
your eyes mine your soul connected by a string a shaking string

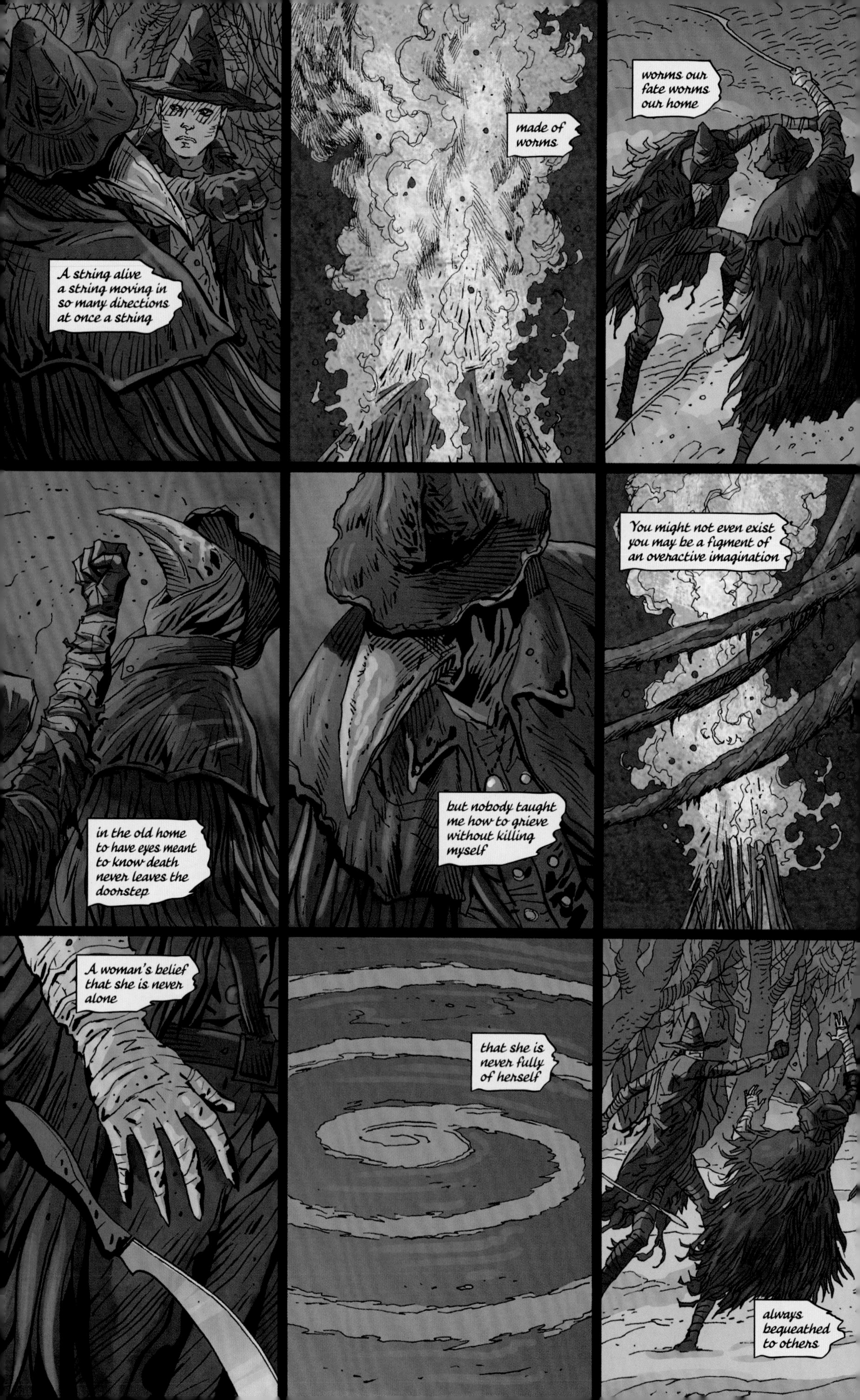
A string alive a string moving in so many directions at once a string
made of worms
worms our fate worms our home
in the old home to have eyes meant to know death never leaves the doorstep
but nobody taught me how to grieve without killing myself
You might not even exist you may be a figment of an overactive imagination
A woman's belief that she is never alone
that she is never fully of herself
always bequeathed to others

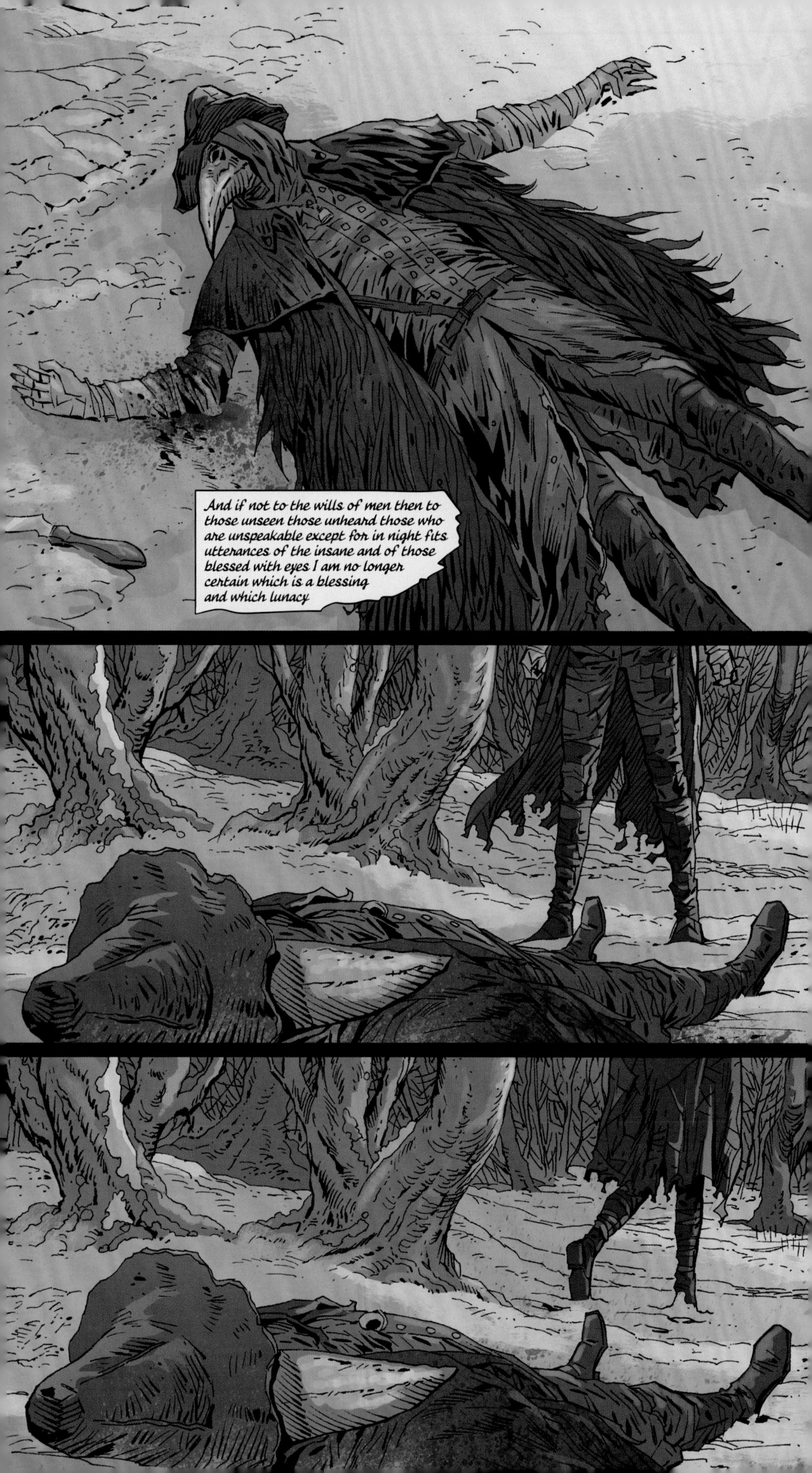
And if not to the wills of men then to those unseen those unheard those who are unspeakable except for in night fits utterances of the insane and of those blessed with eyes I am no longer certain which is a blessing and which lunacy

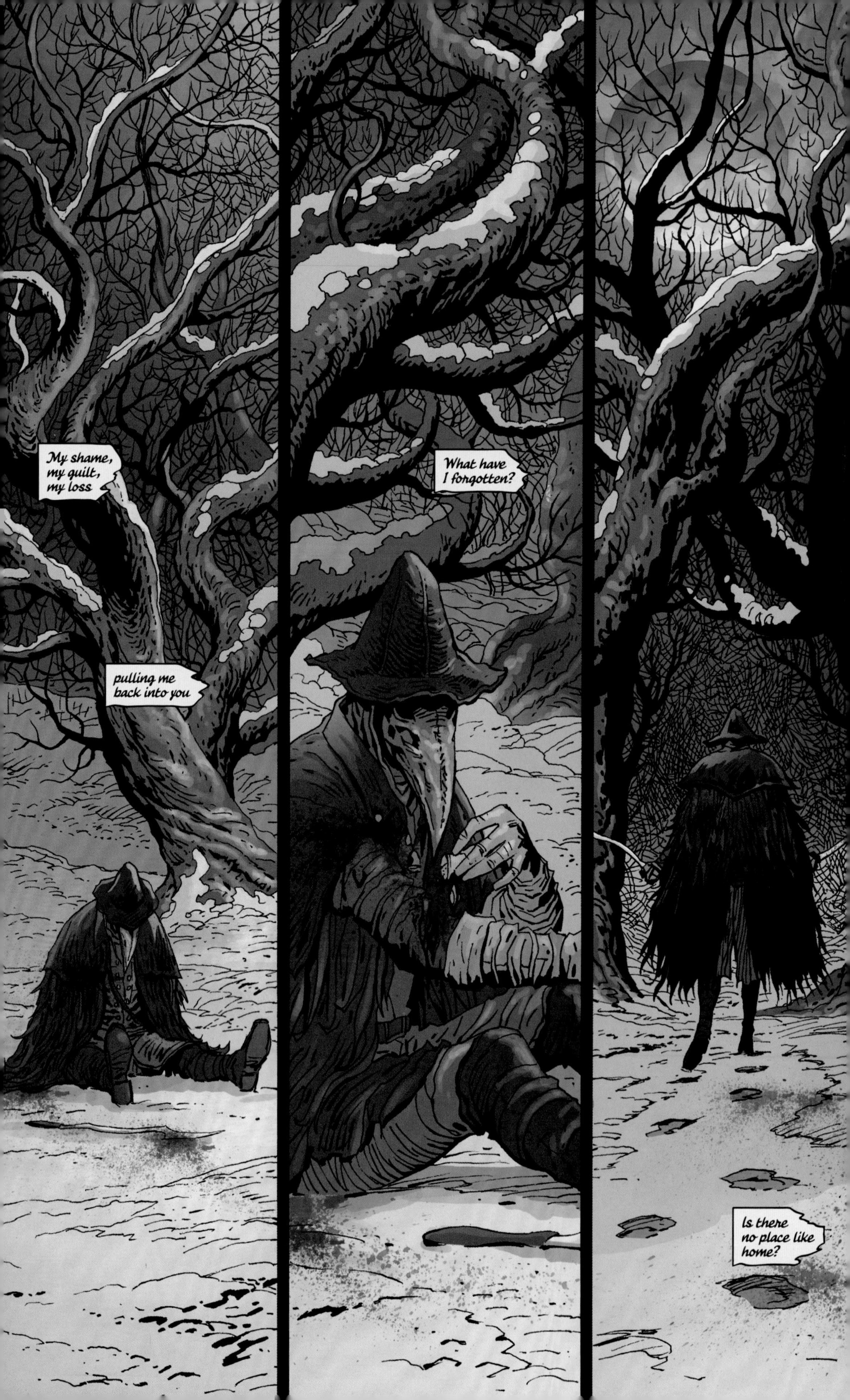
My shame, my guilt, my loss
pulling me back into you
What have I forgotten?
Is there no place like home?

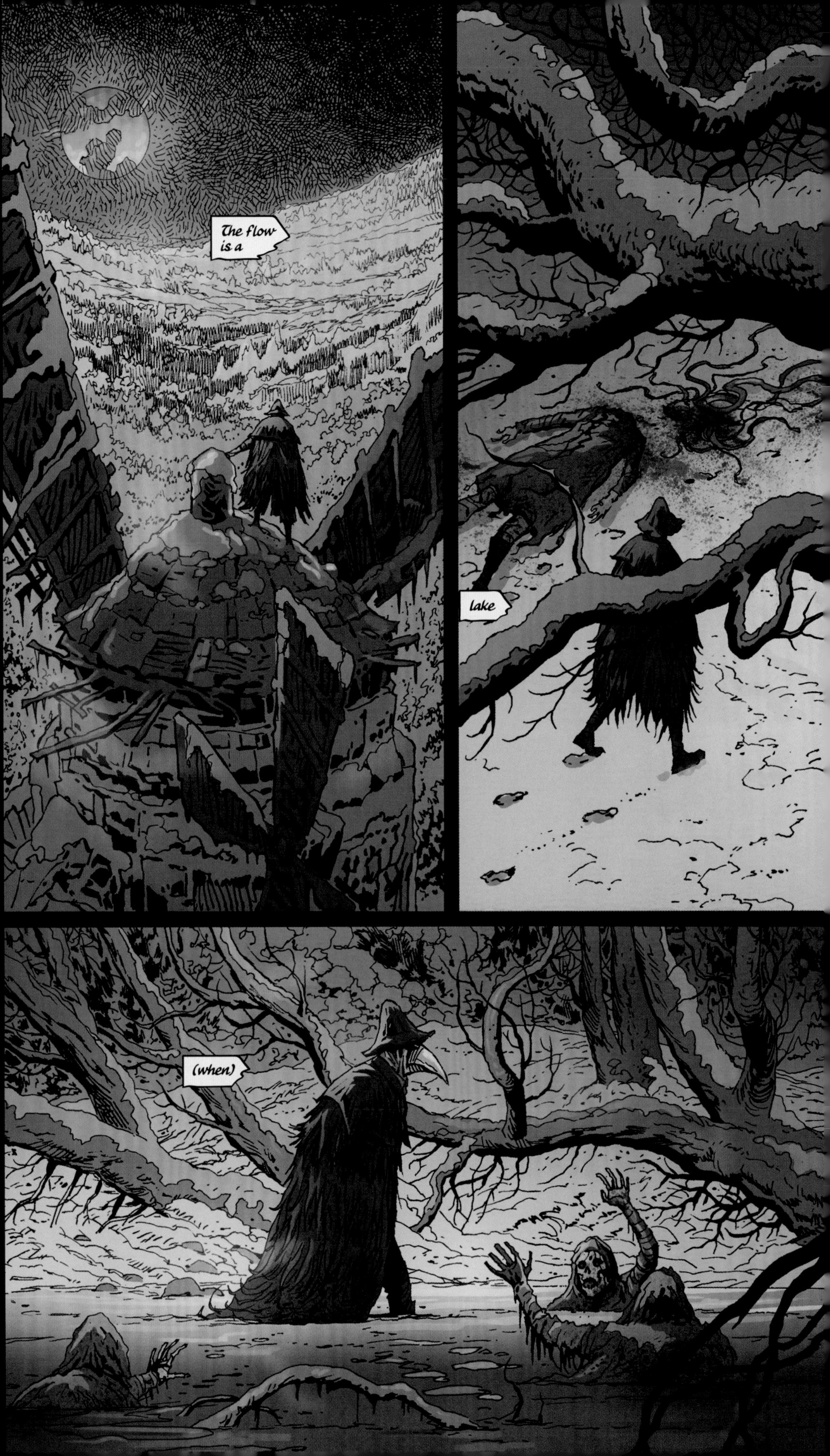
The flow is a
lake
(when)

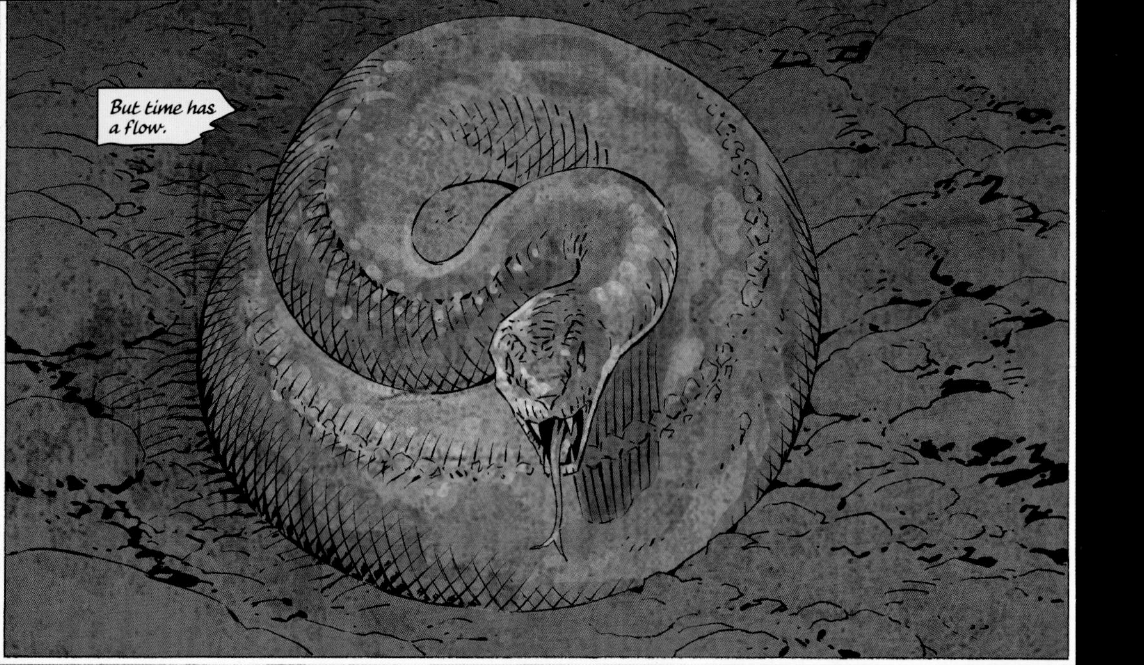
But time has a flow.

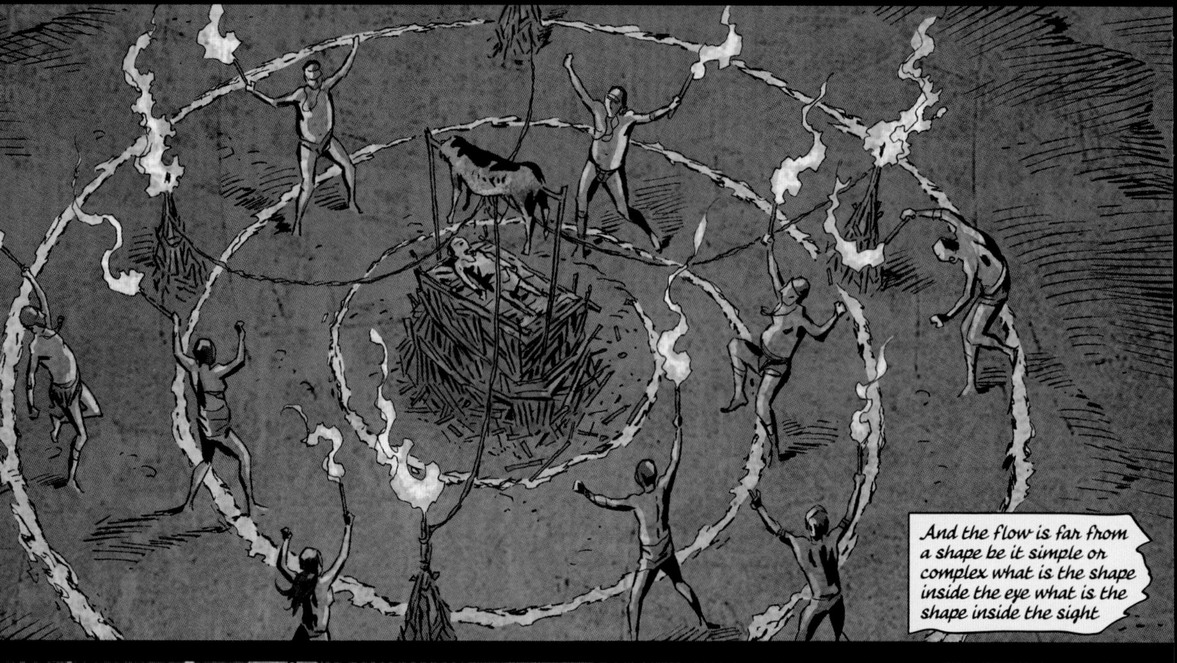
And the flow is far from a shape be it simple or complex what is the shape inside the eye what is the shape inside the sight

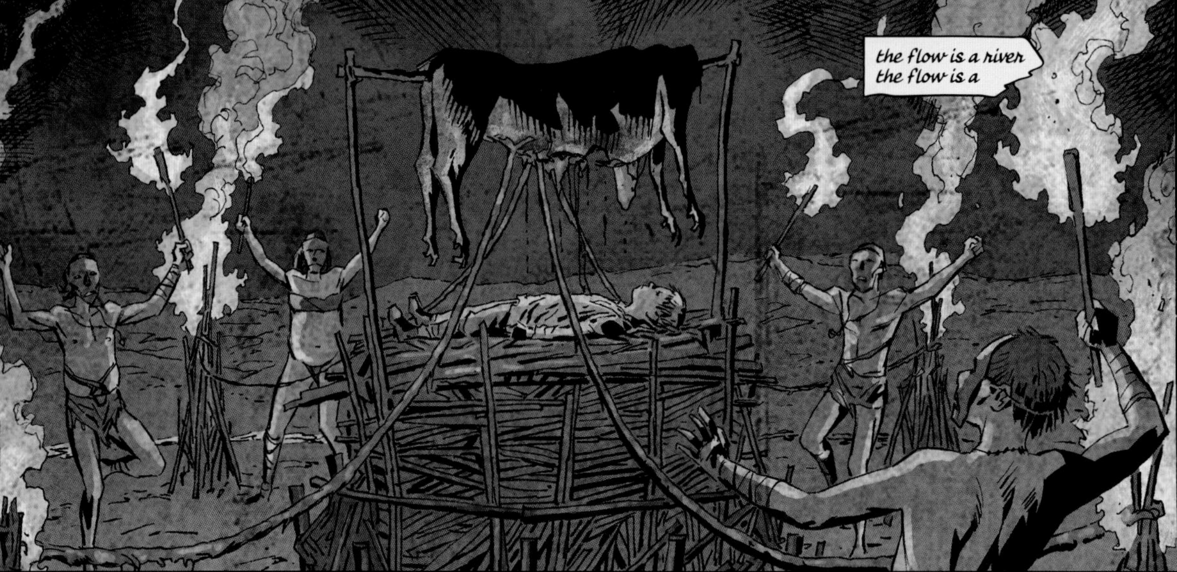
the flow is a river the flow is a

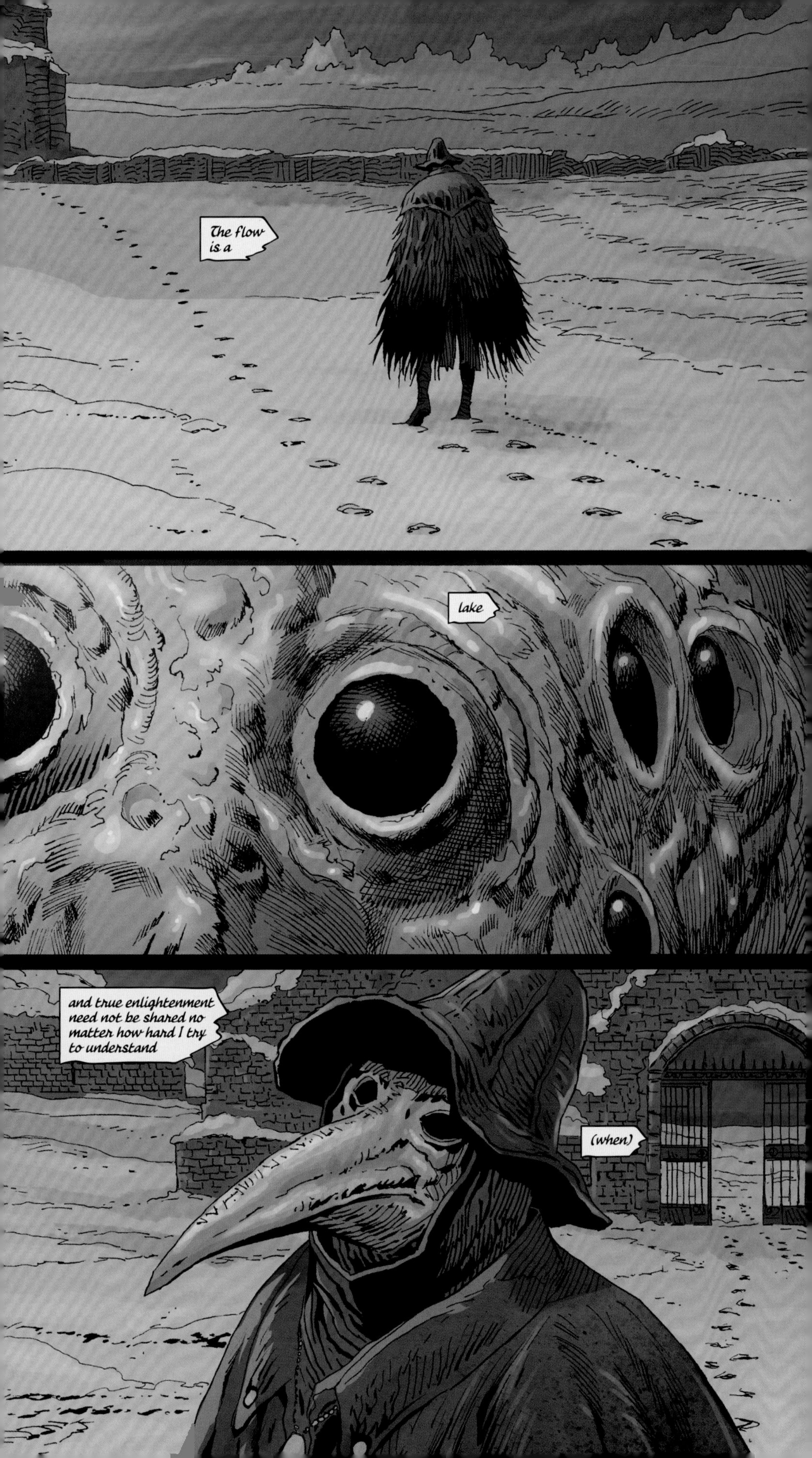
The flow is a
lake
and true enlightenment need not be shared no matter how hard I try to understand
(when)

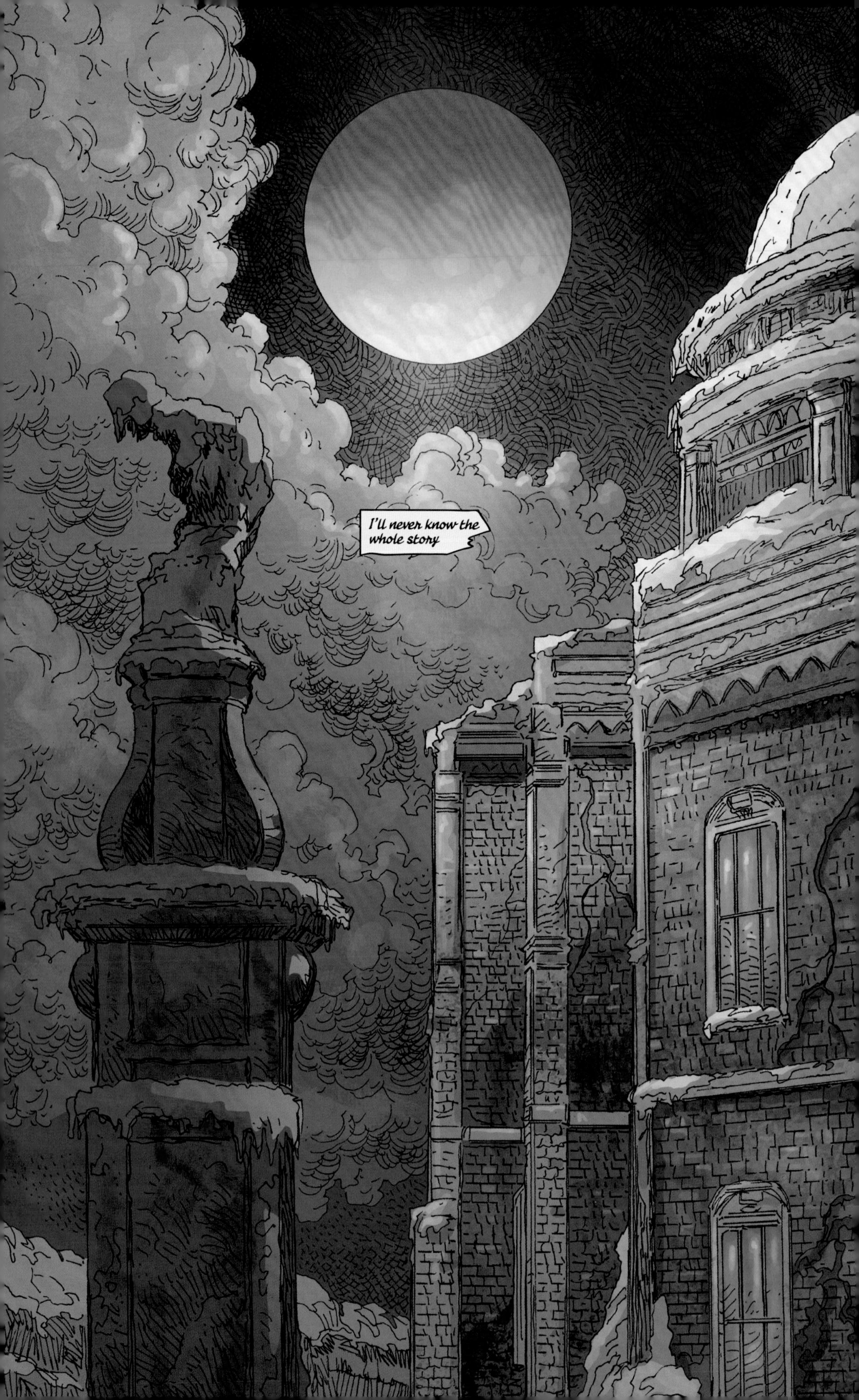
I'll never know the whole story

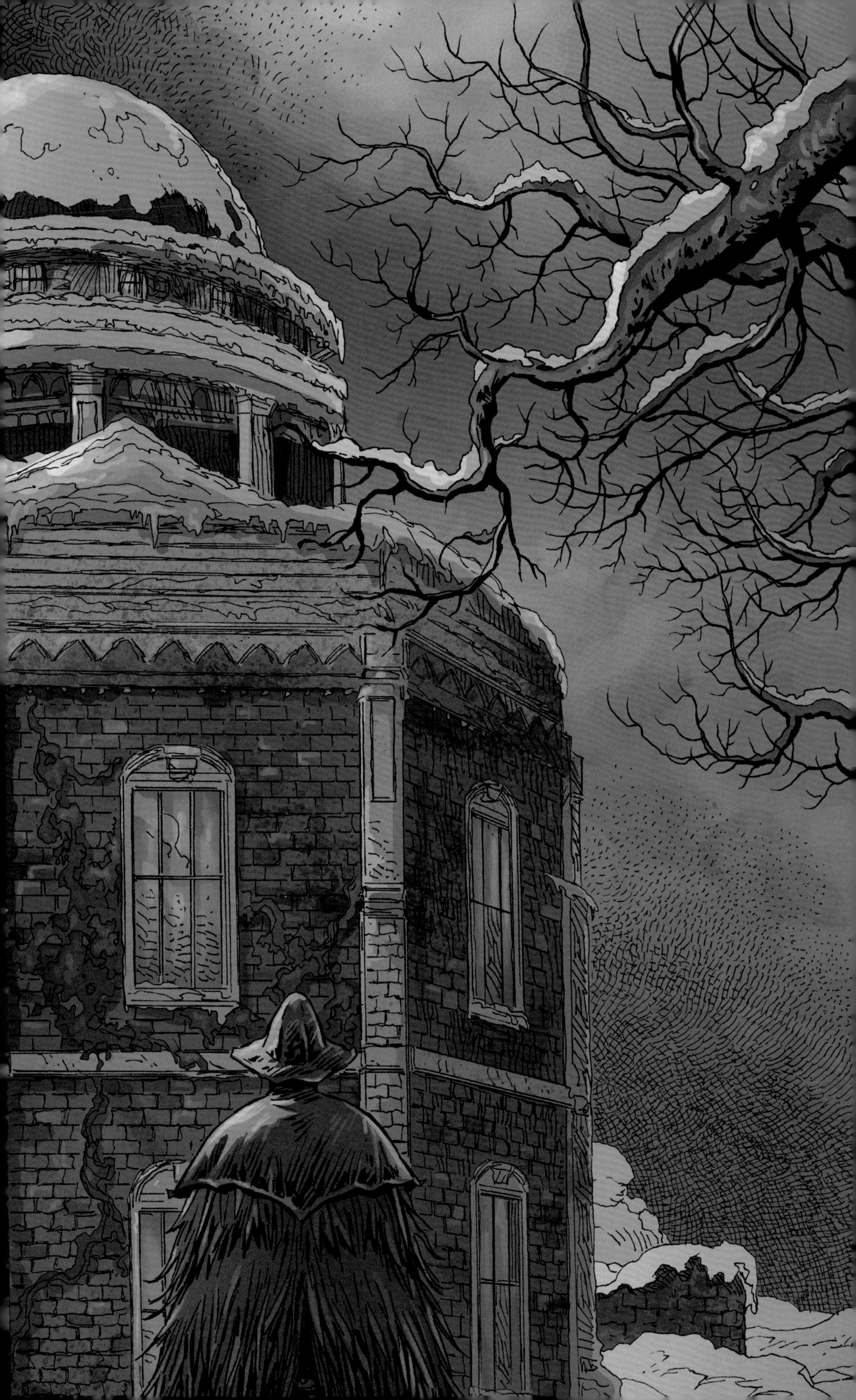

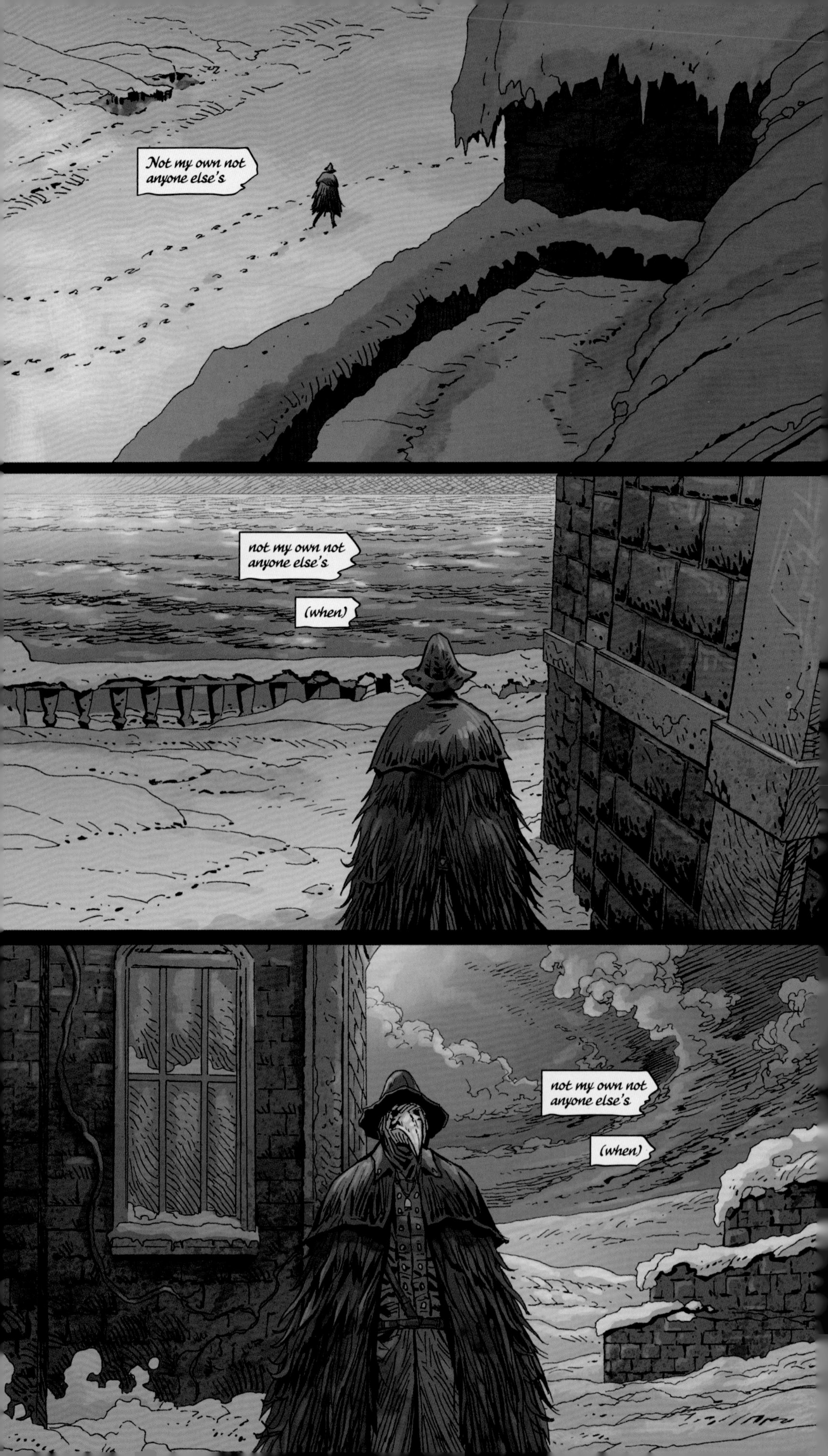
Not my own not anyone else's
not my own not anyone else's
(when)
not my own not anyone else's
(when)

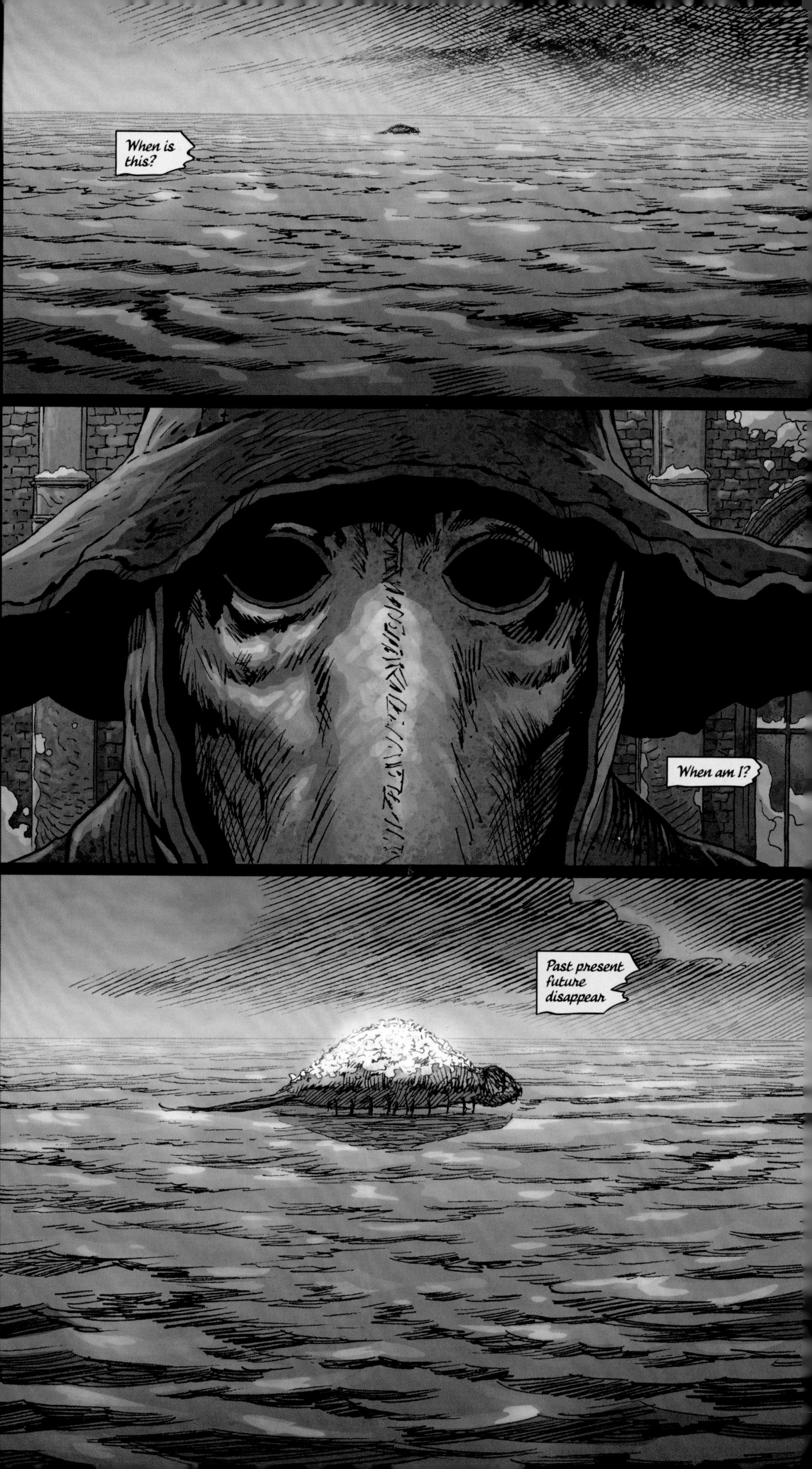
When is this?
When am I?
Past present future disappear

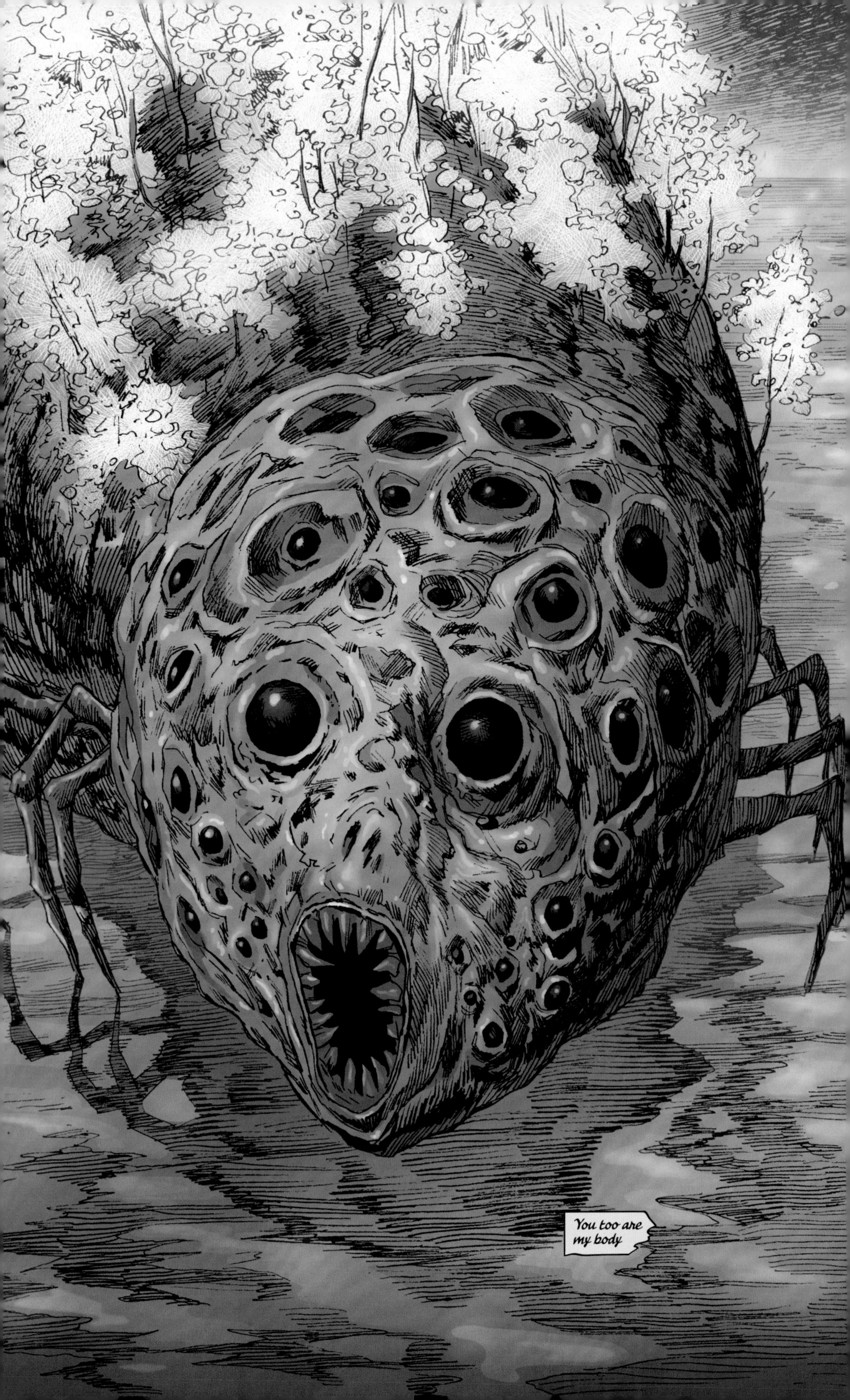
You too are my body

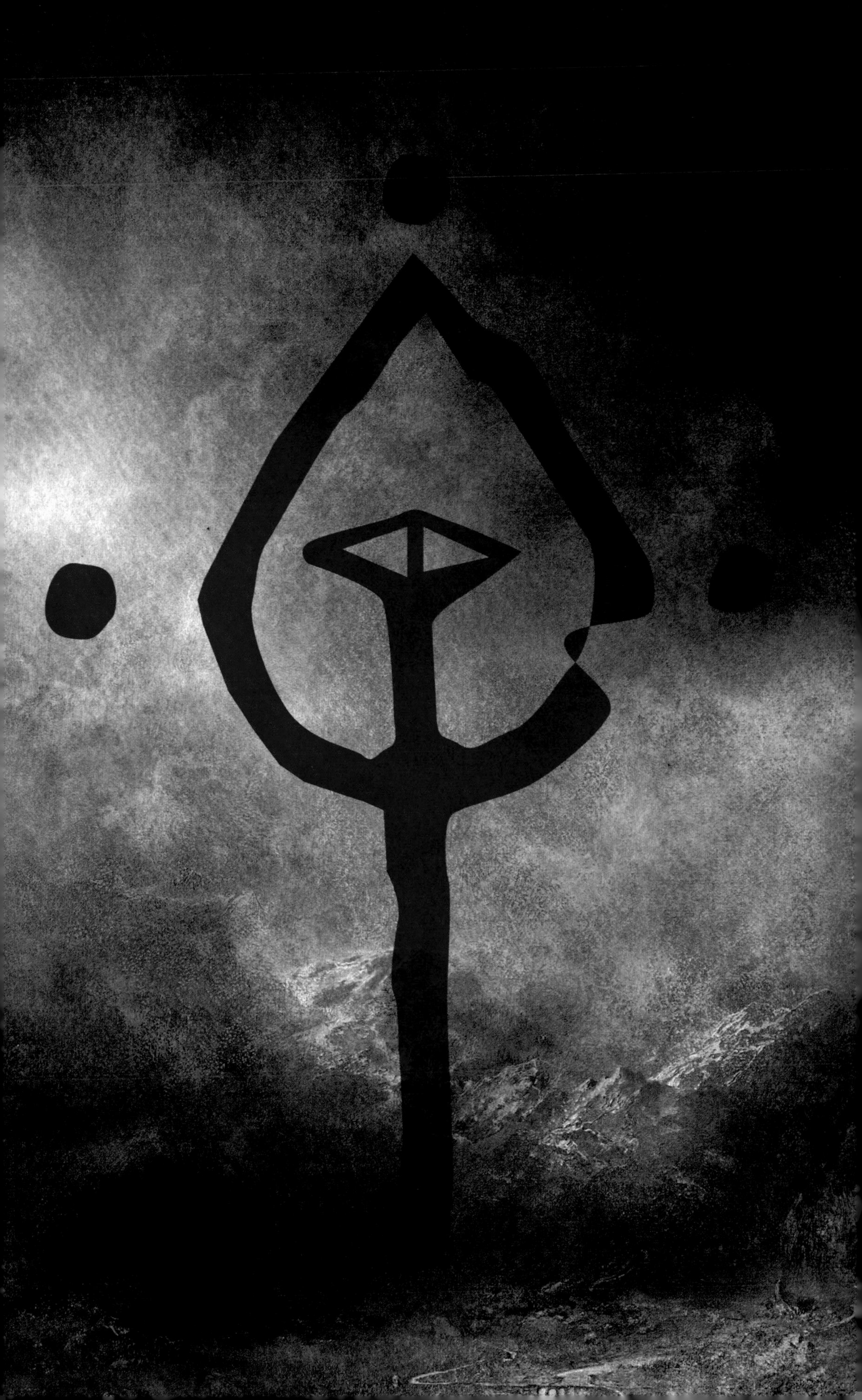

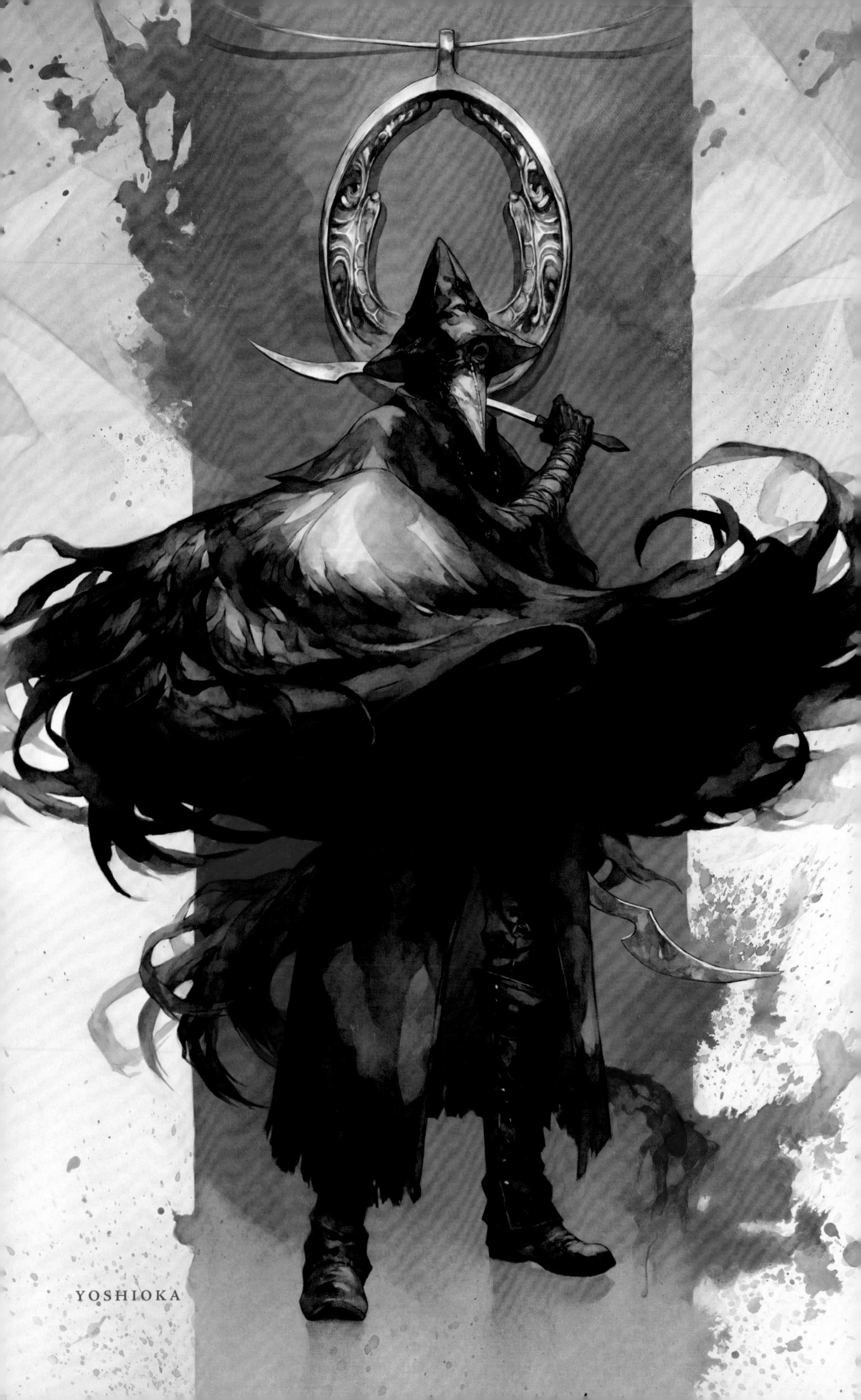

YOSHIOKA

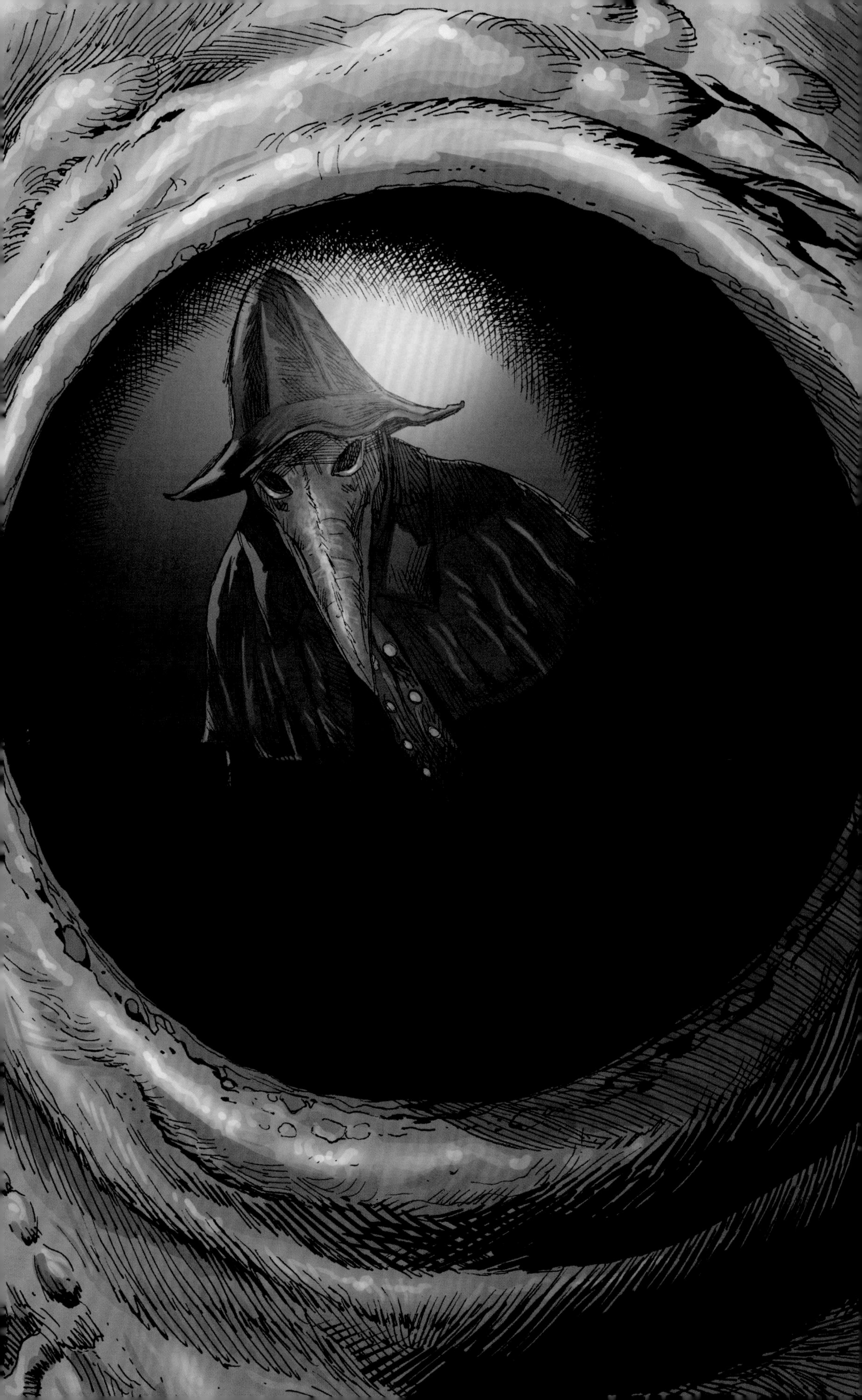

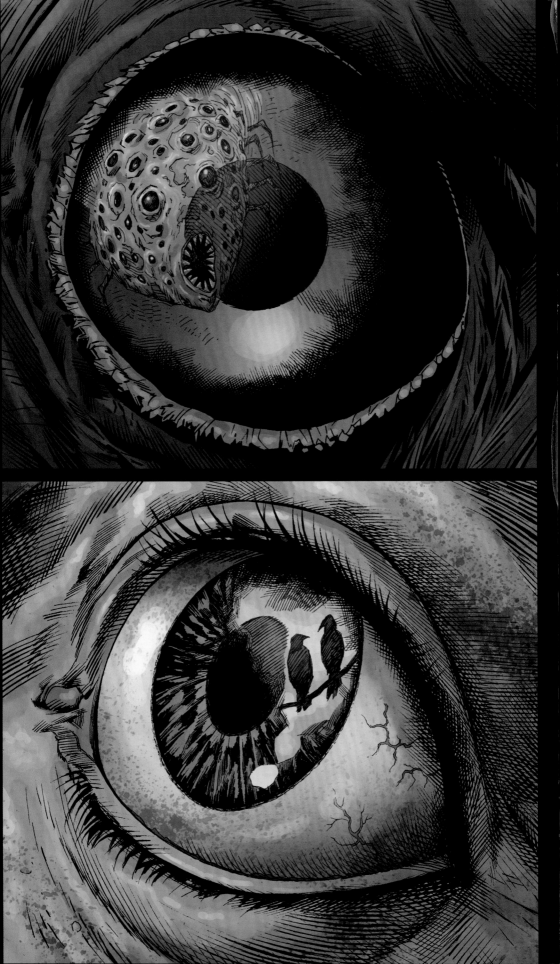

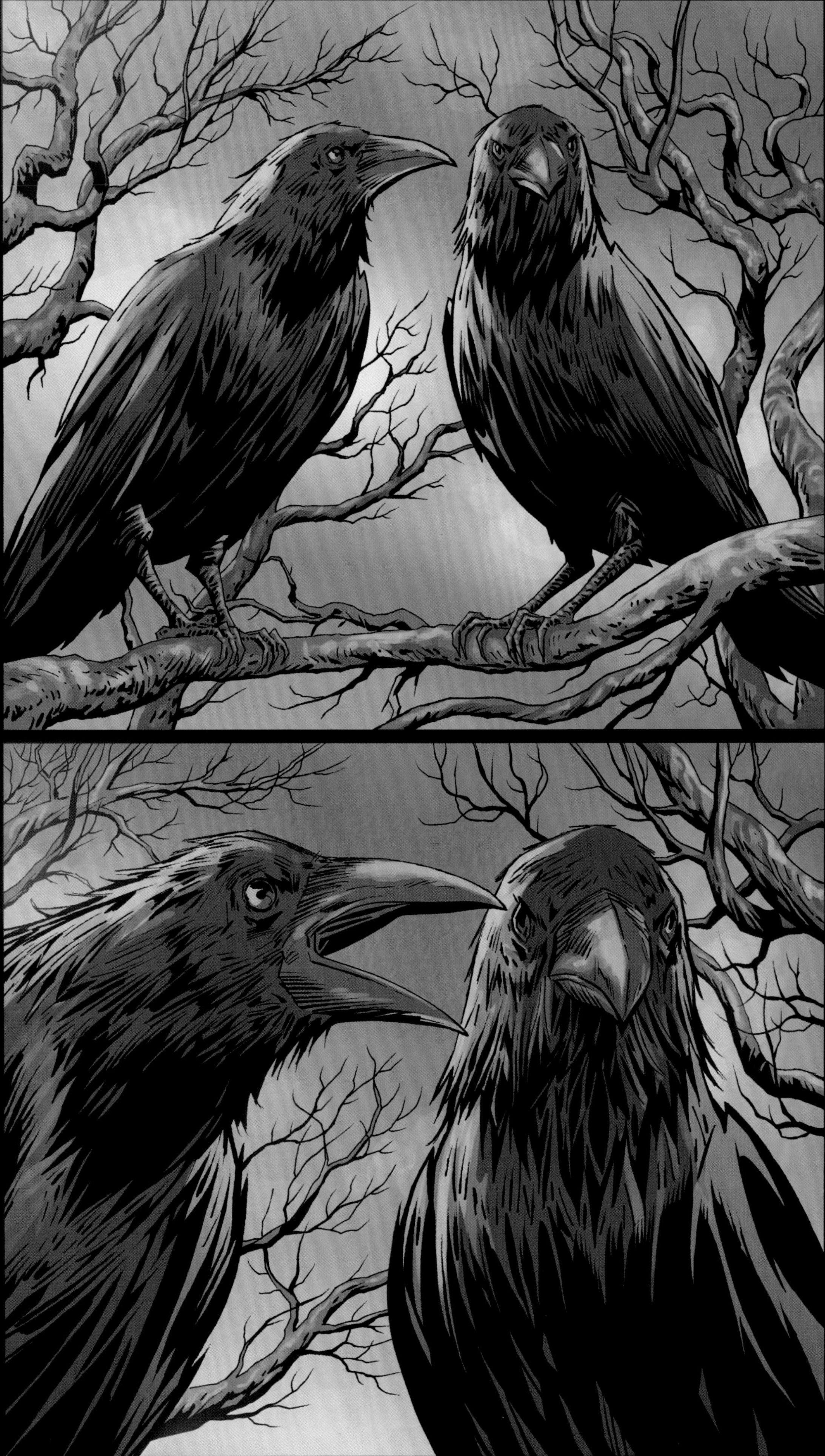

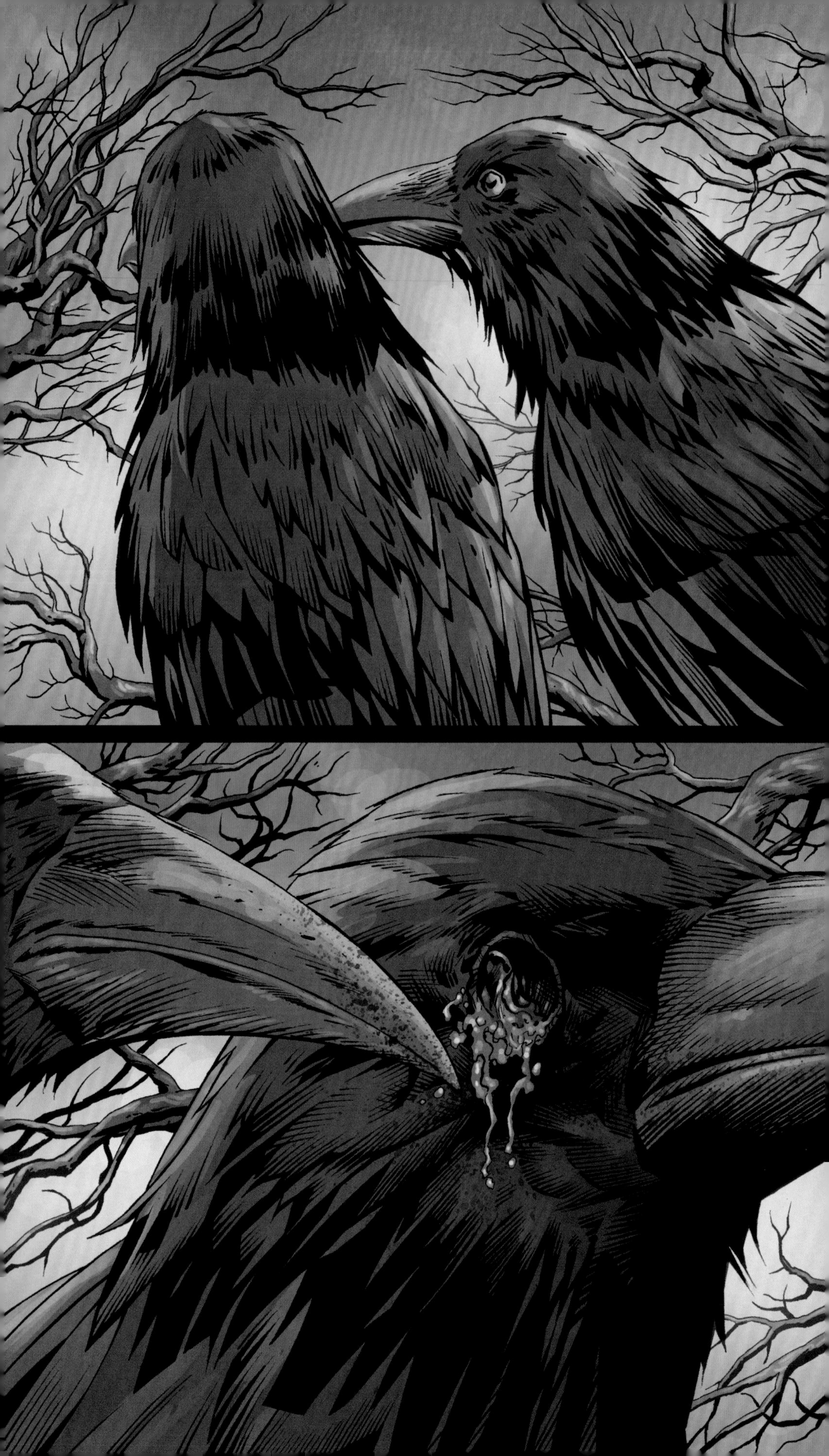

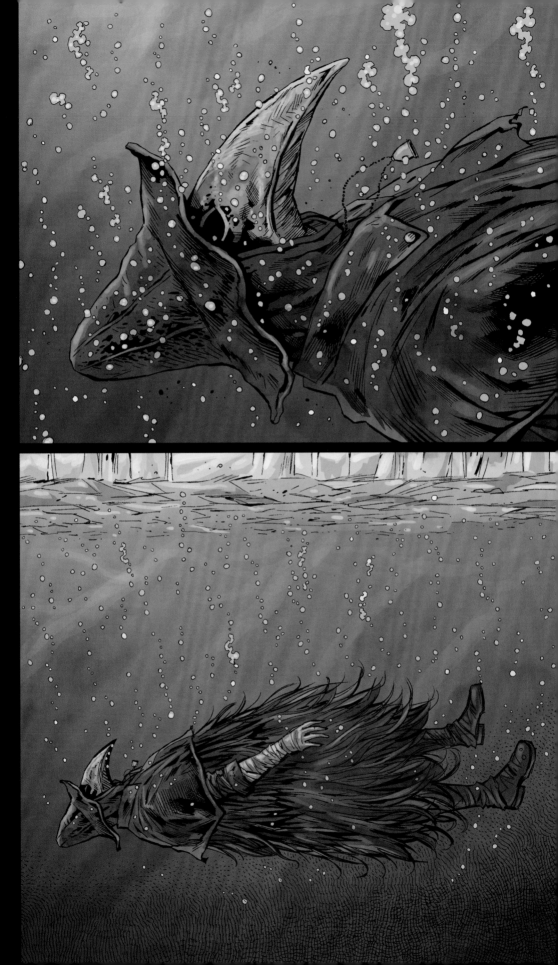

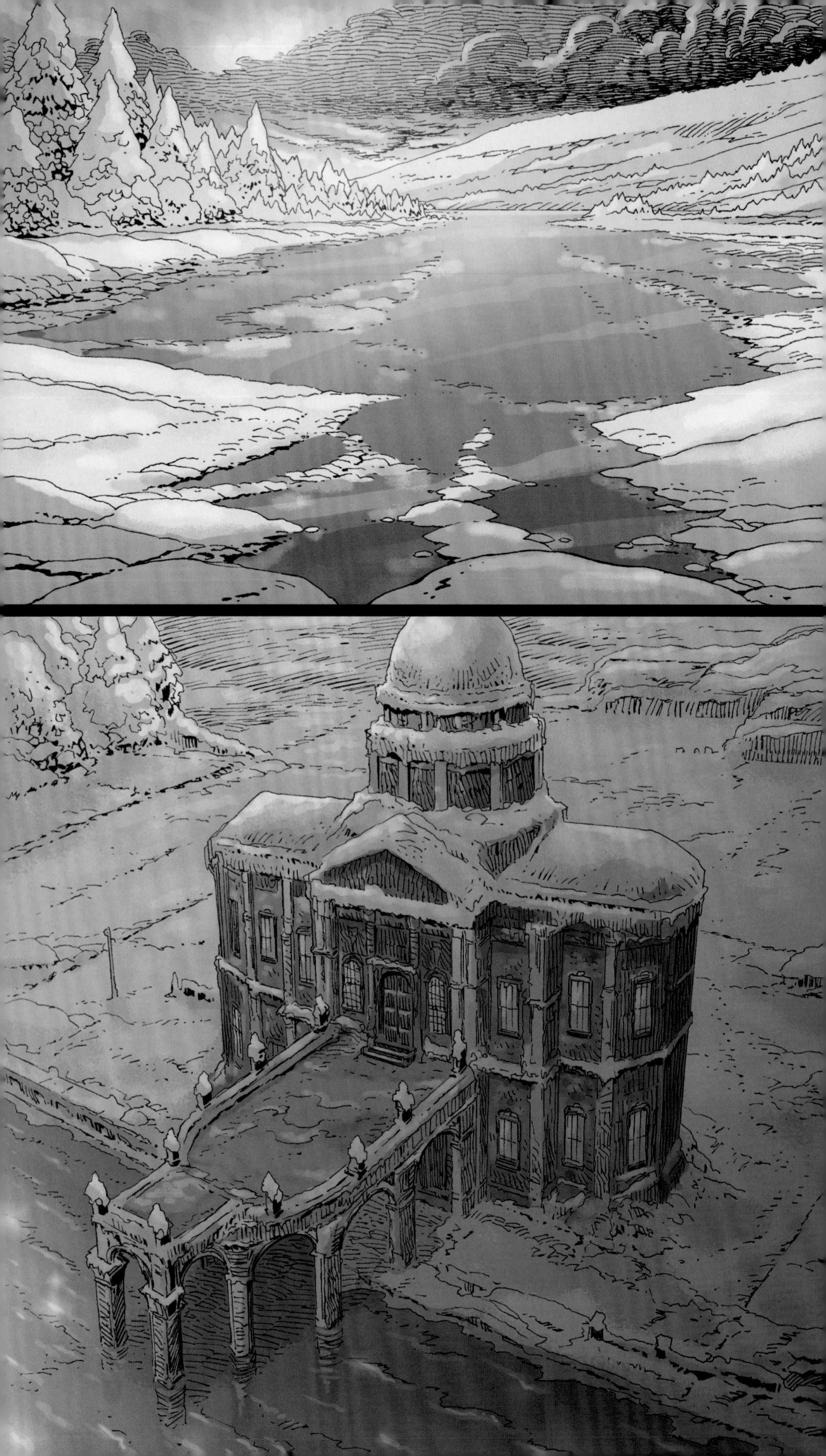

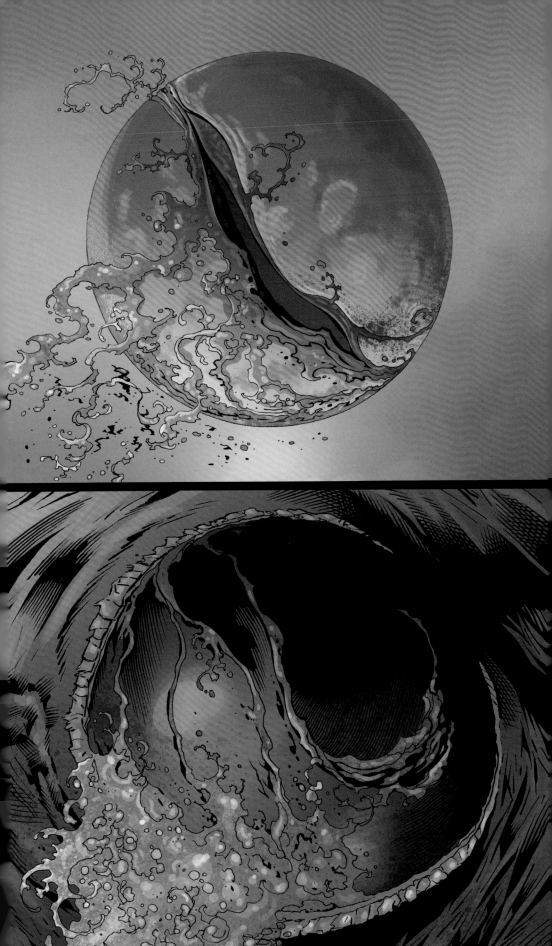

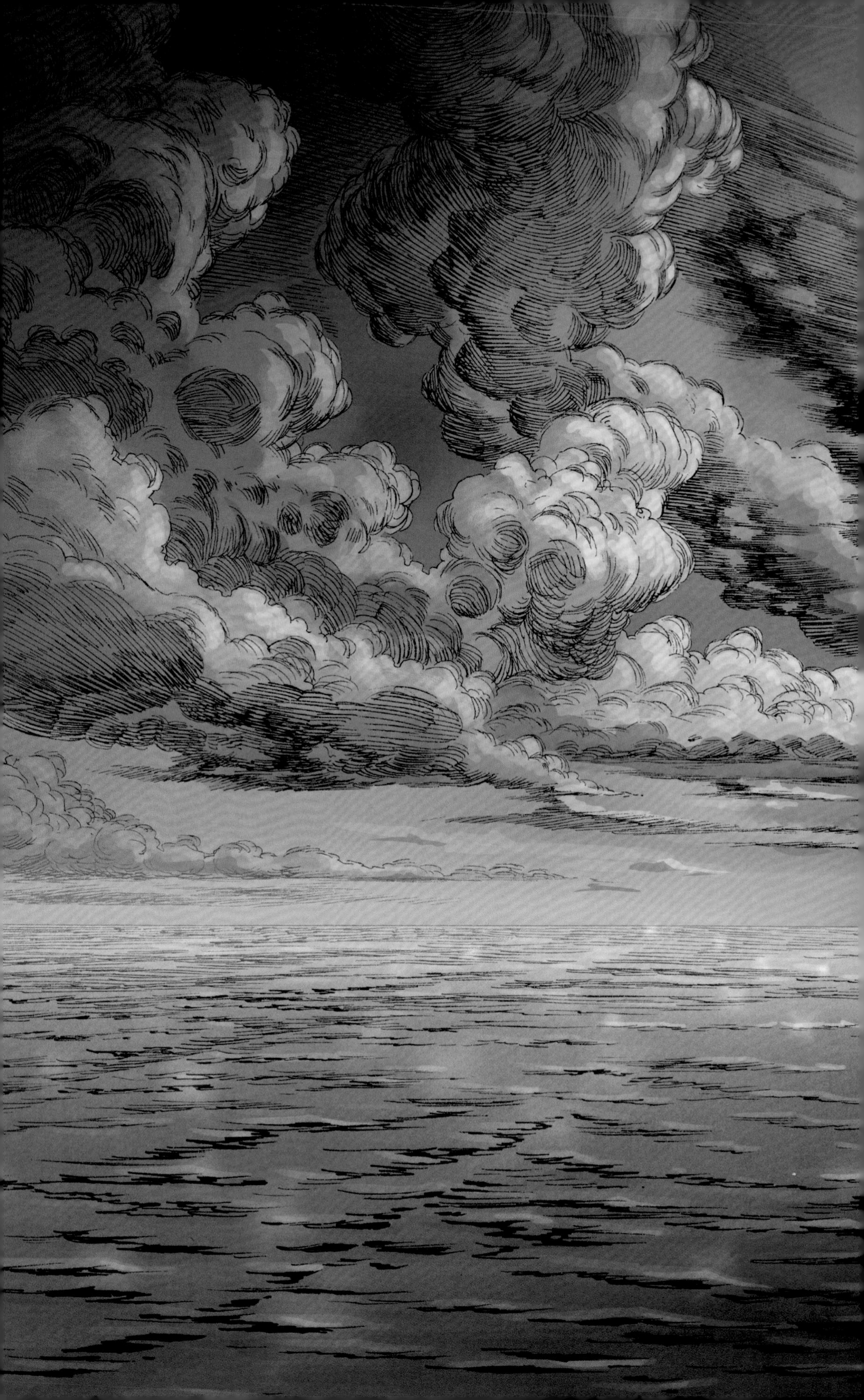

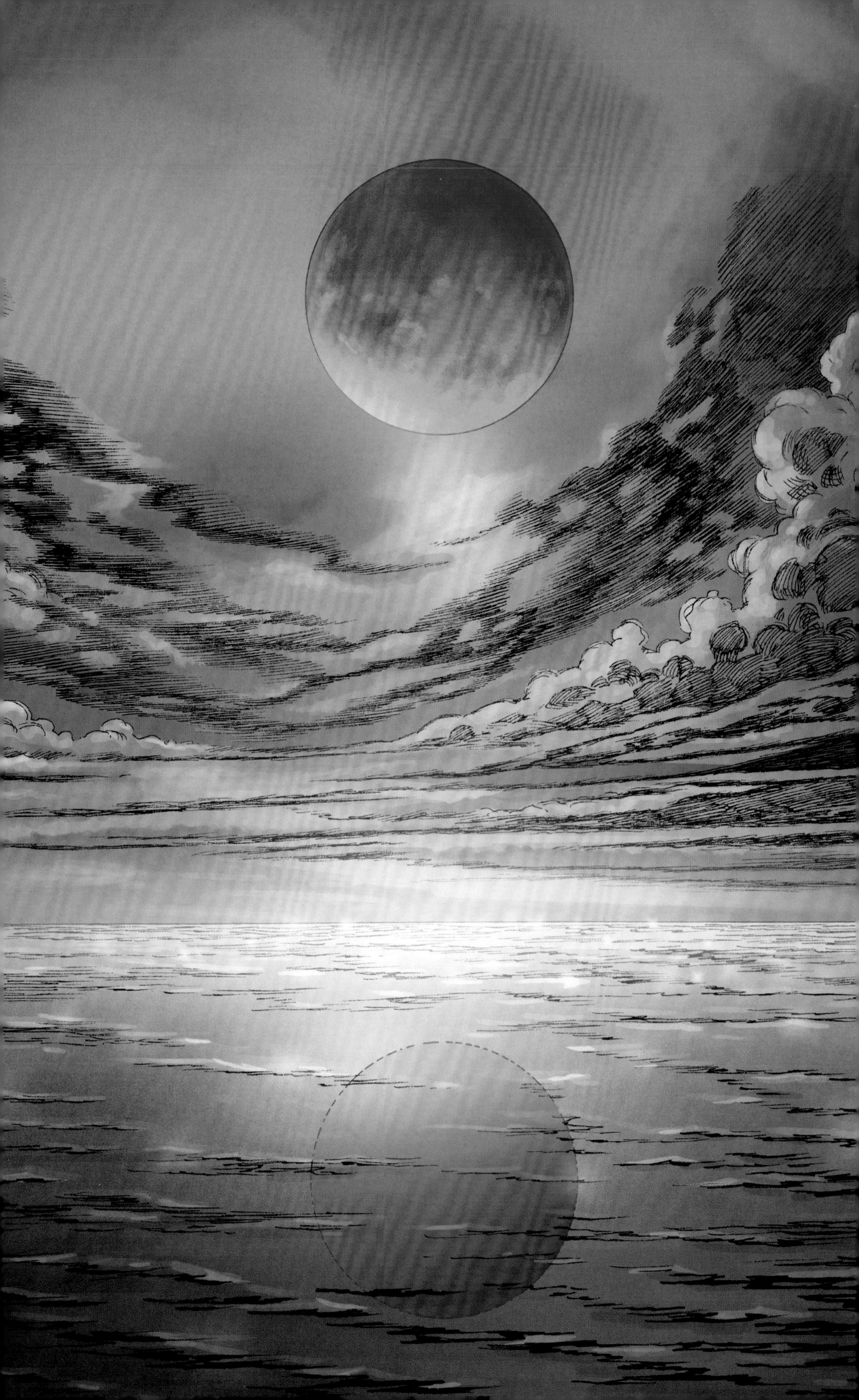

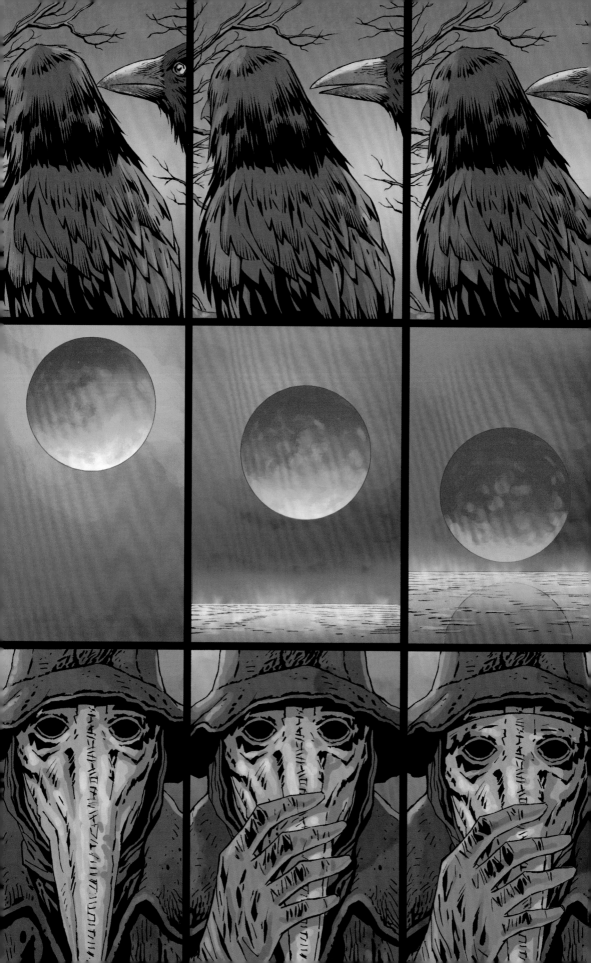

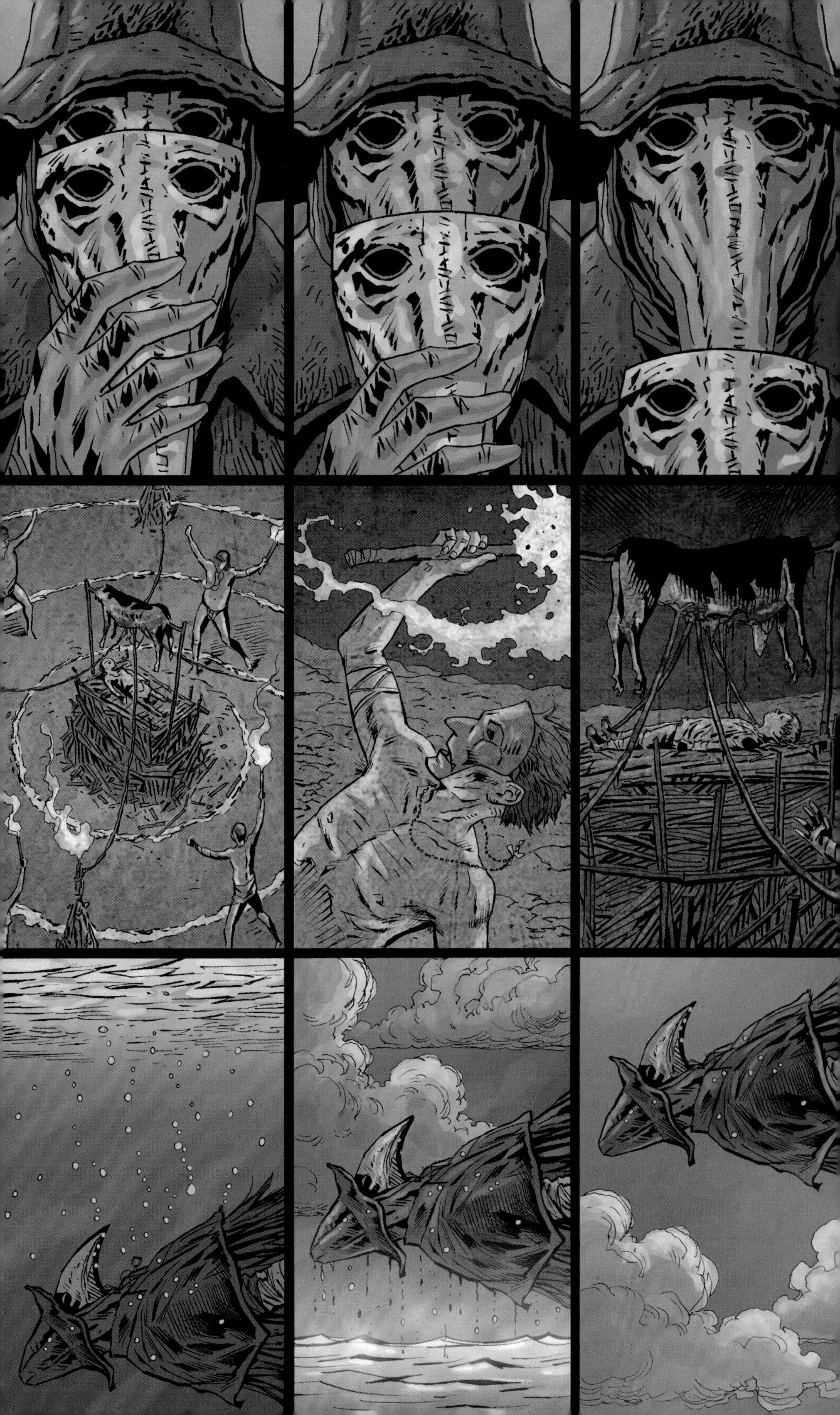

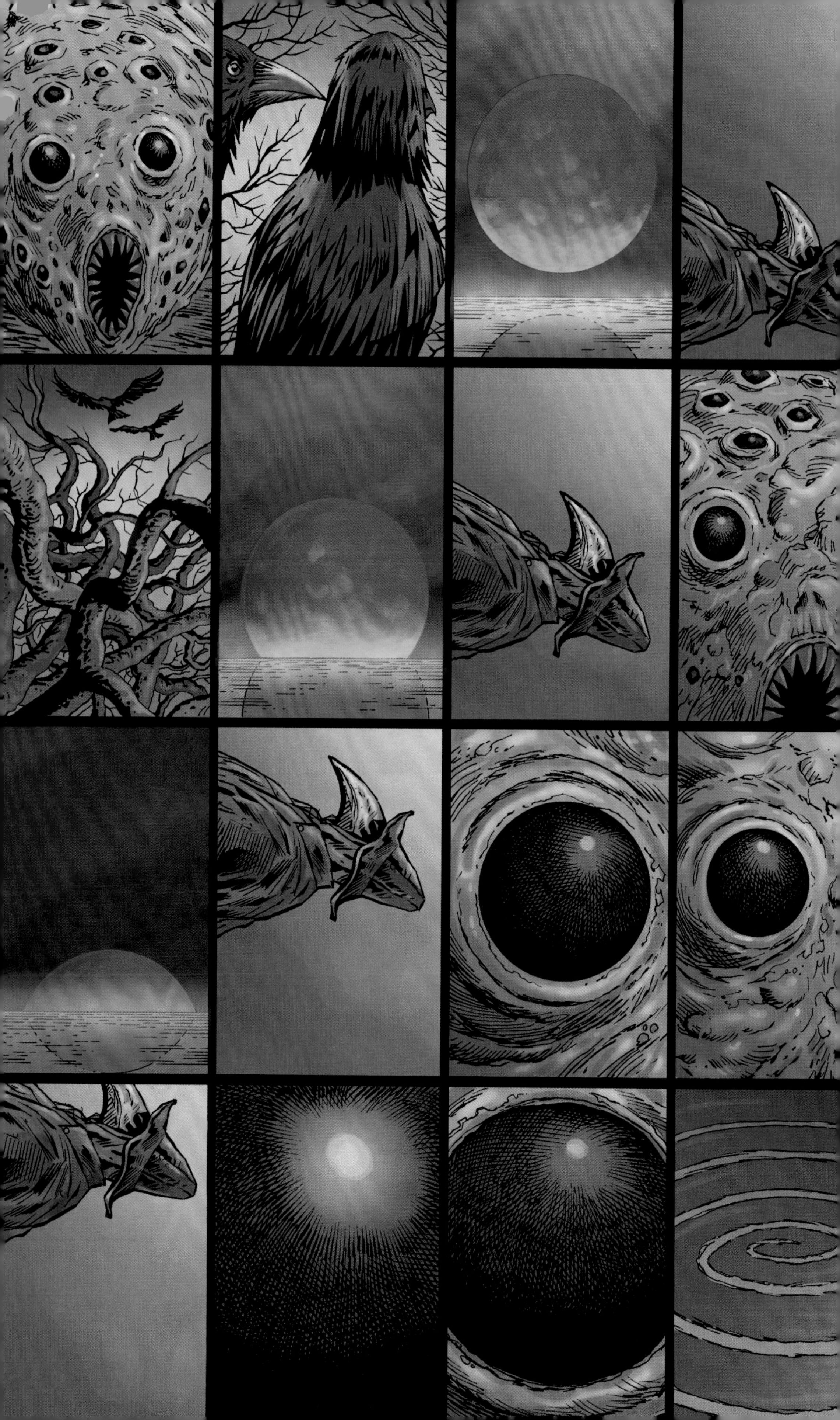

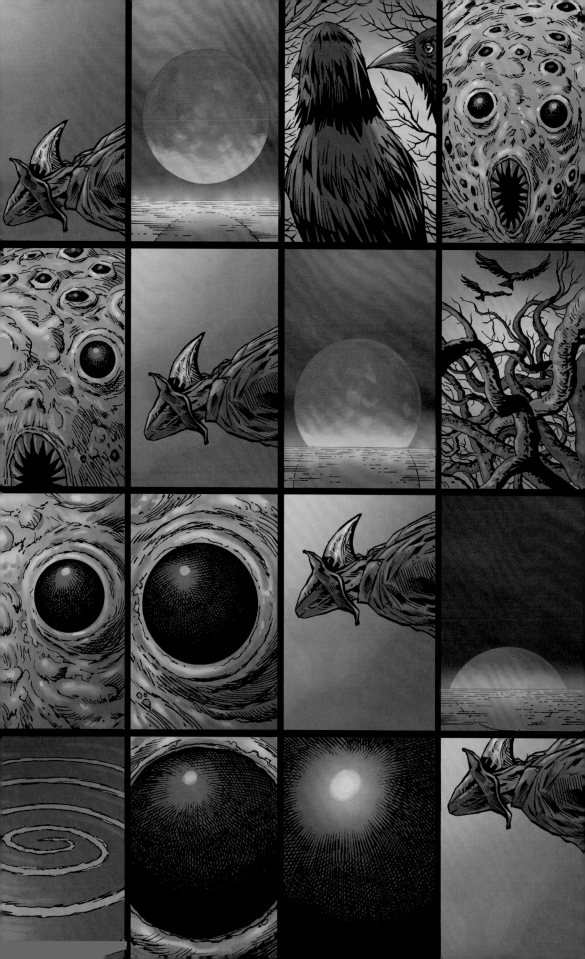

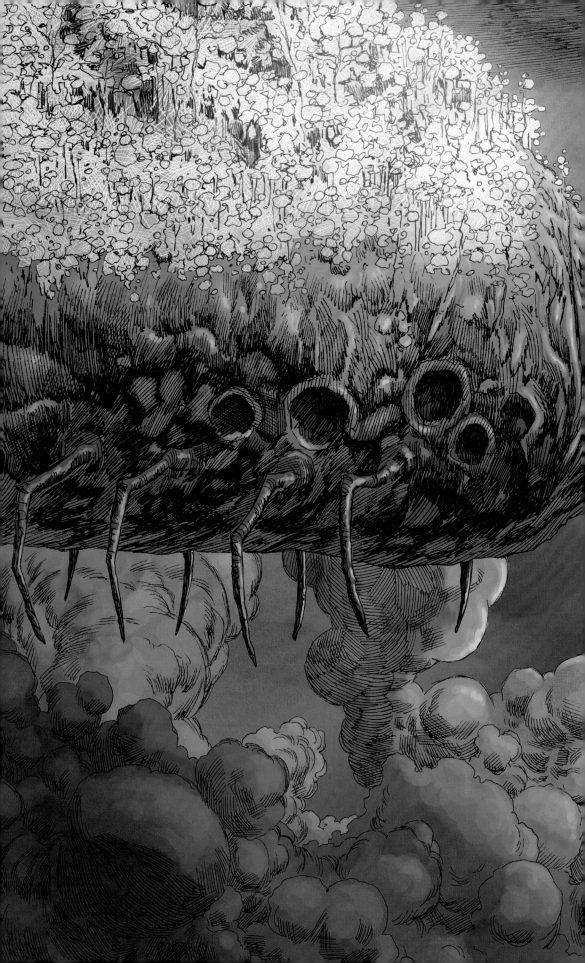

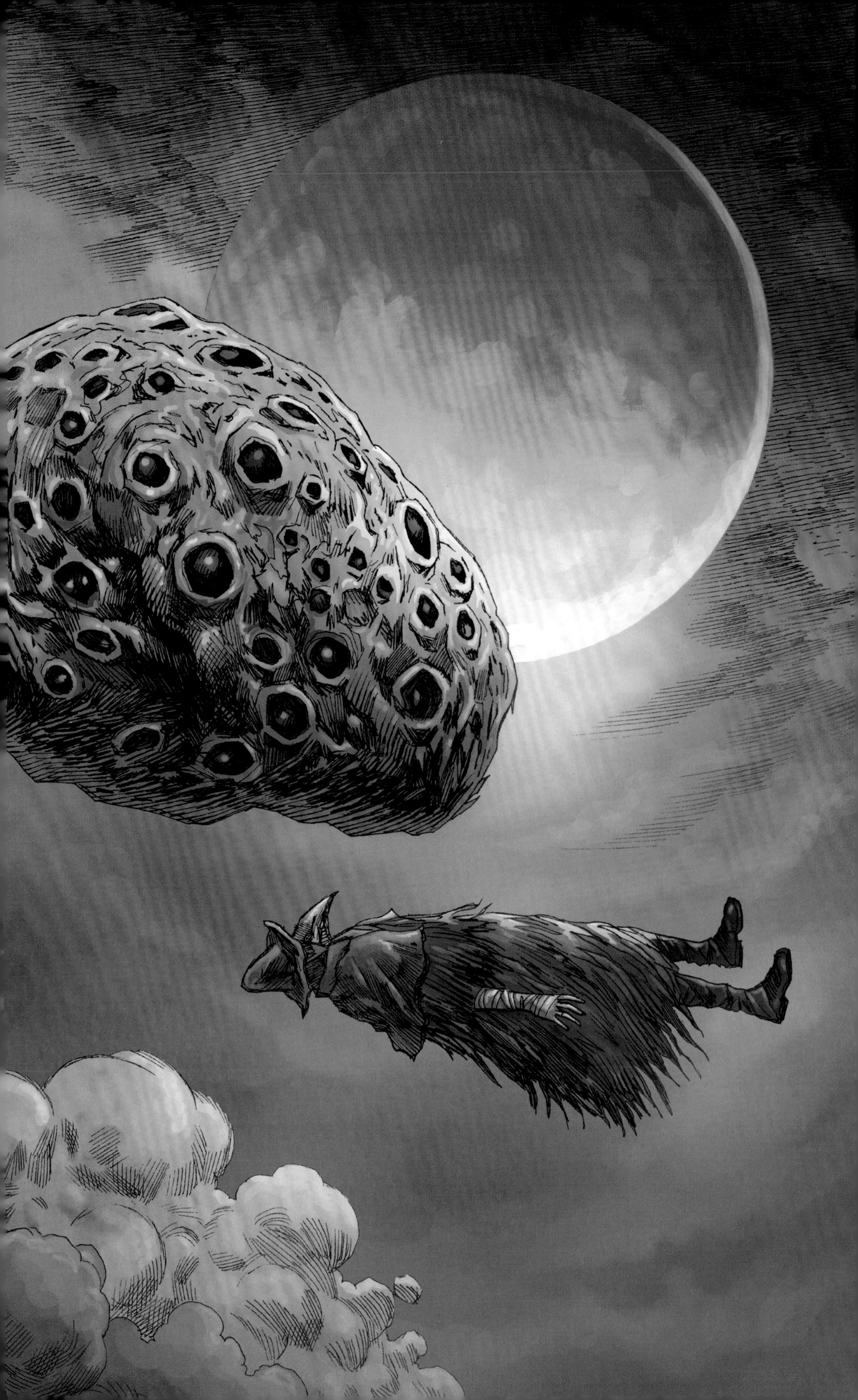

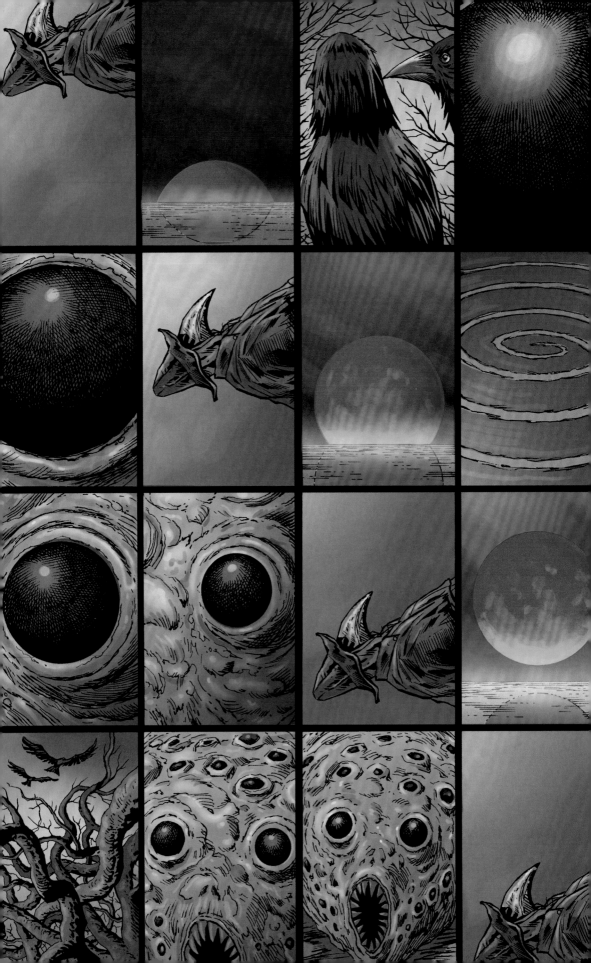

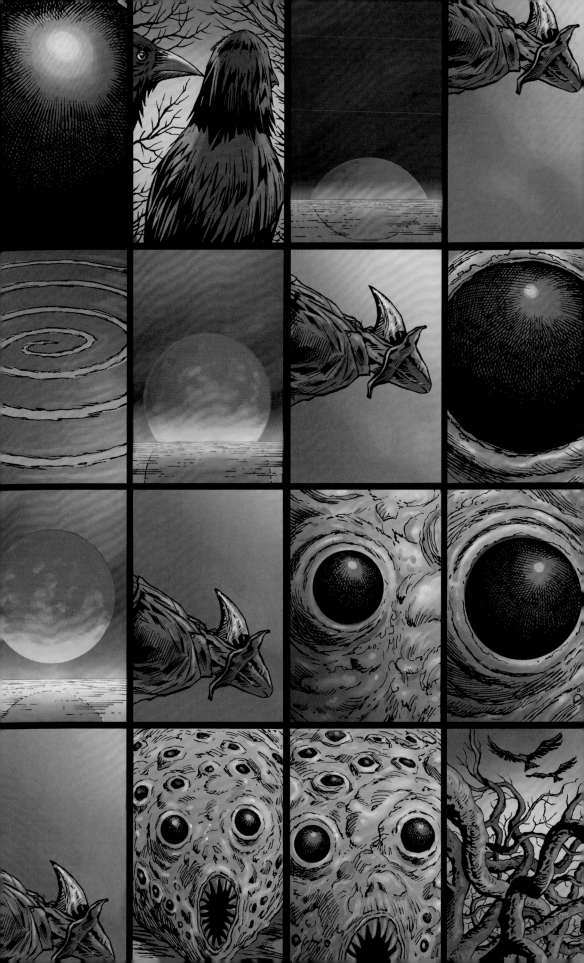

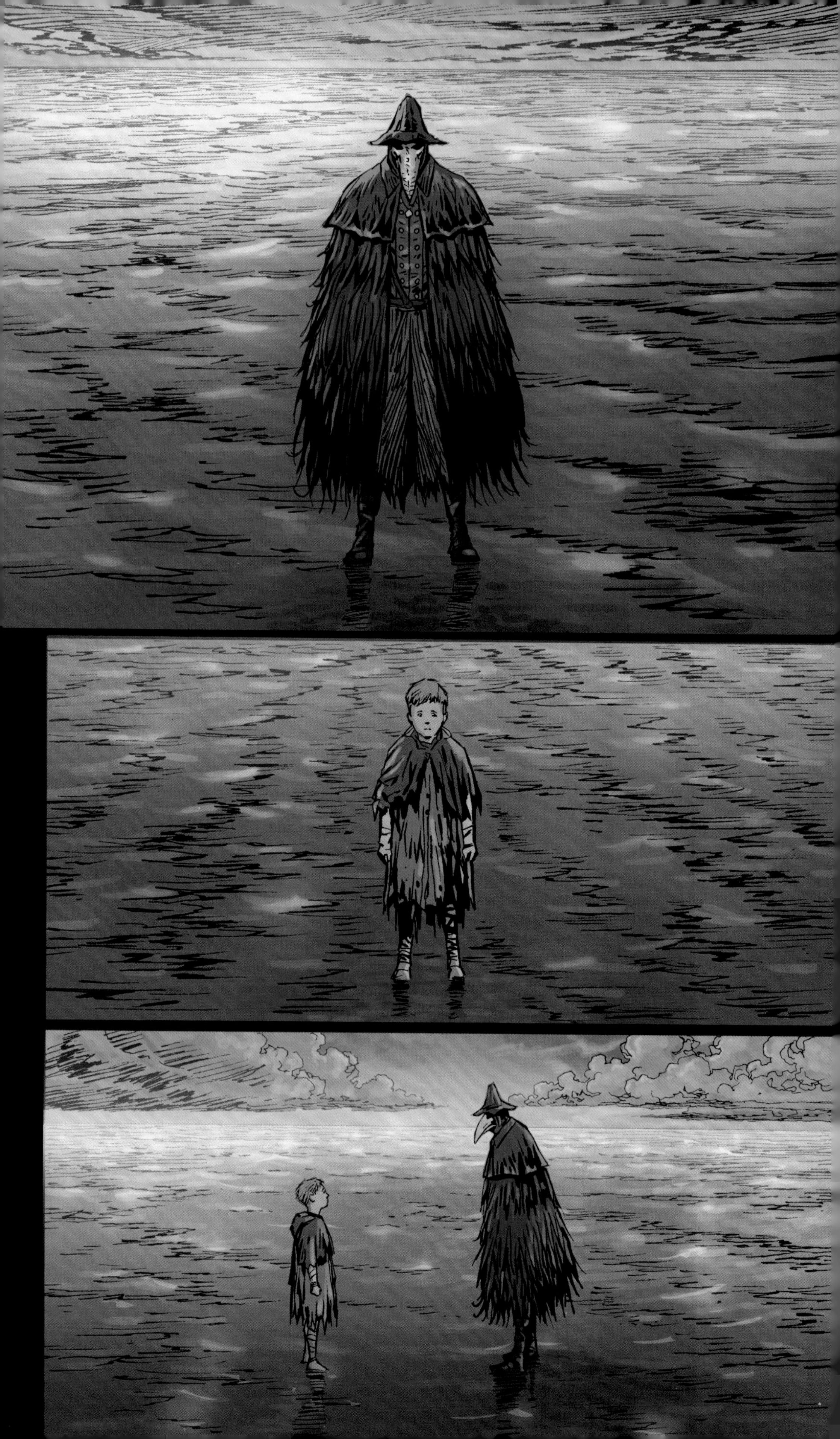

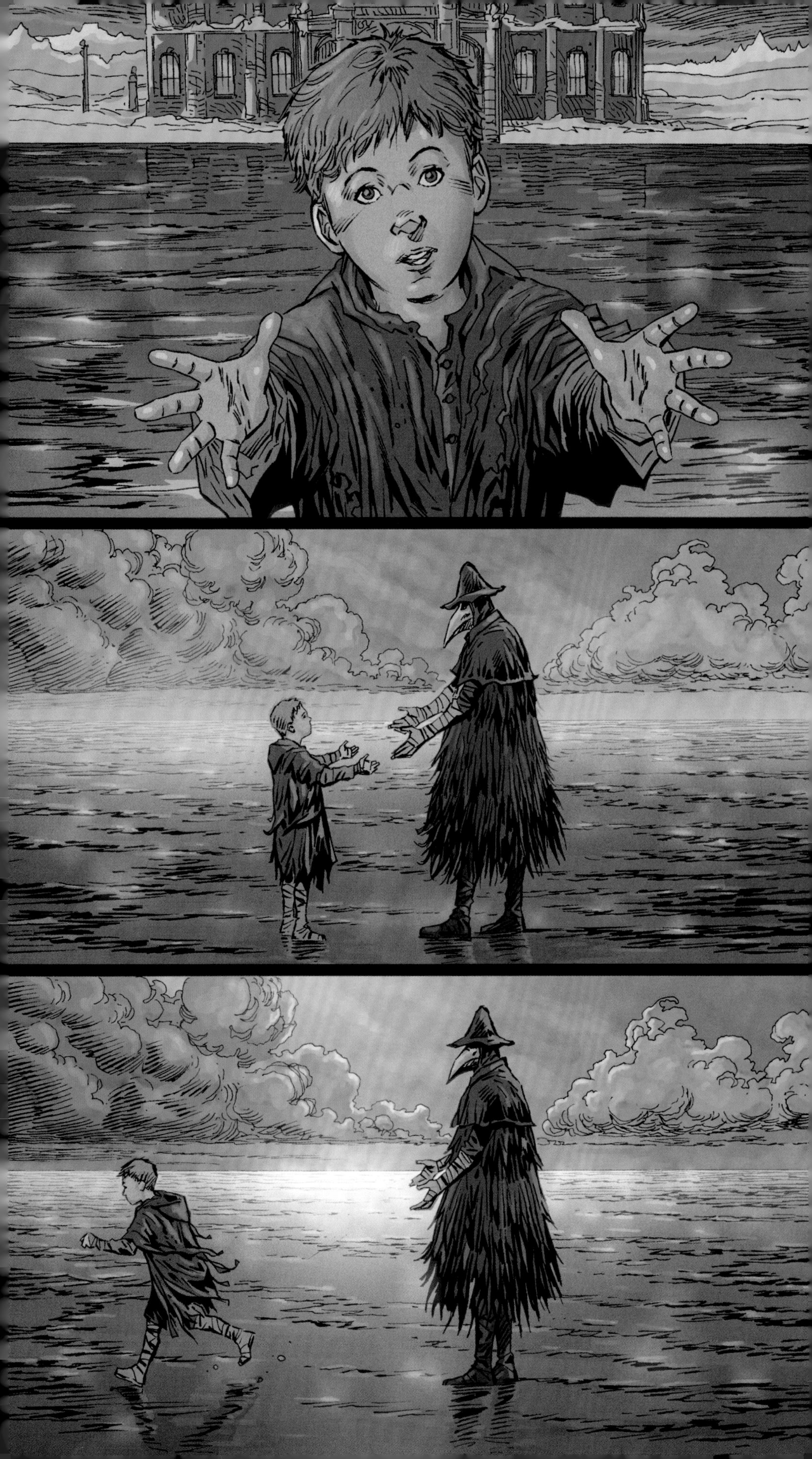

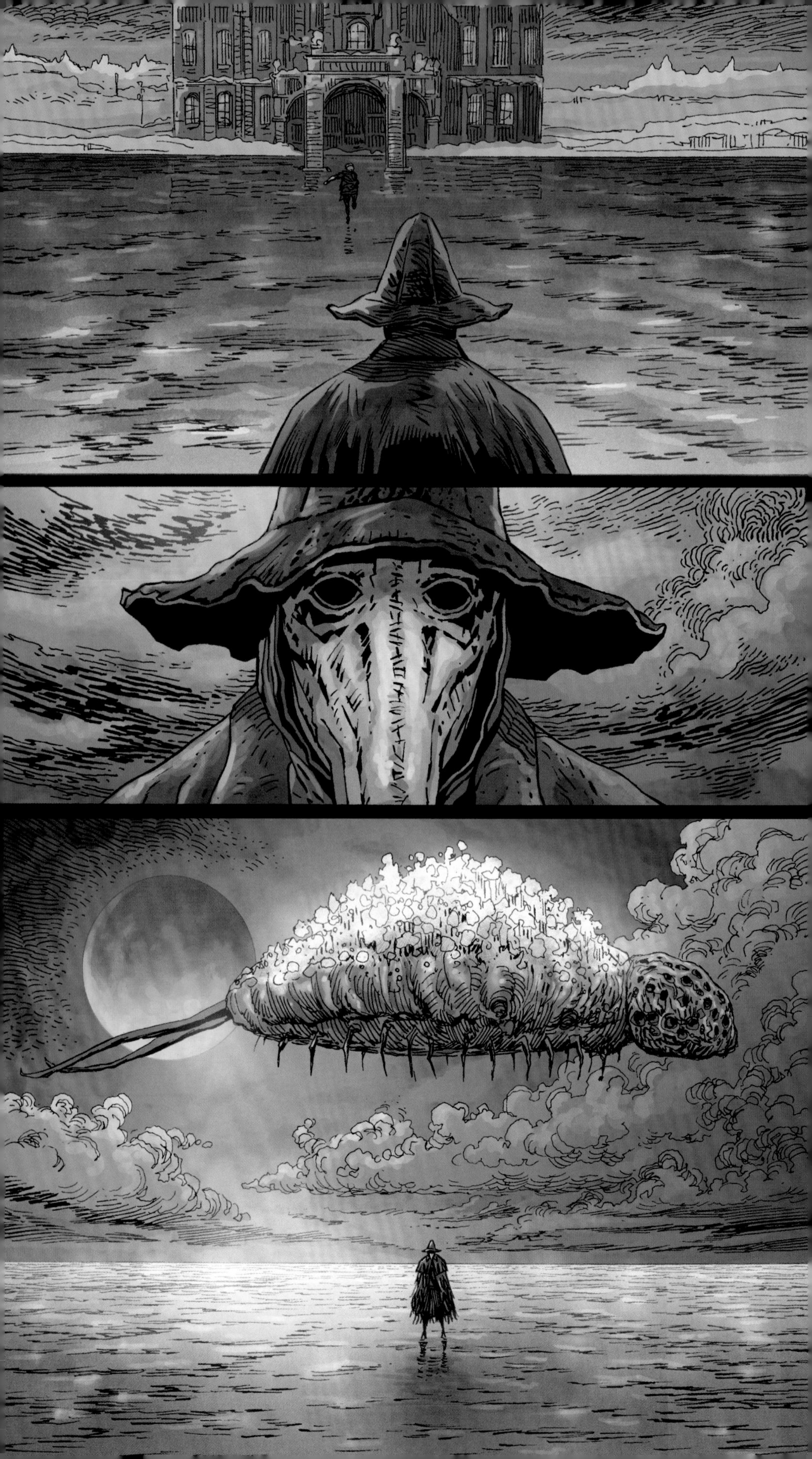

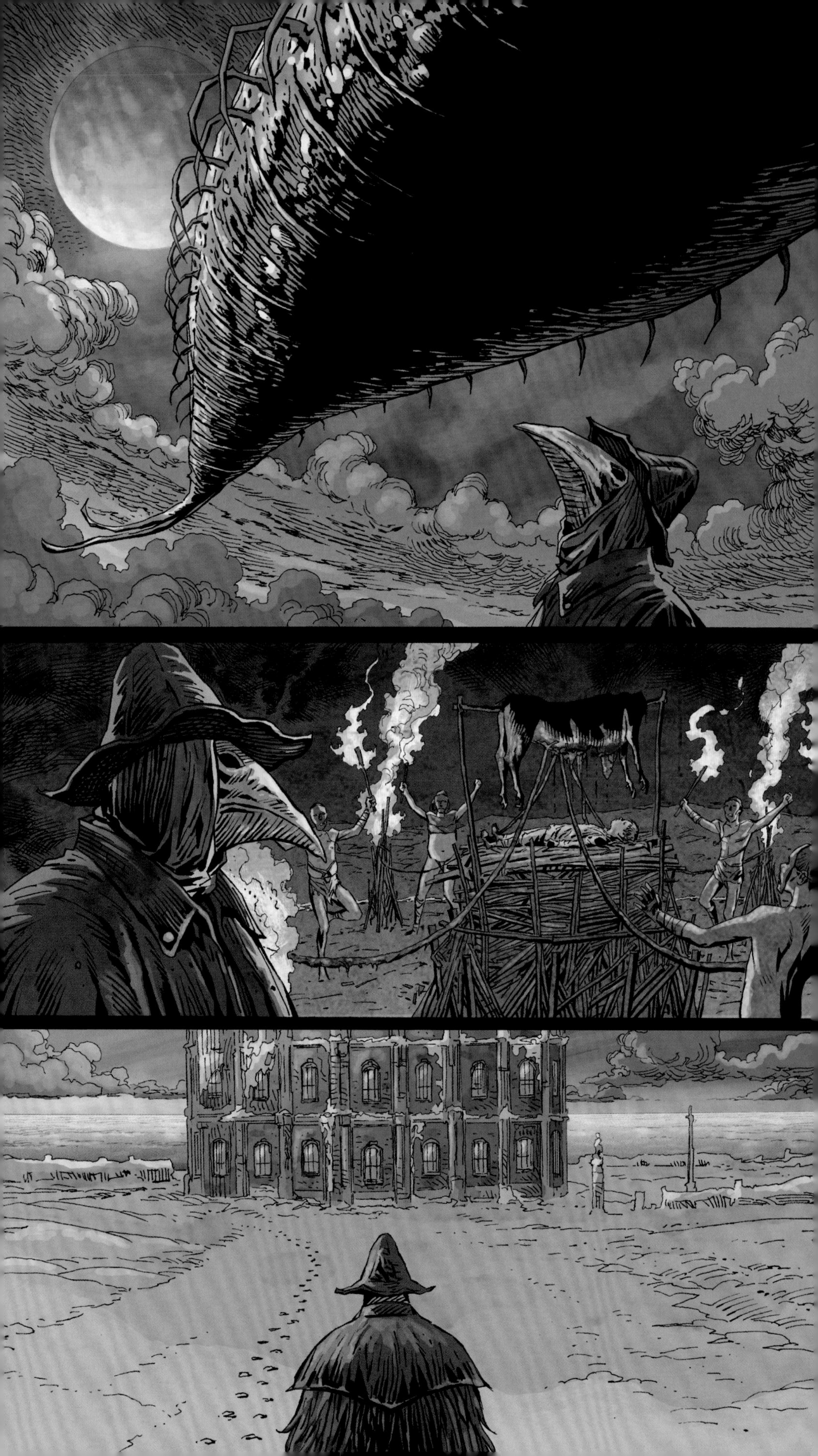

YOU ARE
GRANTED
EYES.

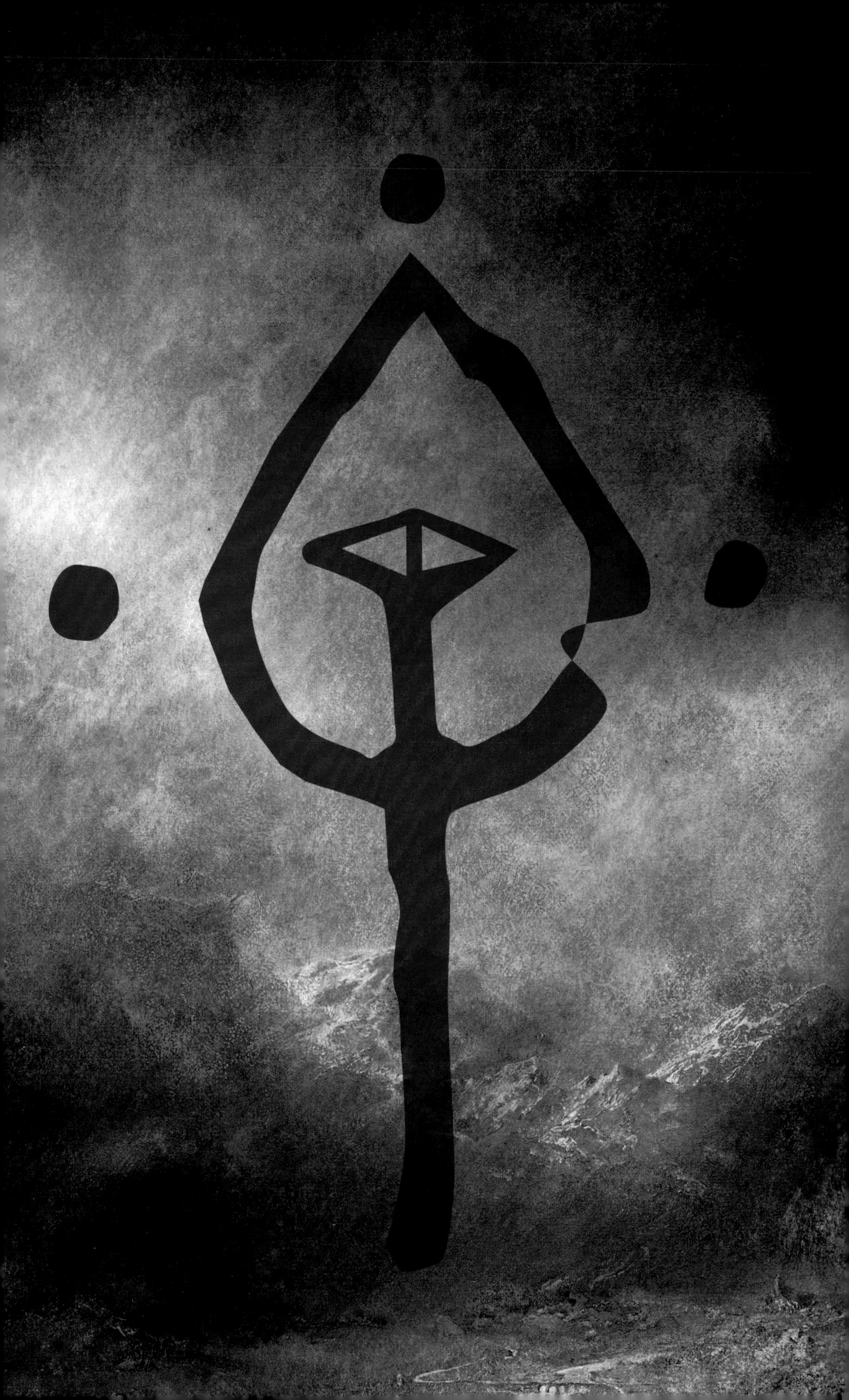

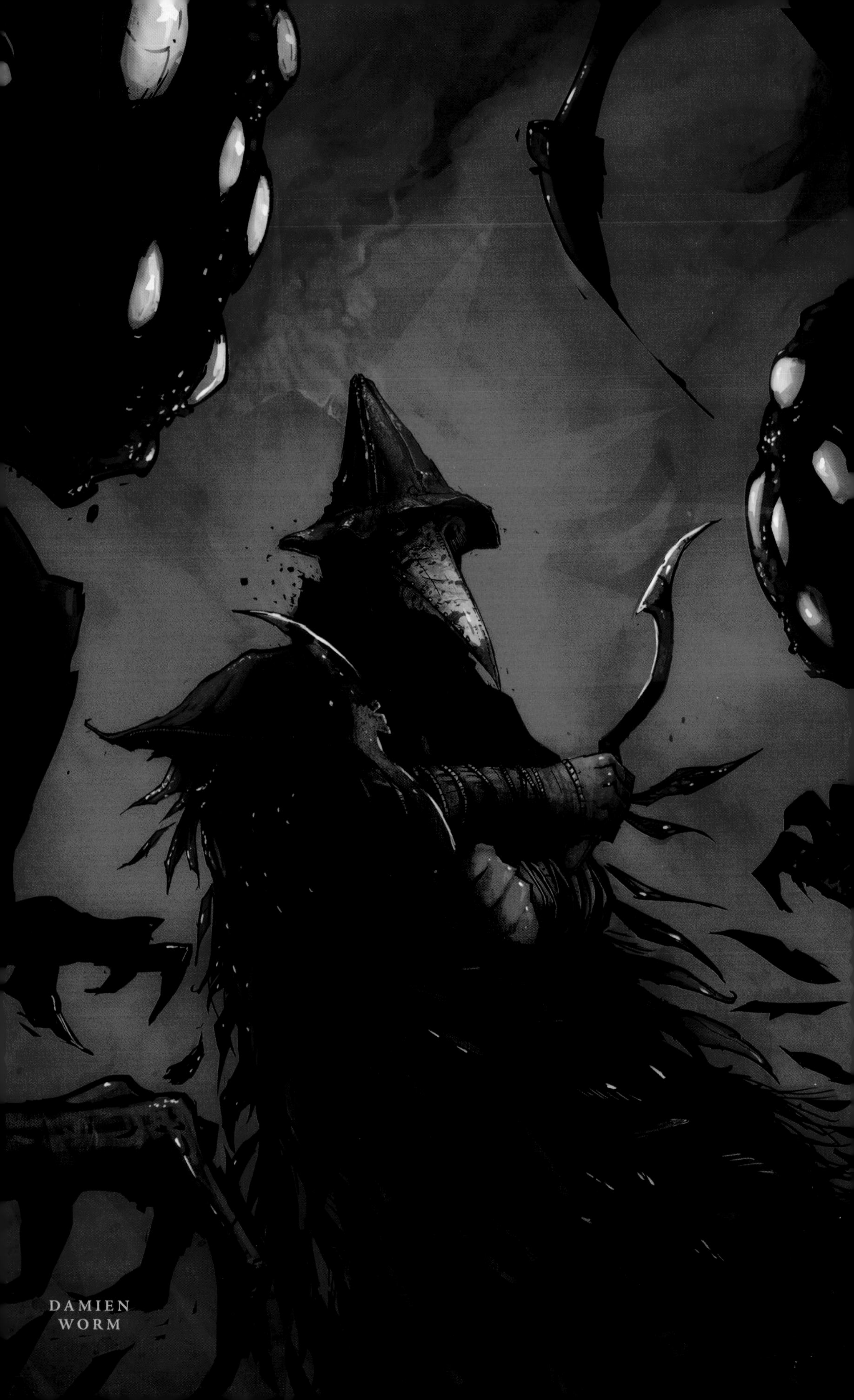
DAMIEN
WORM

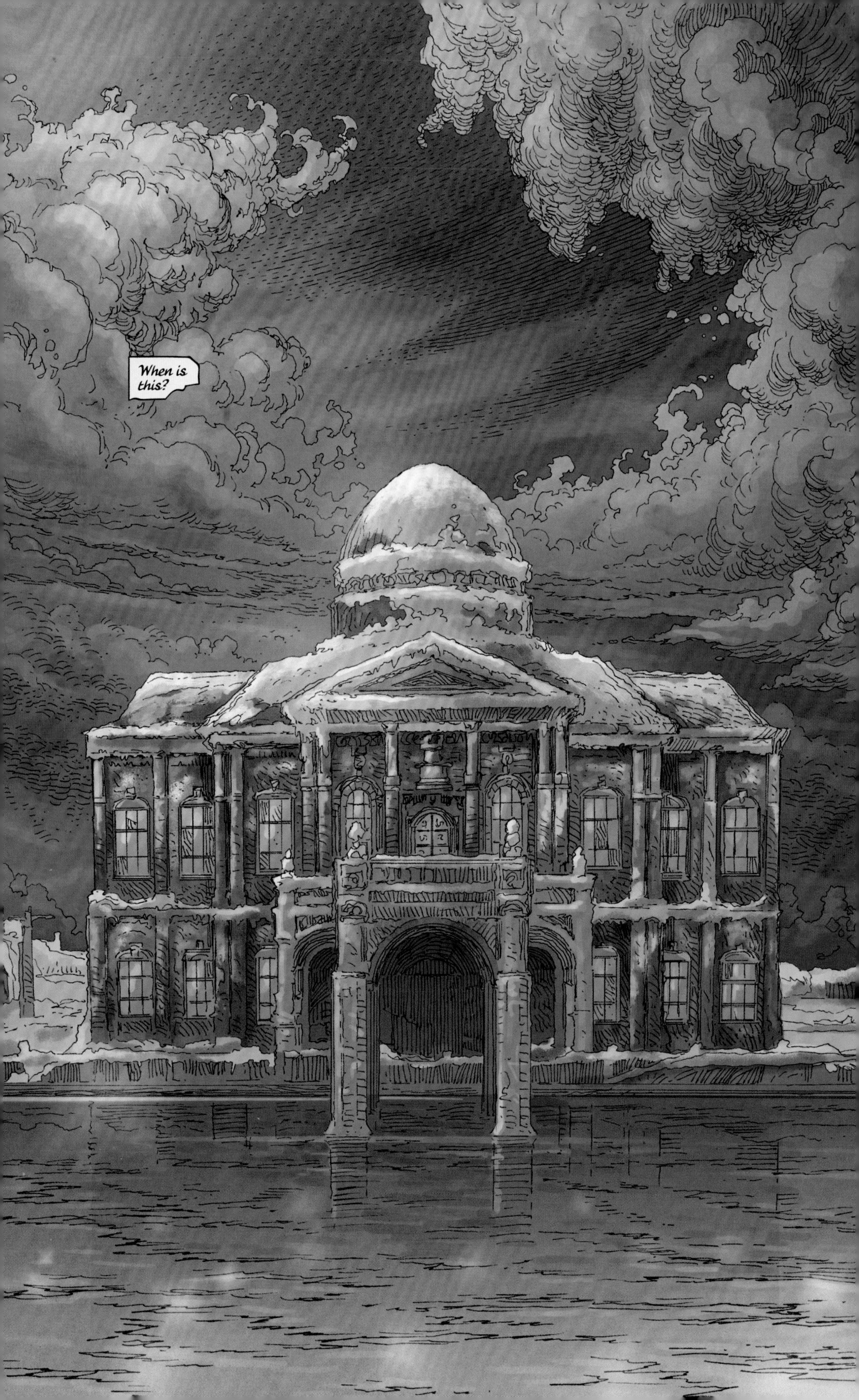
When is this?

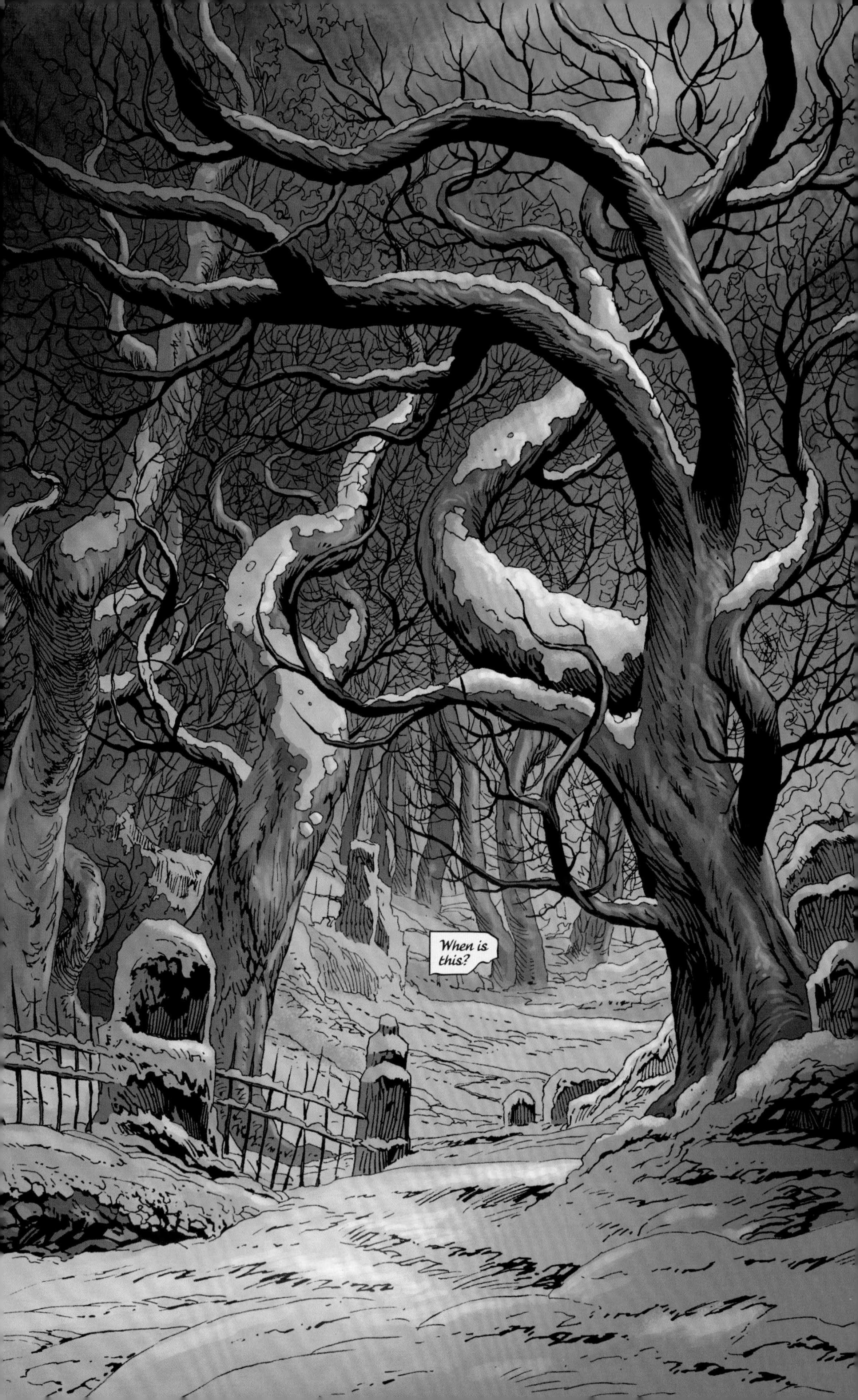
When is this?

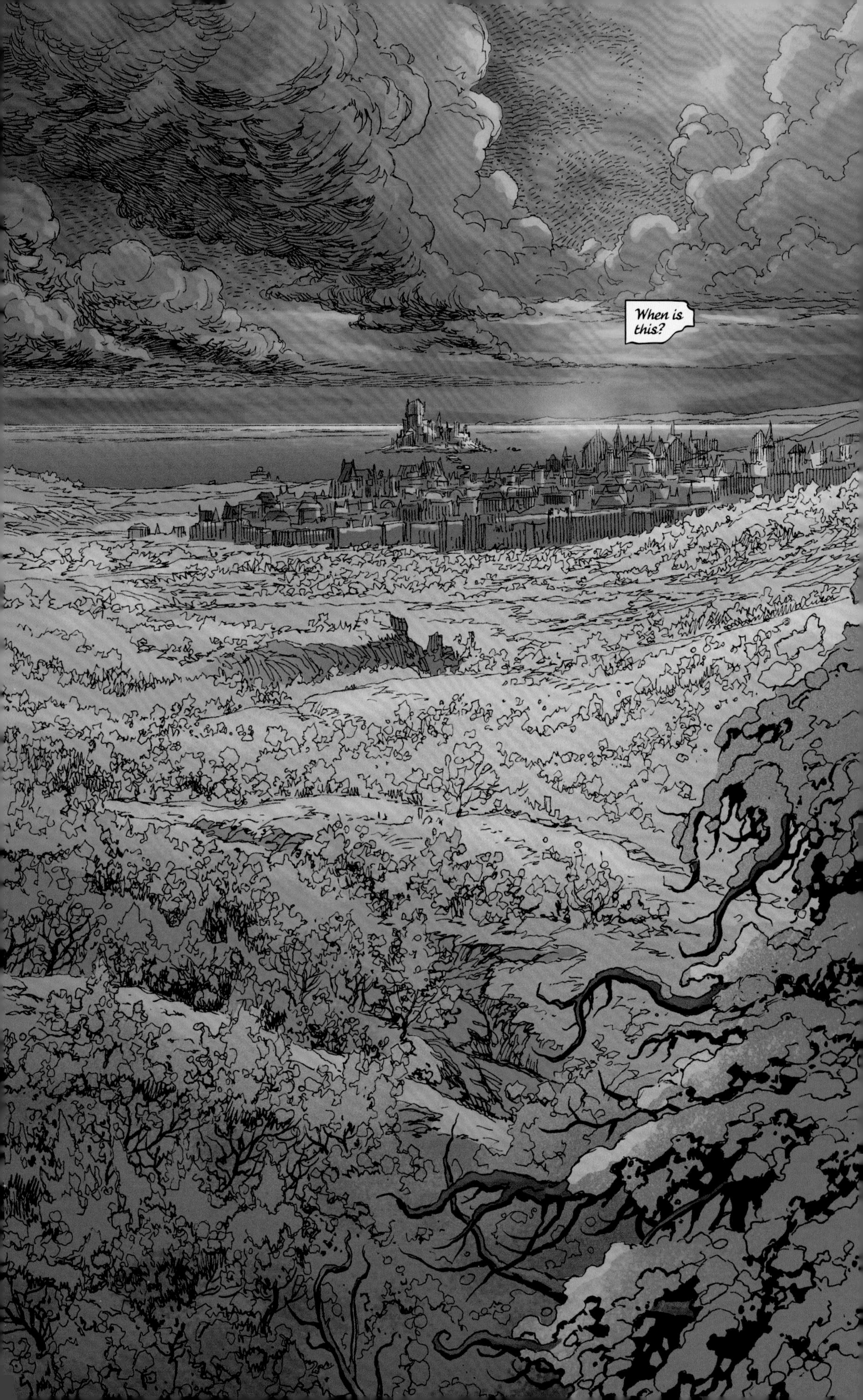
When is this?

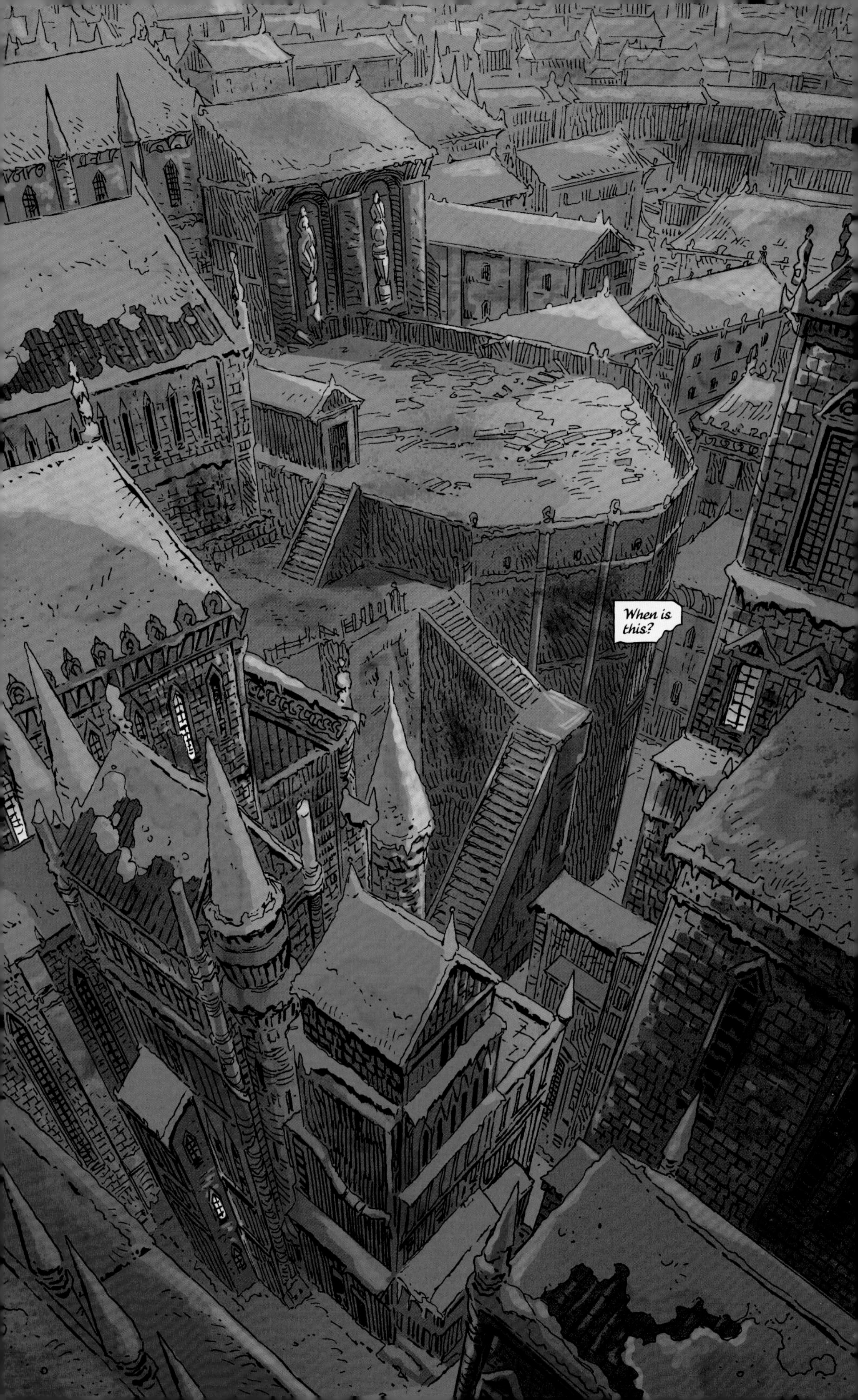
When is this?

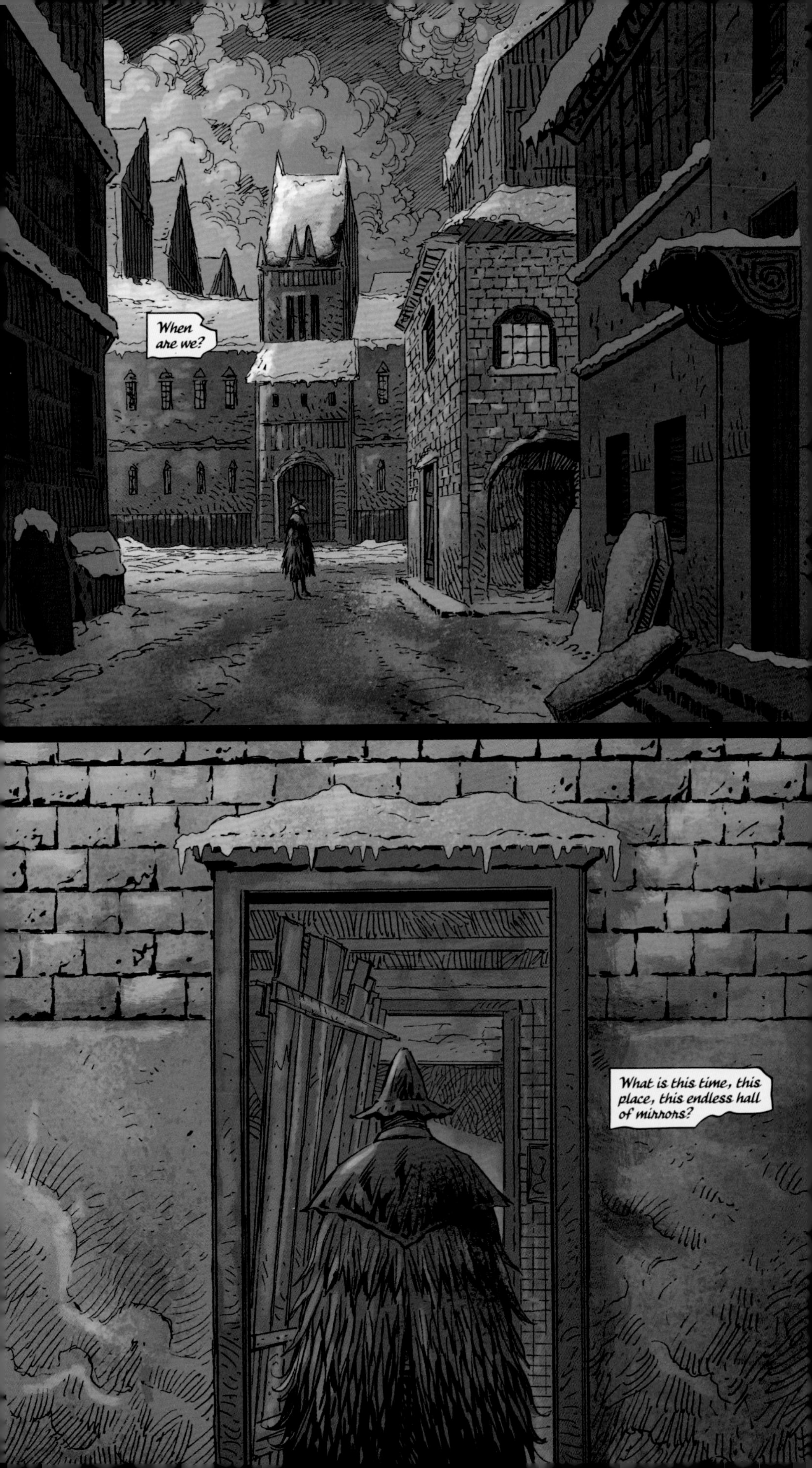
When are we?
What is this time, this place, this endless hall of mirrors?

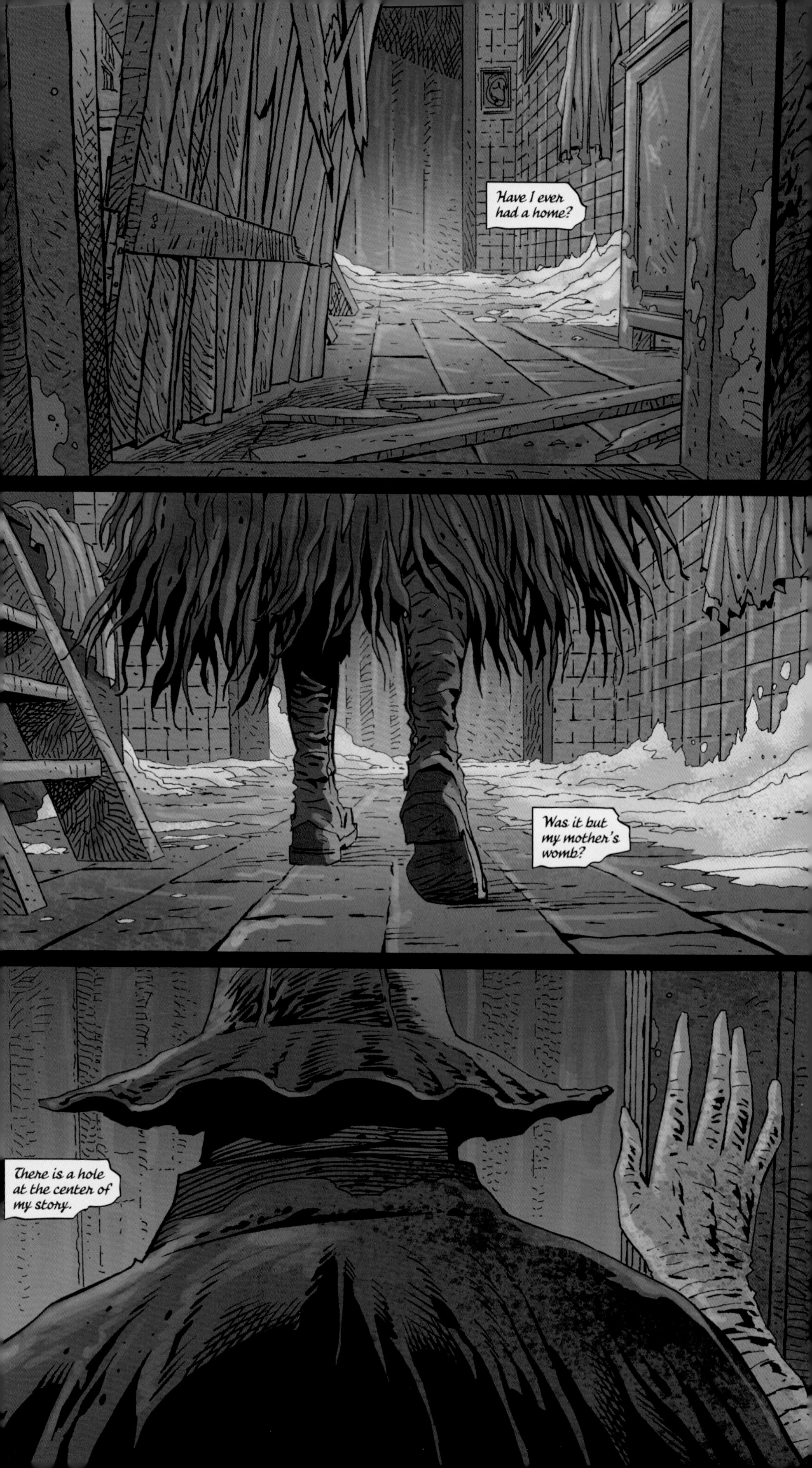
Have I ever had a home?
Was it but my mother's womb?
There is a hole at the center of my story.

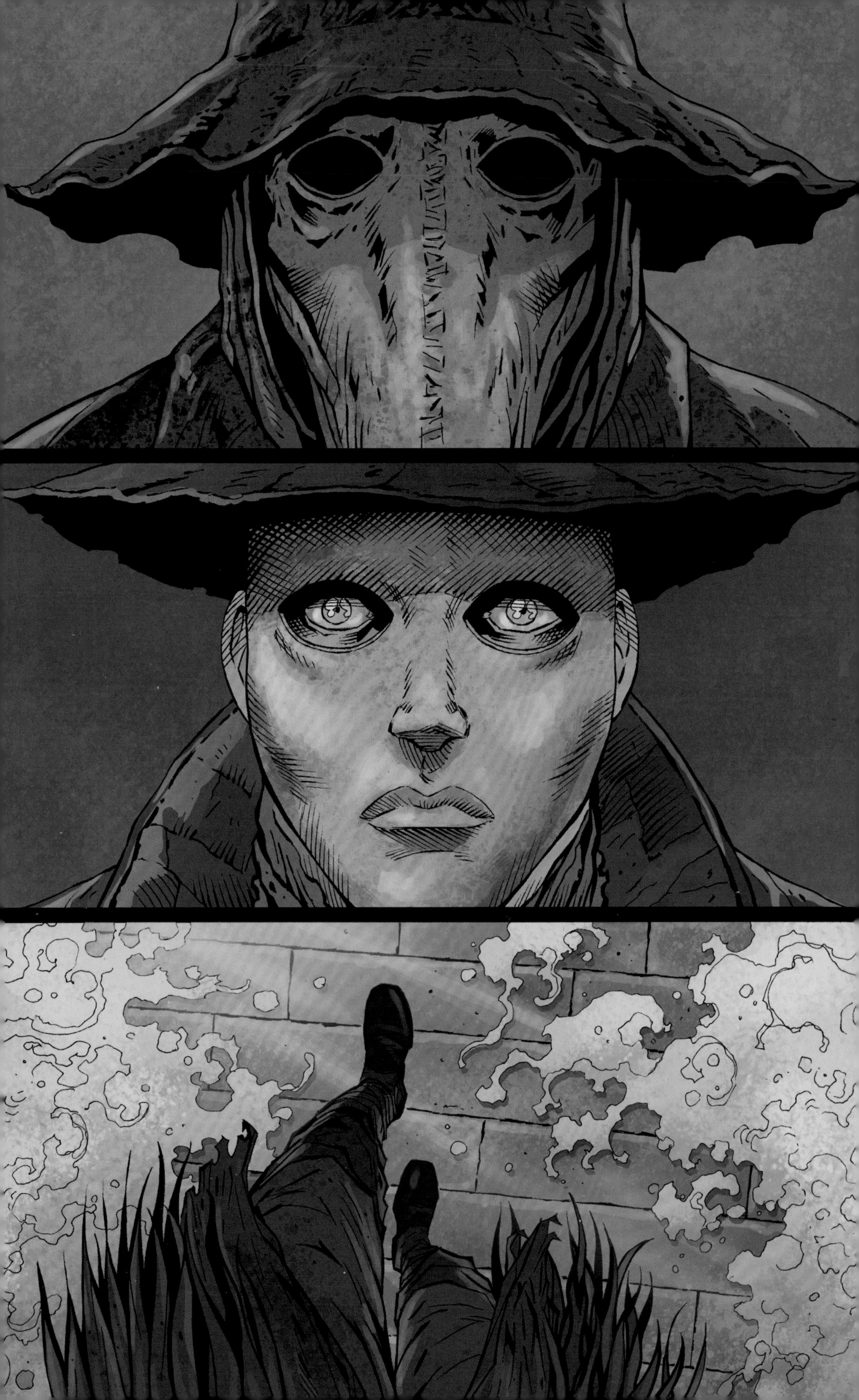

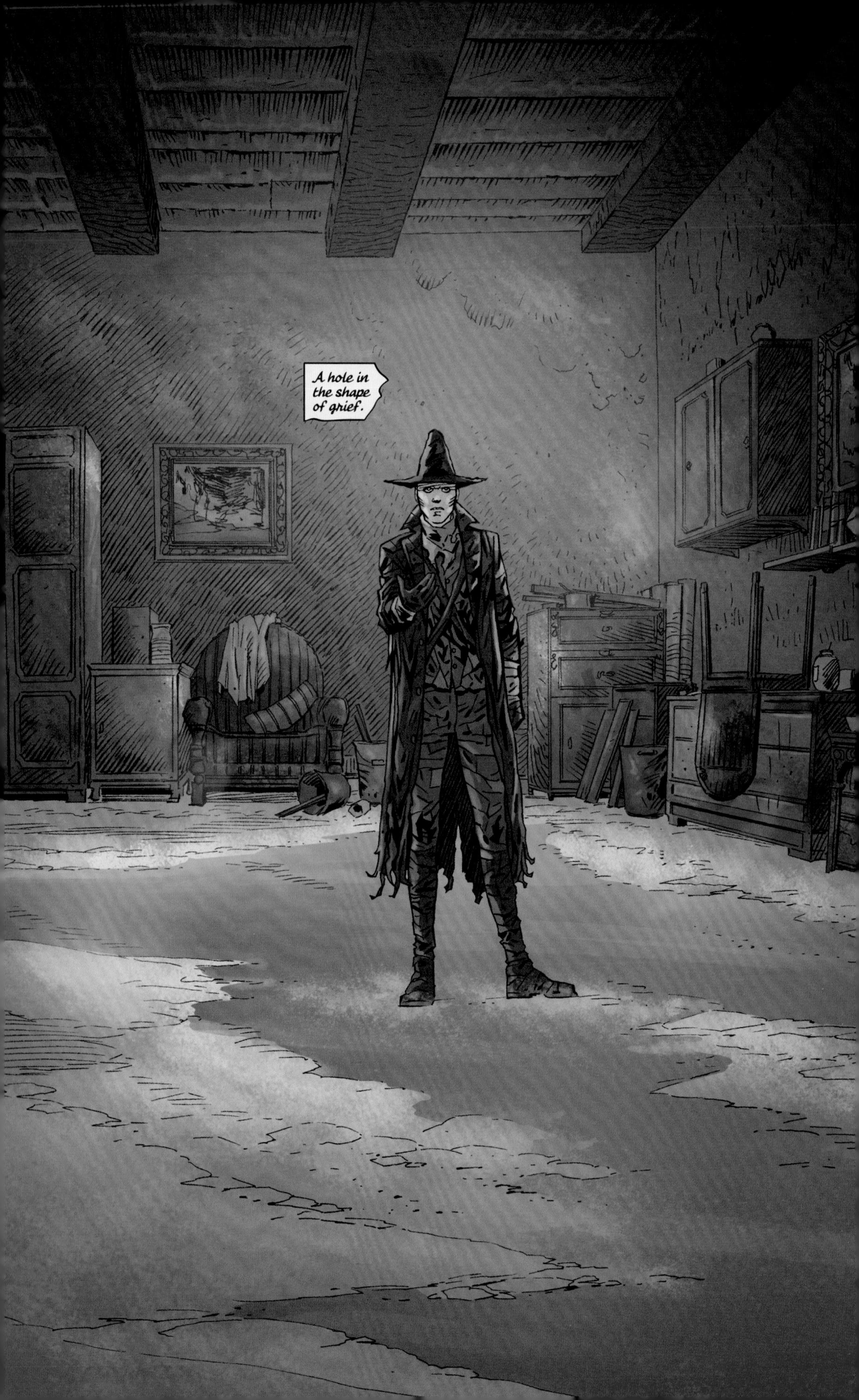
A hole in the shape of grief.

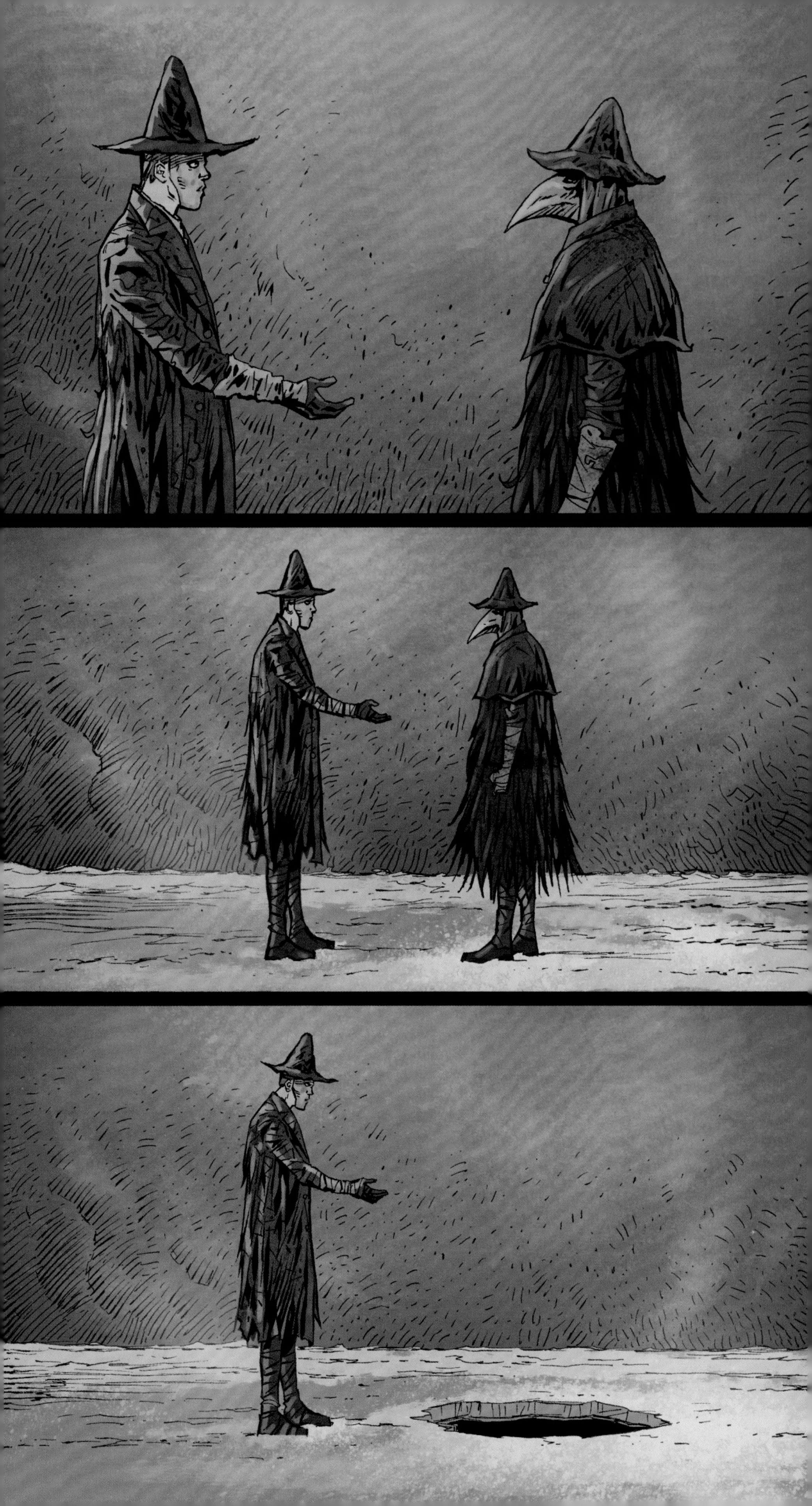

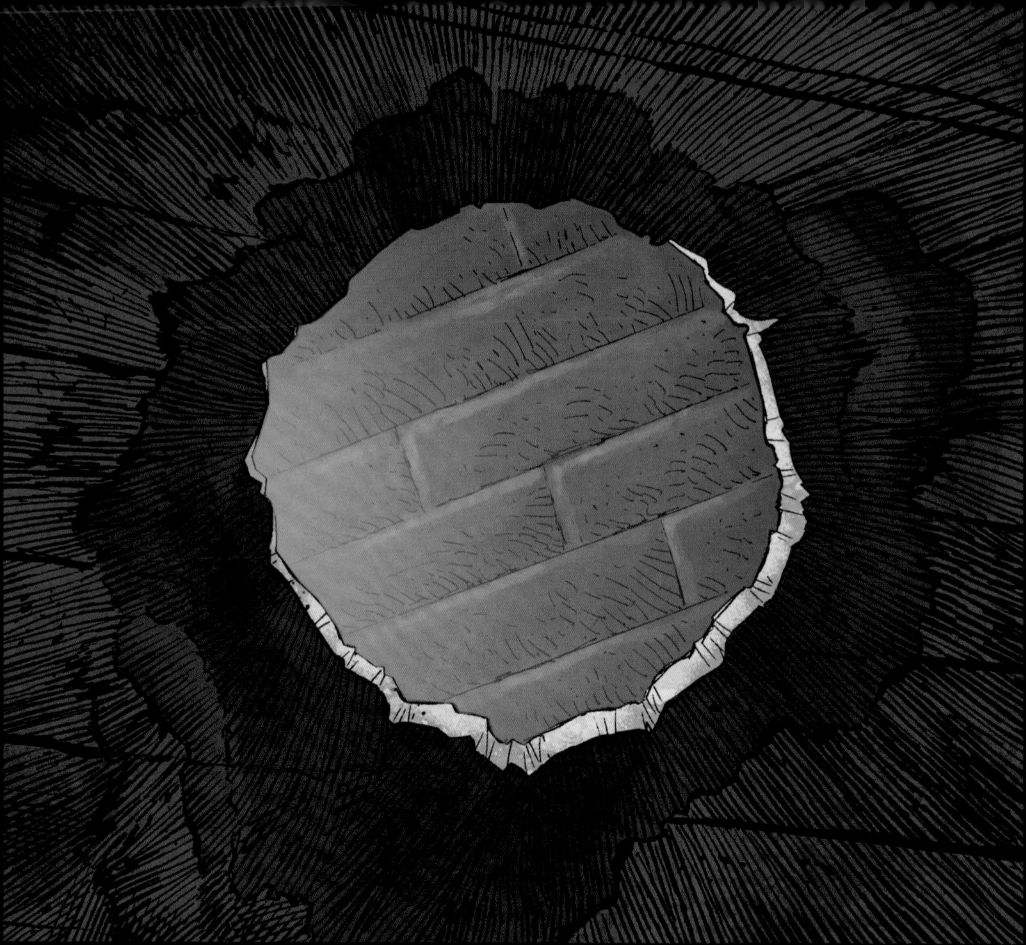
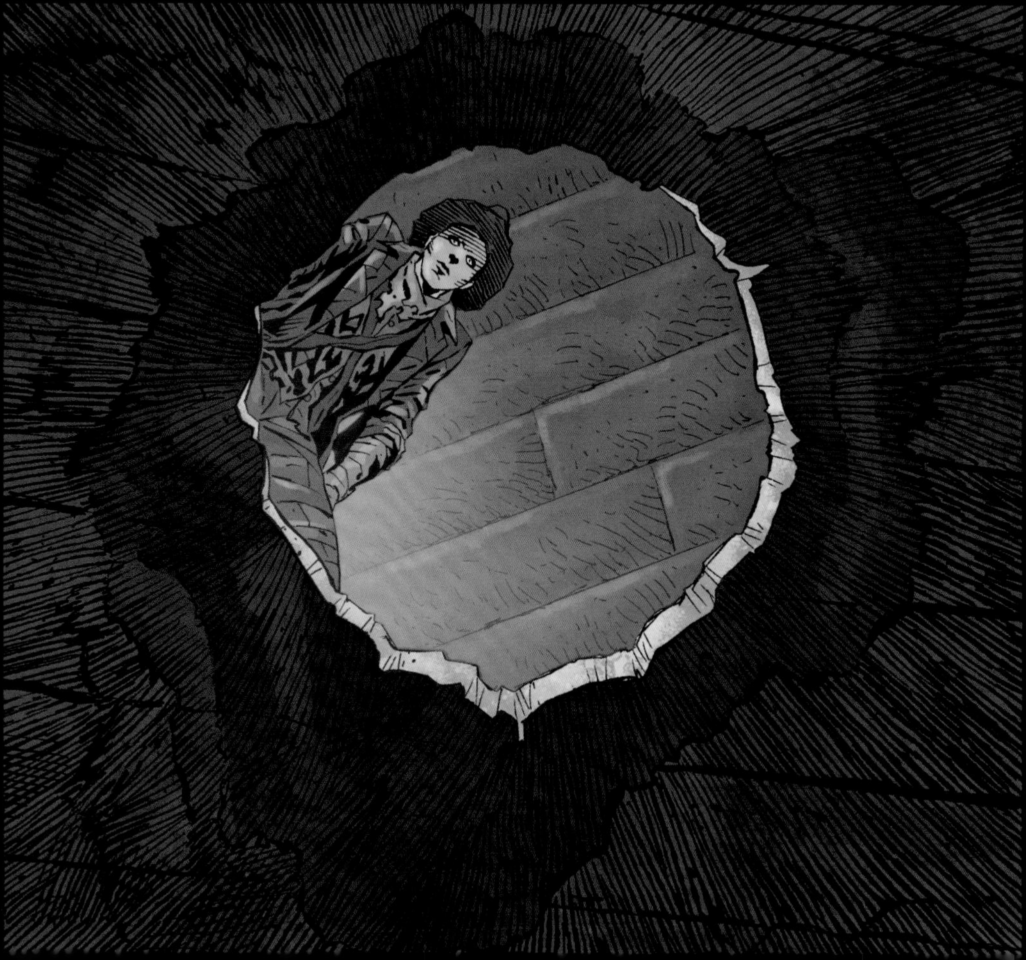

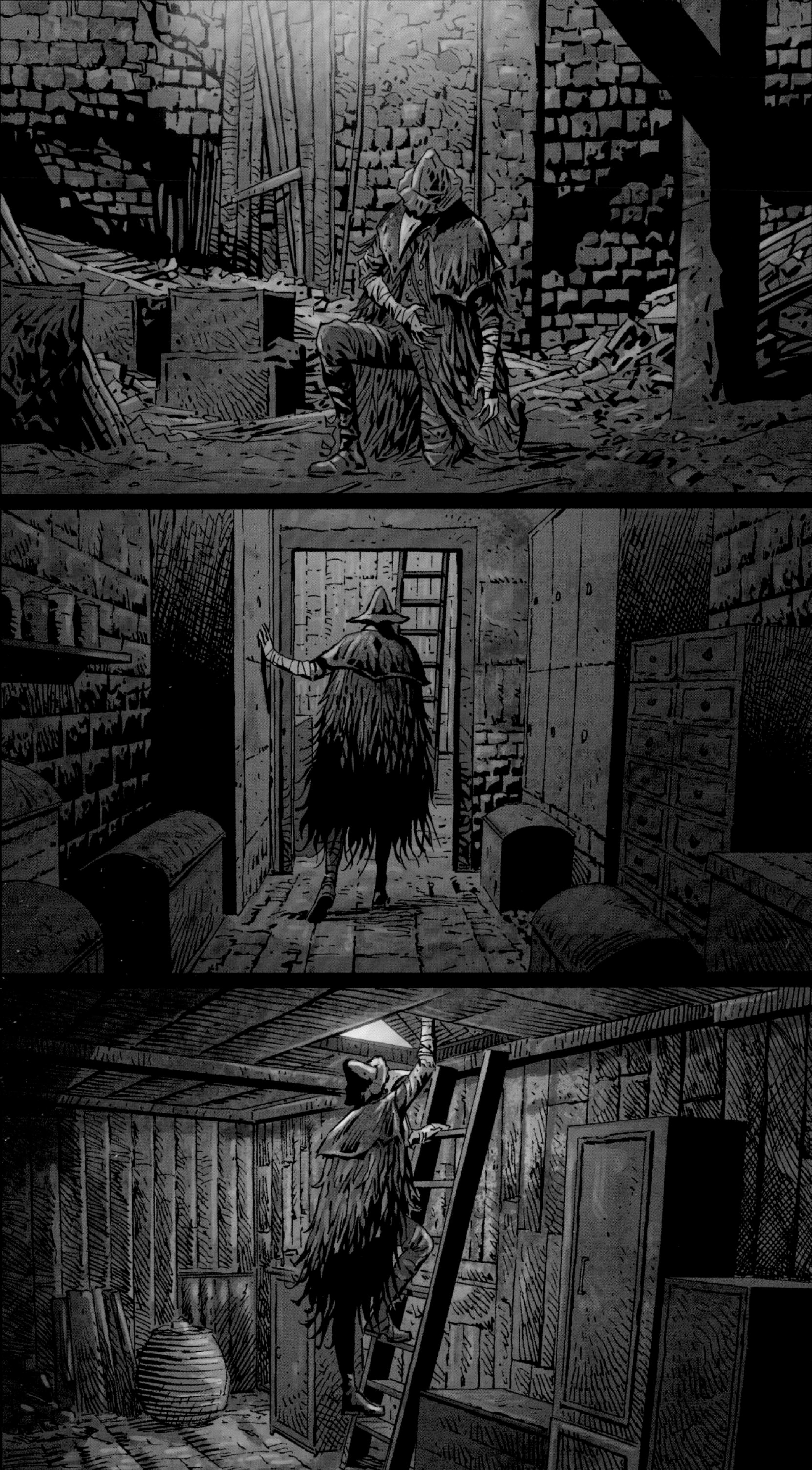

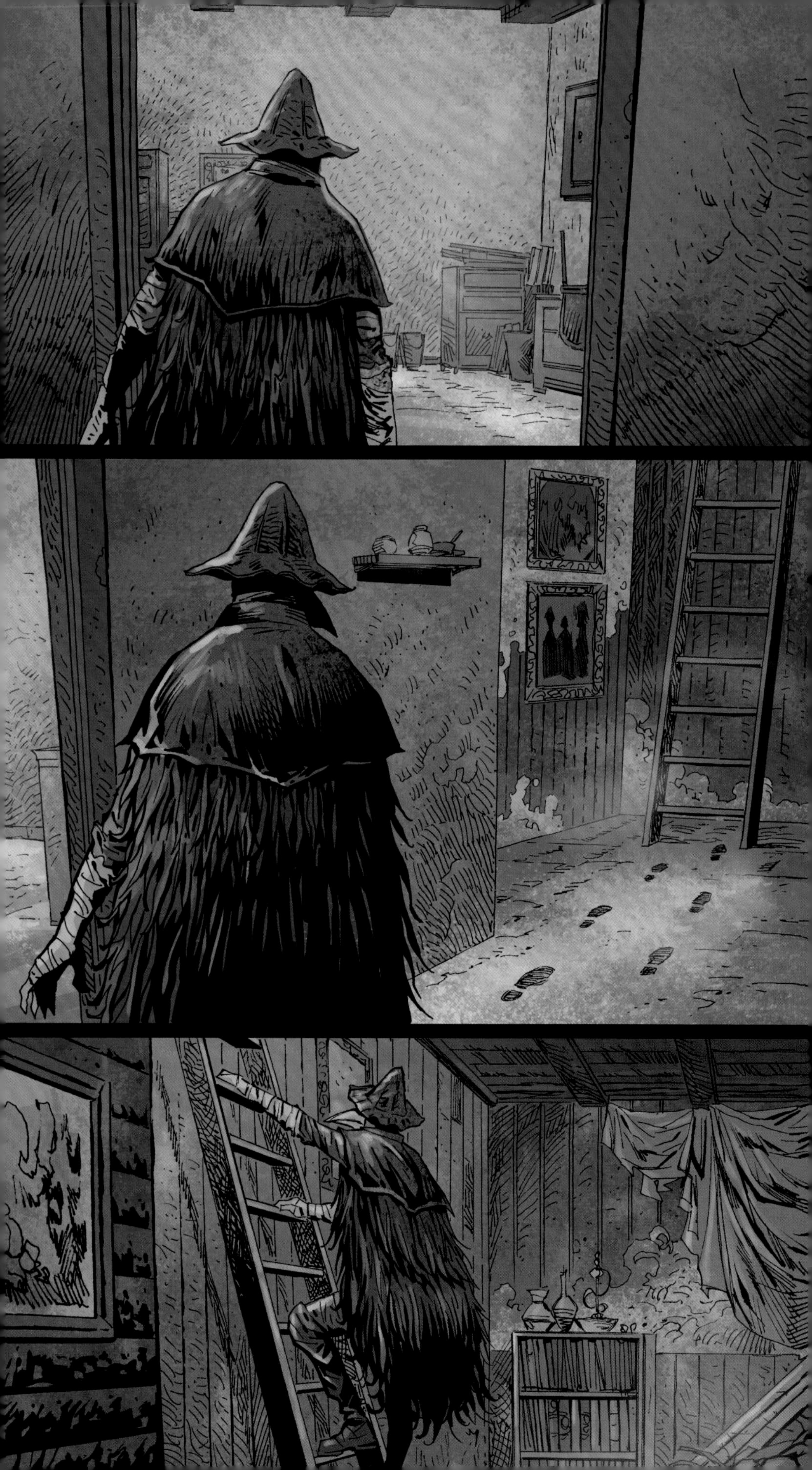

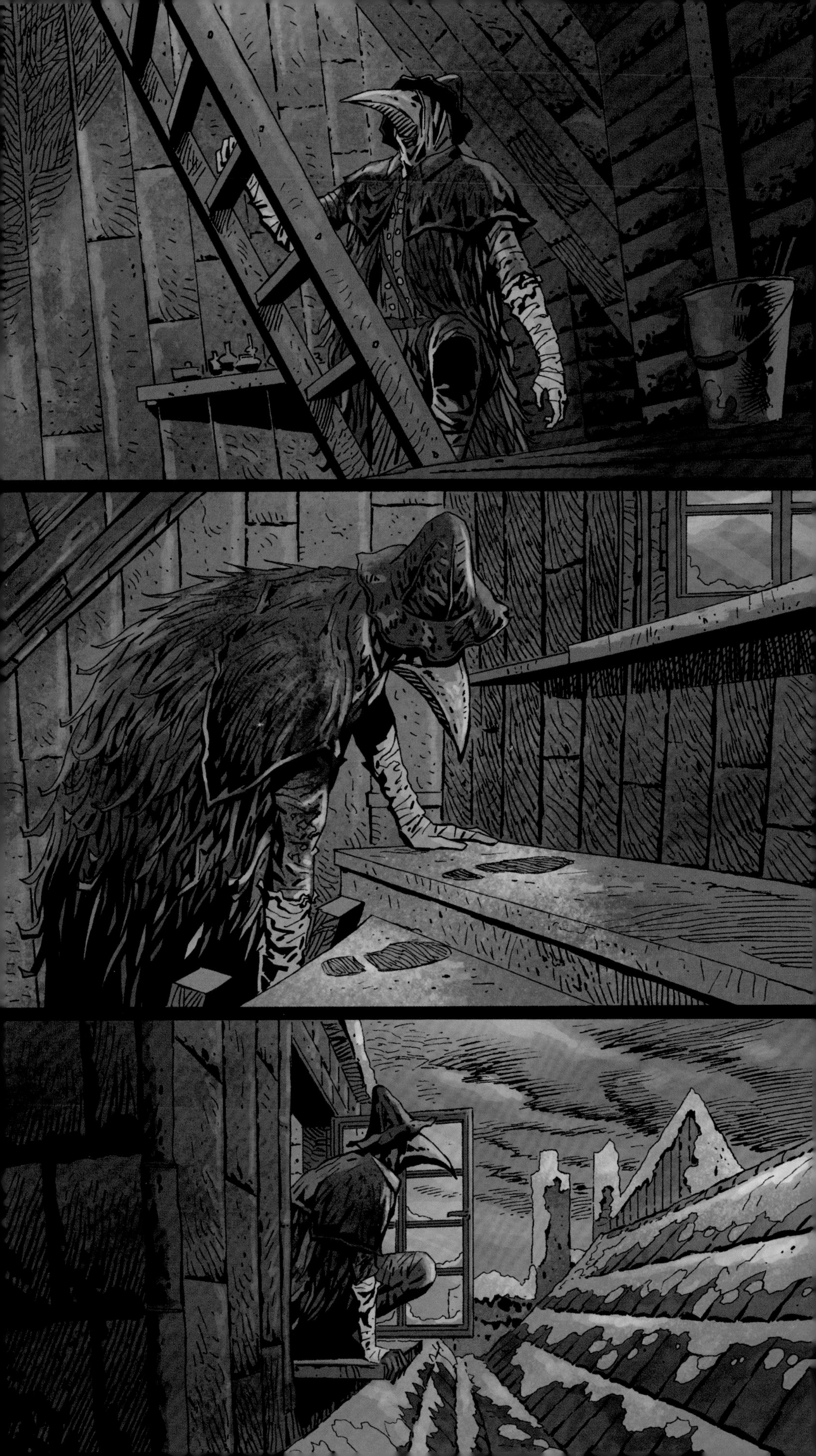

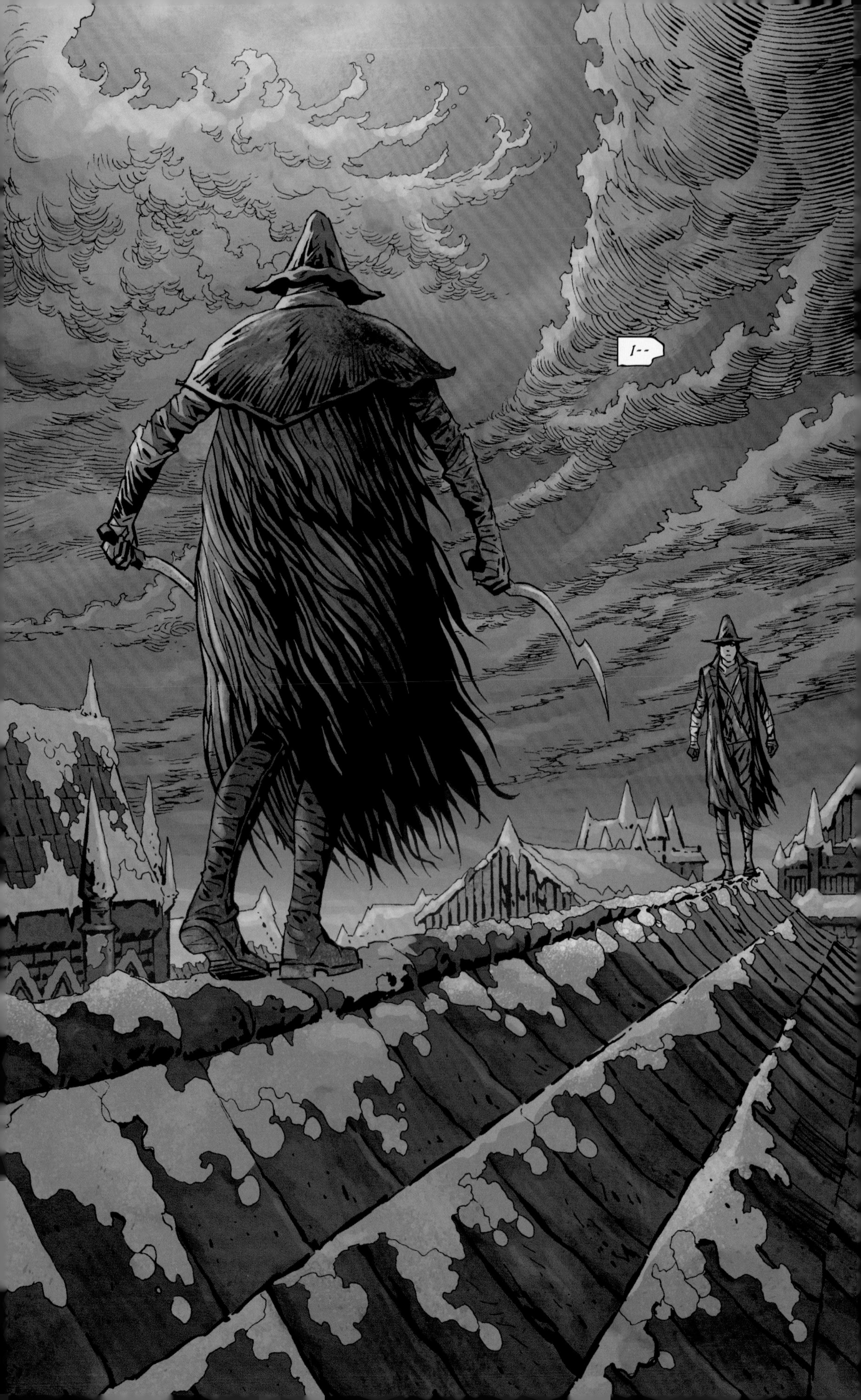
I--

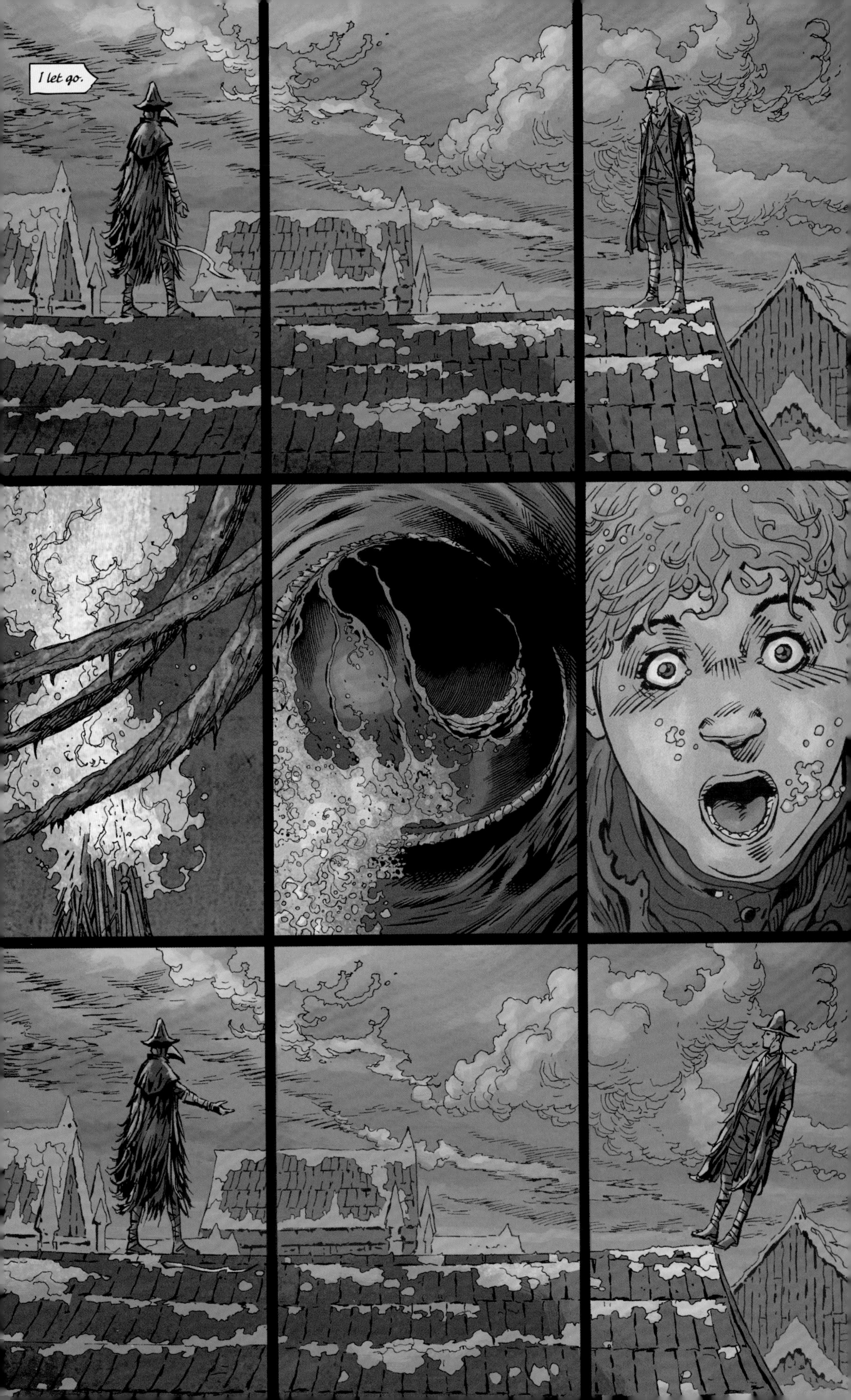
I let go.

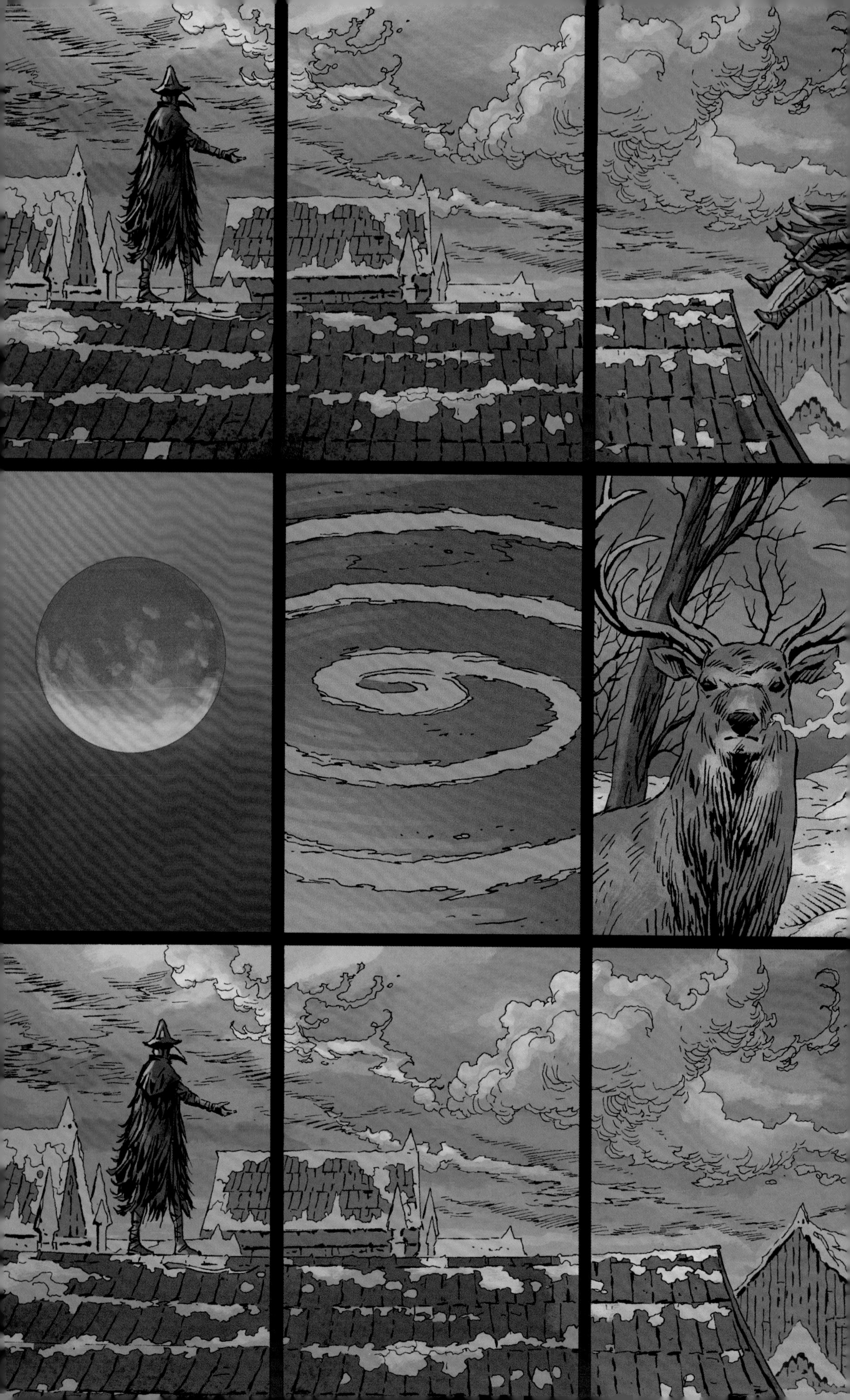

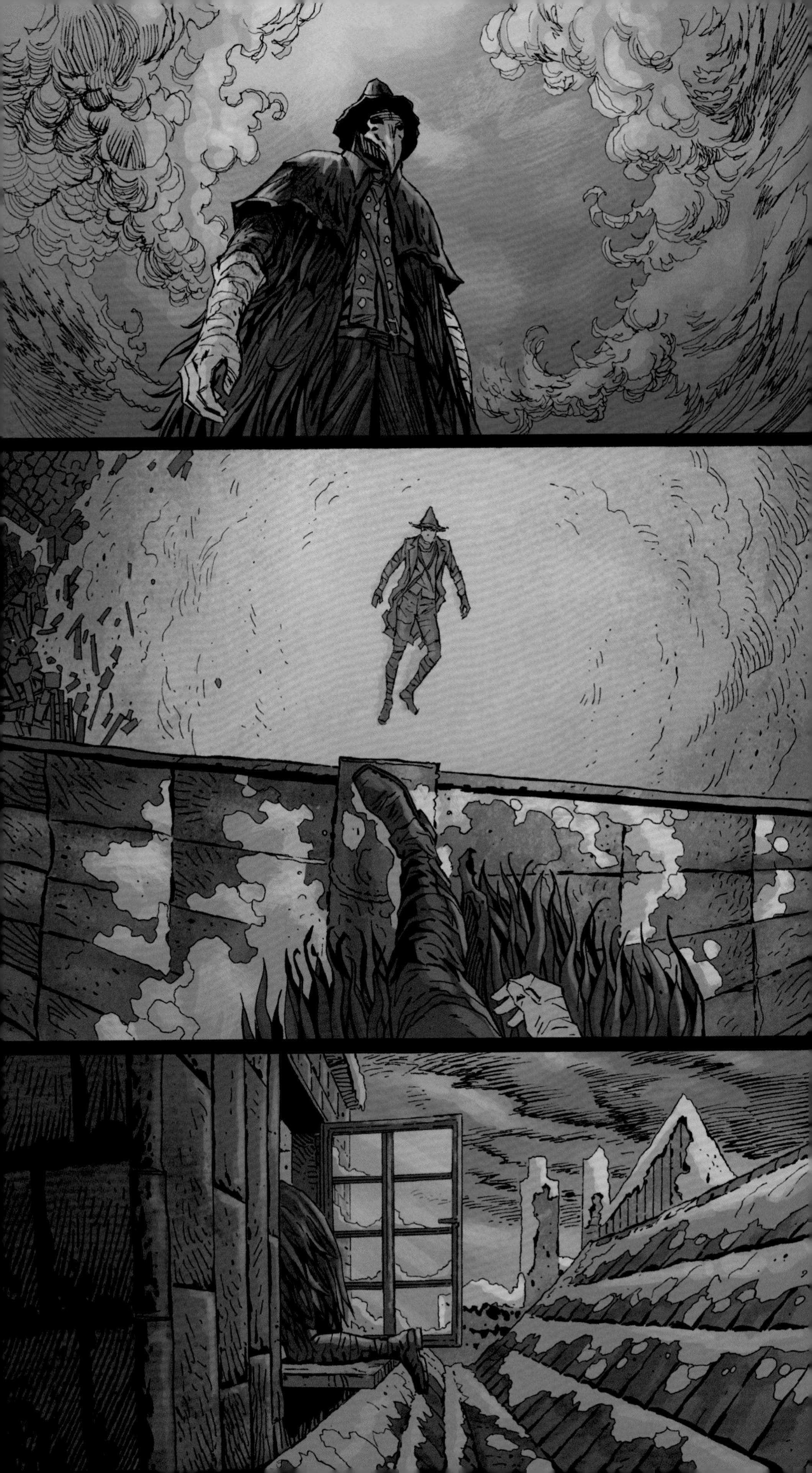

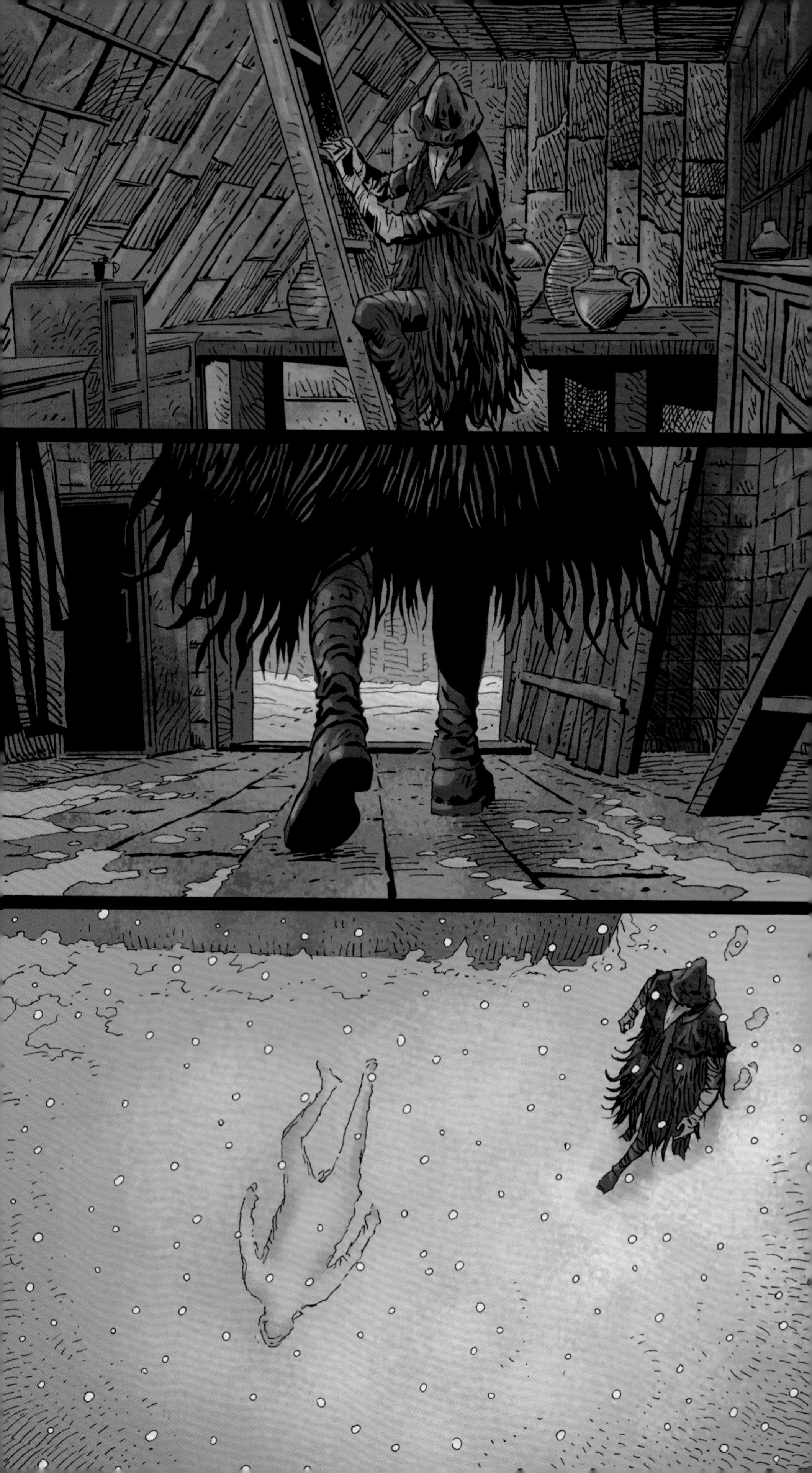

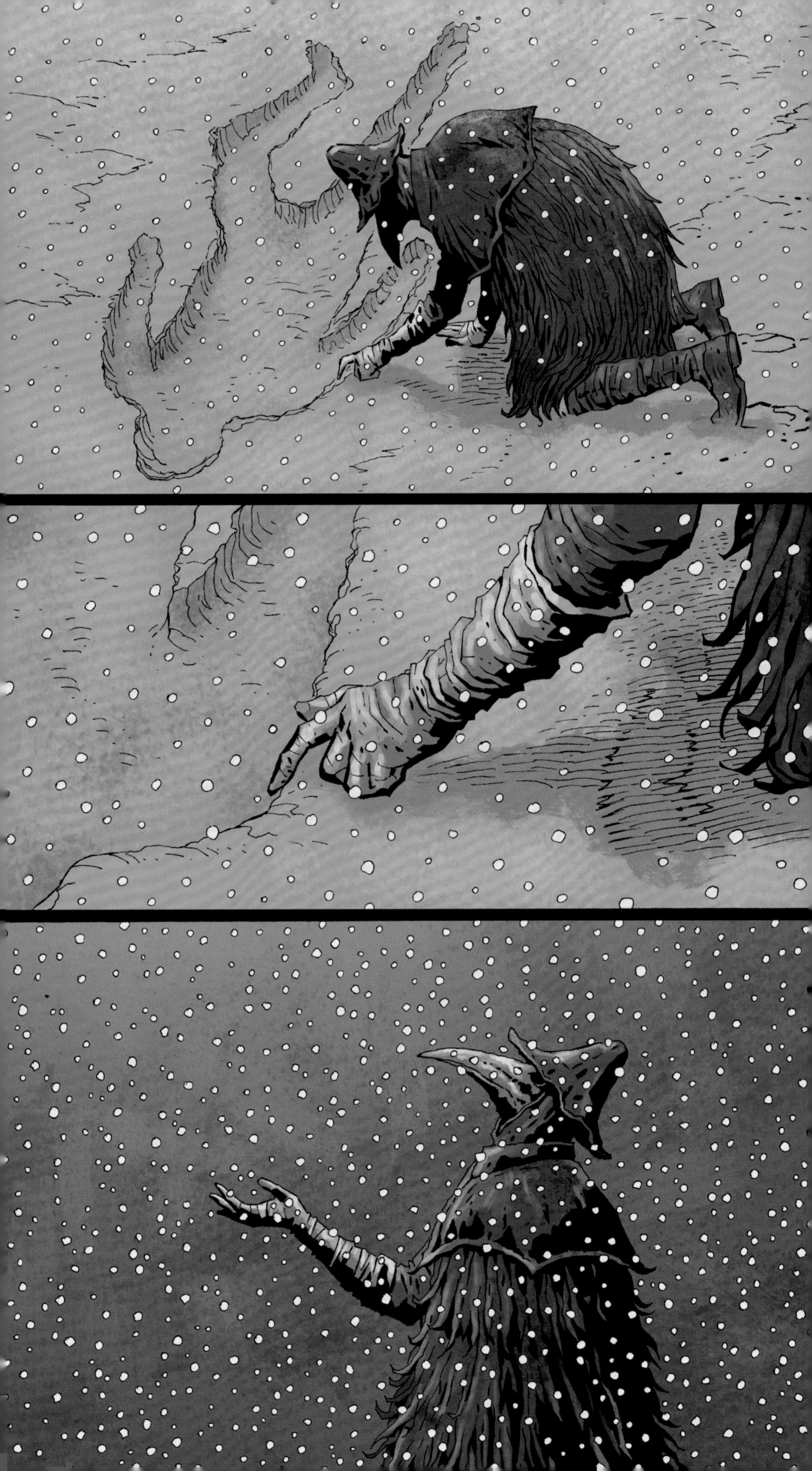

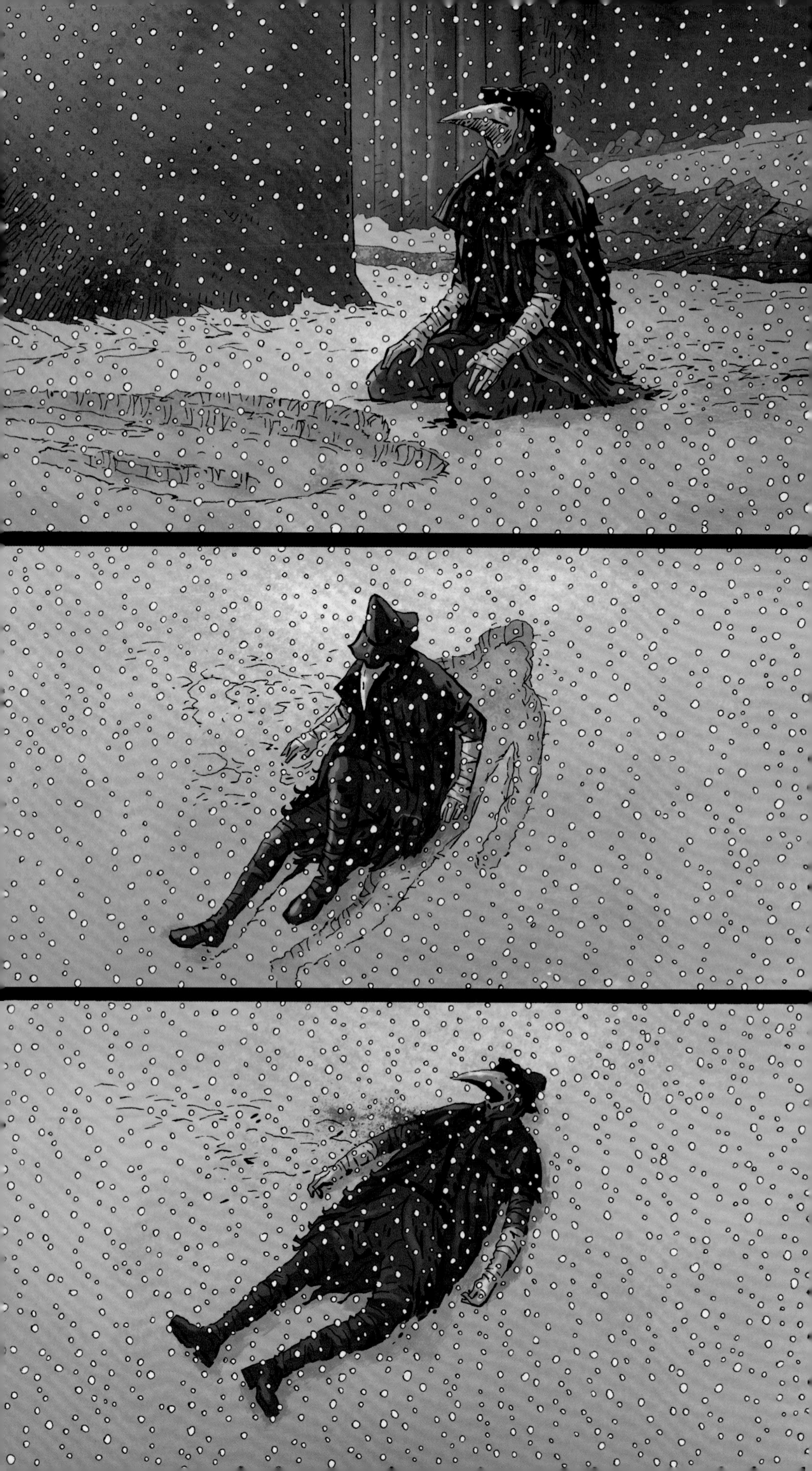

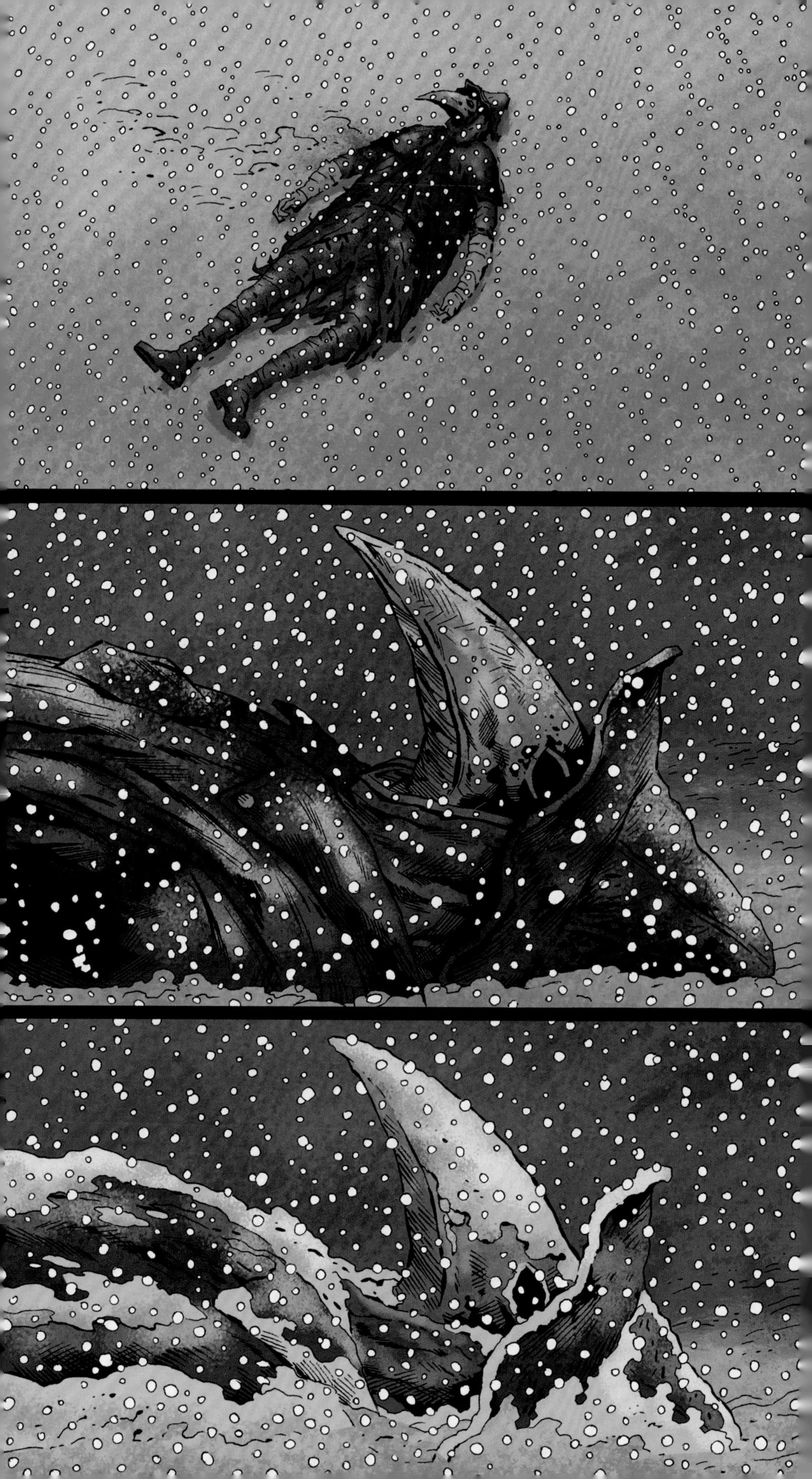

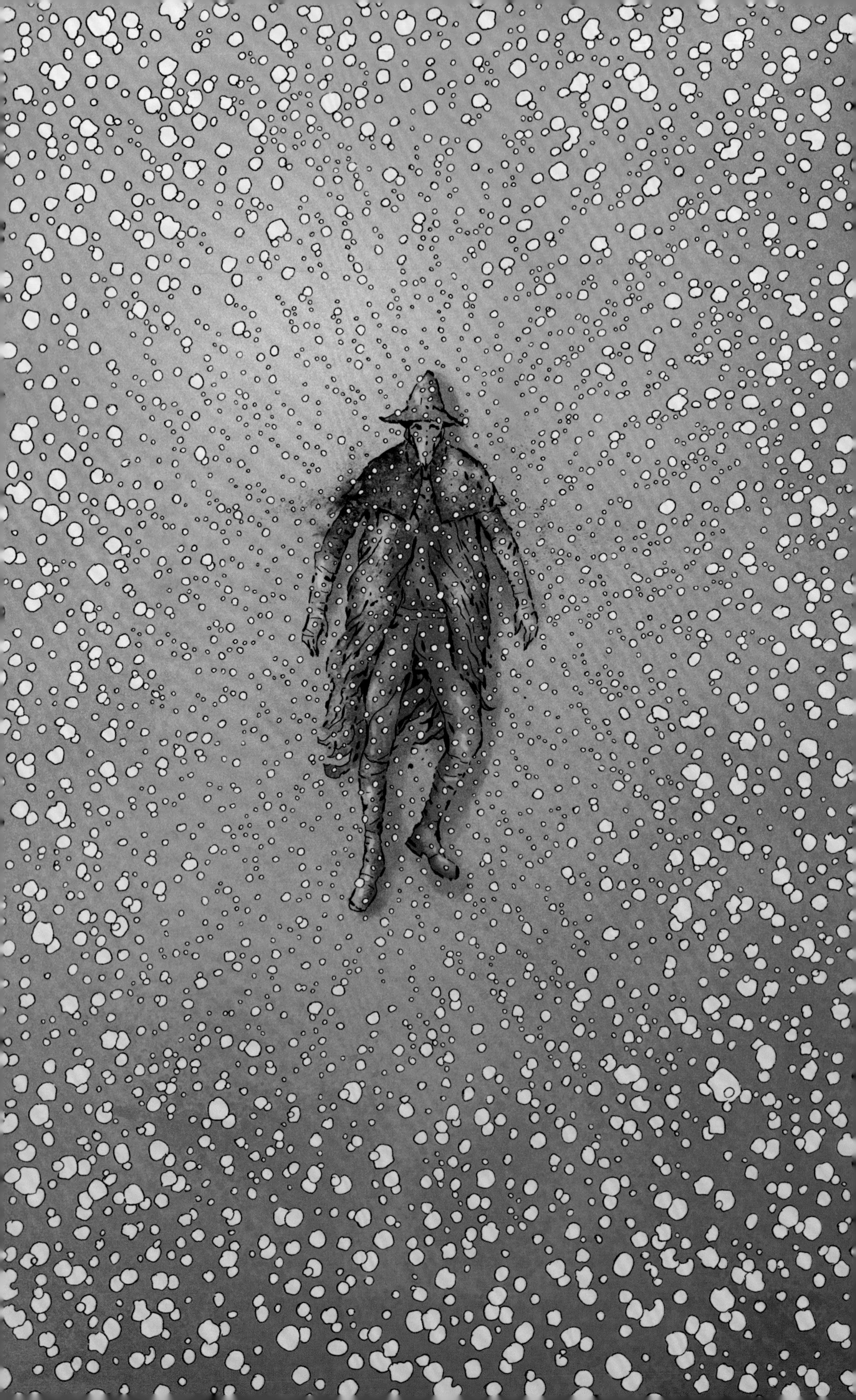

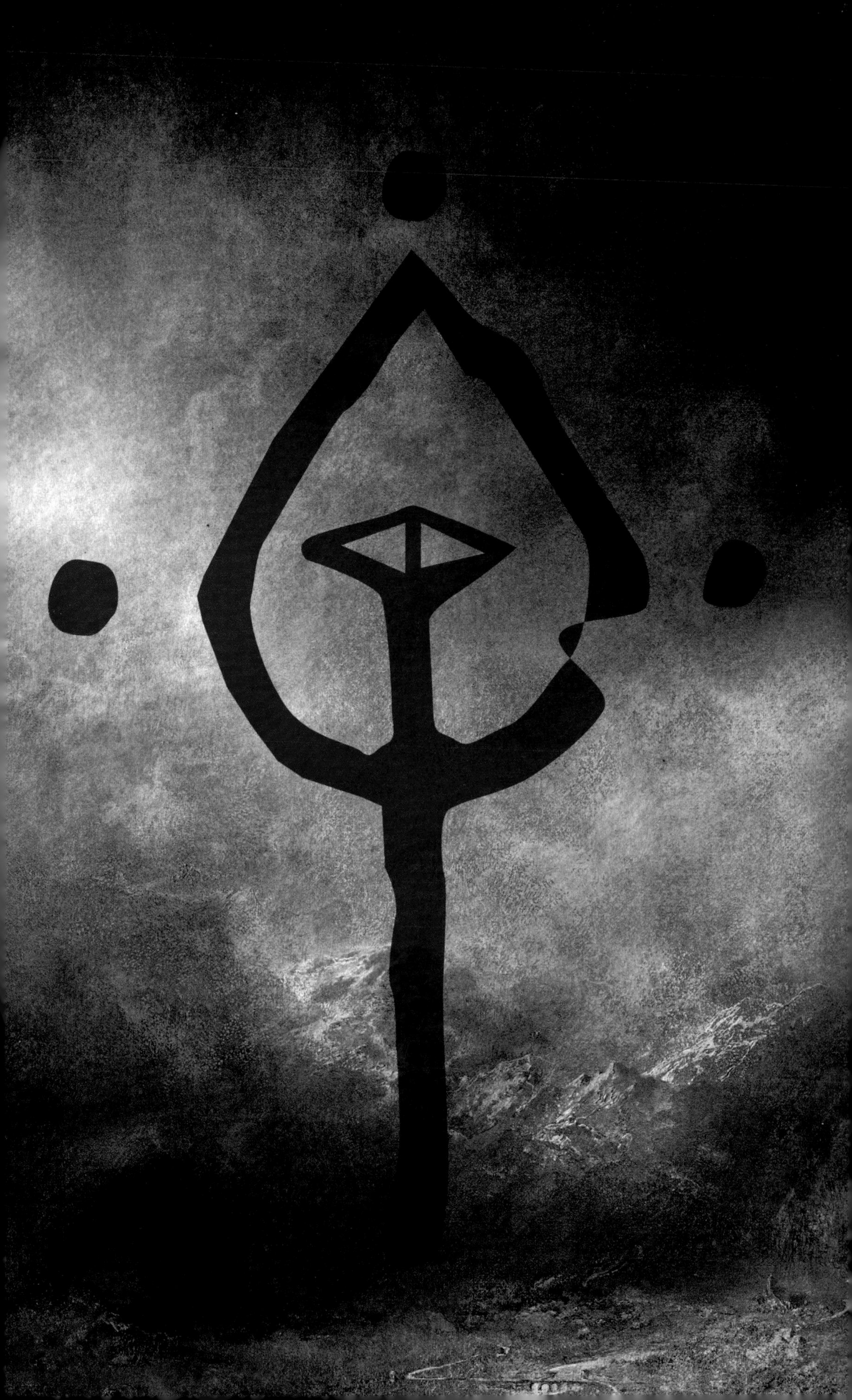

# Bloodborne

## COVER GALLERY

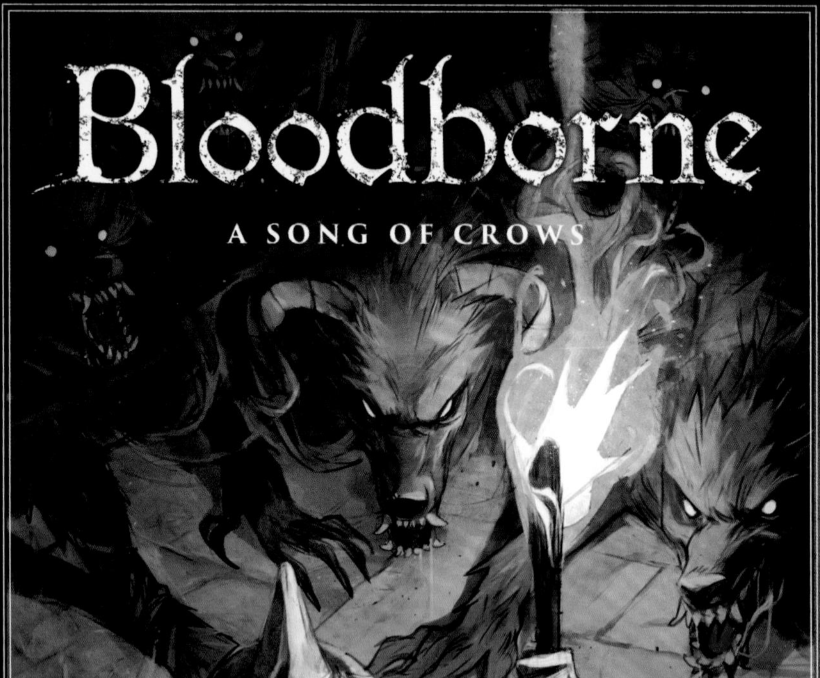
Bloodborne
A SONG OF CROWS
SHAVRIN '18
KOT | KOWALSKI | SIMPSON

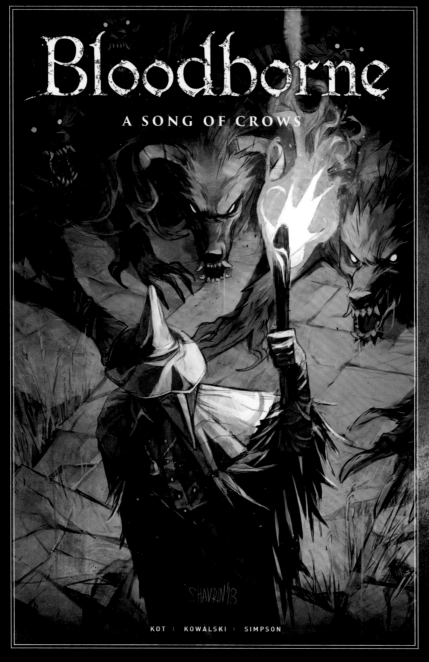

ISSUE #9 COVER B
IVAN SHAVRIN

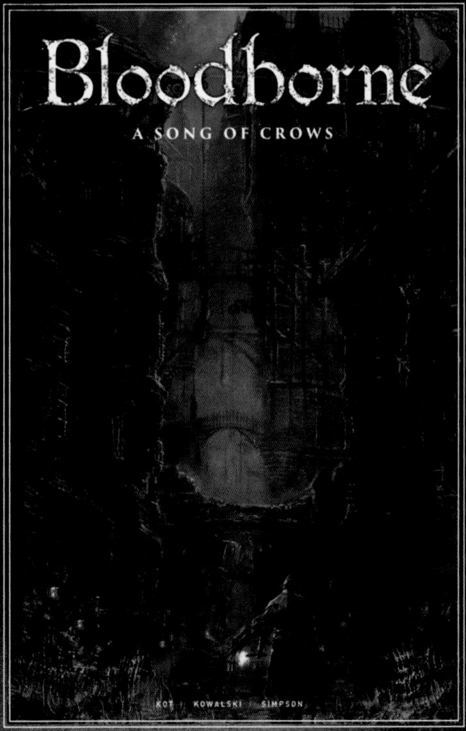
Bloodborne
A SONG OF CROWS
KOT | KOWALSKI | SIMPSON

ISSUE #9 COVER C
GAME ART

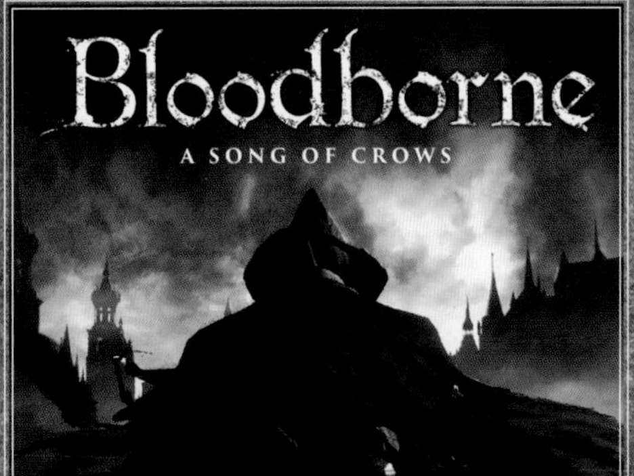
Bloodborne
A SONG OF CROWS
KOT | KOWALSKI | SIMPSON

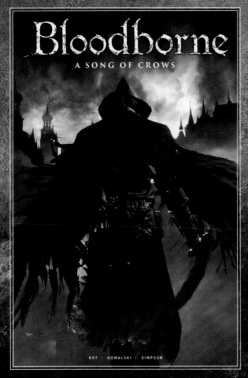

ISSUE #10 COVER B
GAME ART

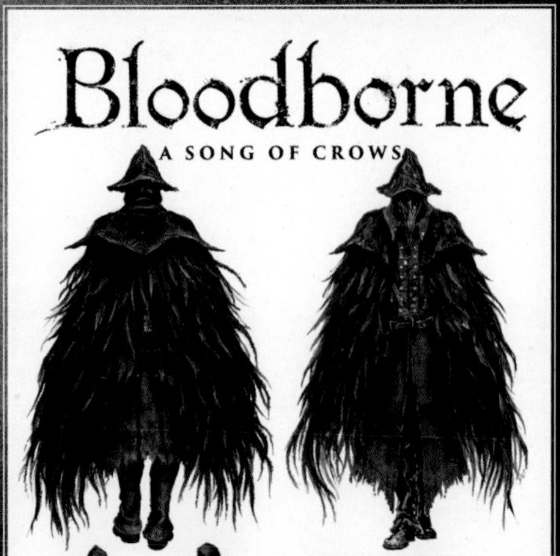
Bloodborne
A SONG OF CROWS
KOT | KOWALSKI | SIMPSON

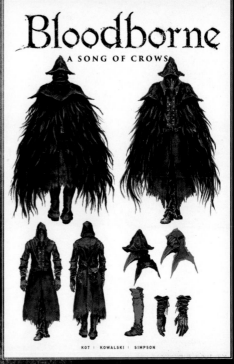

ISSUE #10 COVER C
CHARACTER CONCEPT

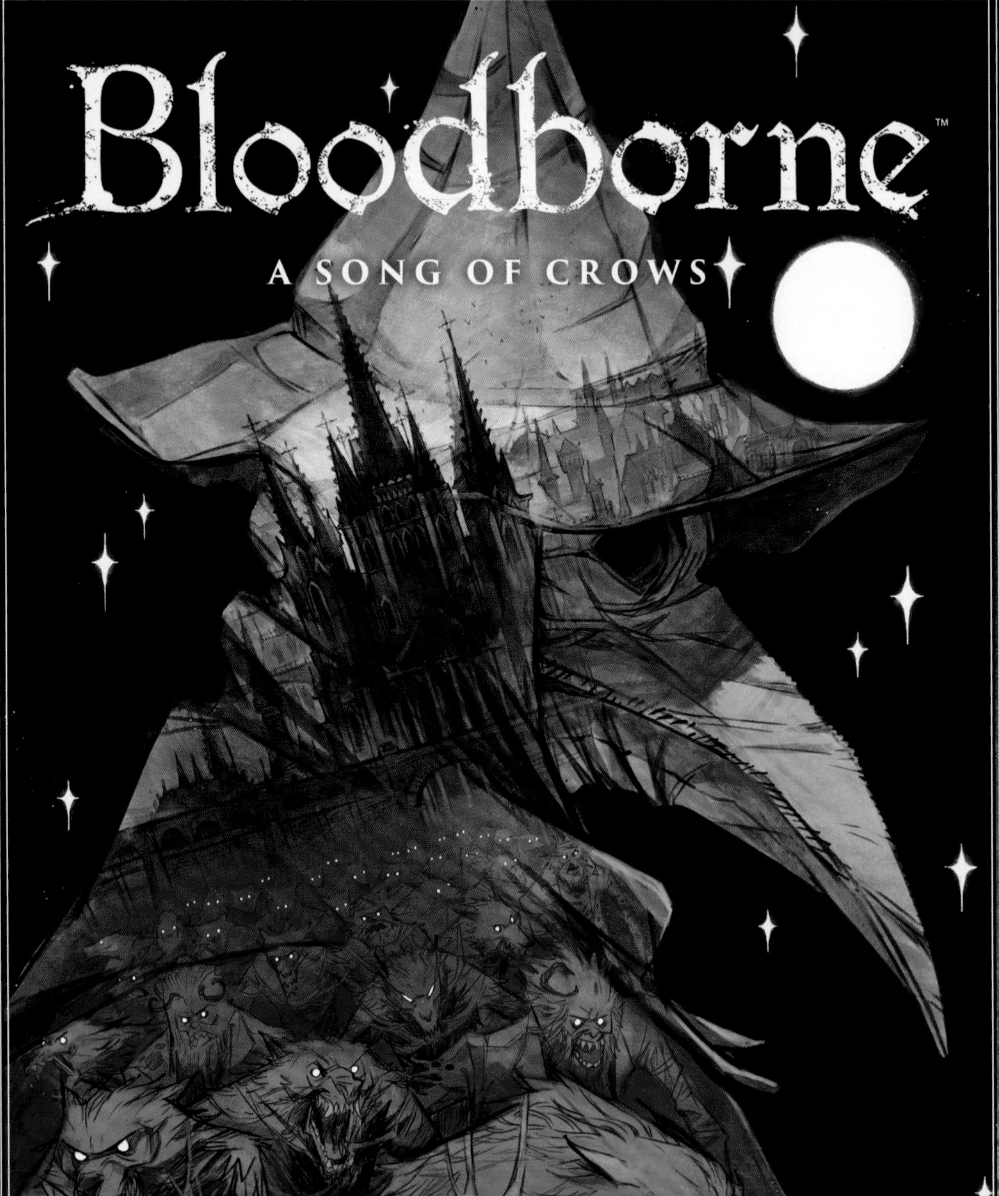
Bloodborne™
A SONG OF CROWS
KOT | KOWALSKI | SIMPSON
SHAVRIN '18
SUGGESTED FOR MATURE READERS
IVAN SHAVRIN

ISSUE #11 COVER B
IVAN SHAVRIN

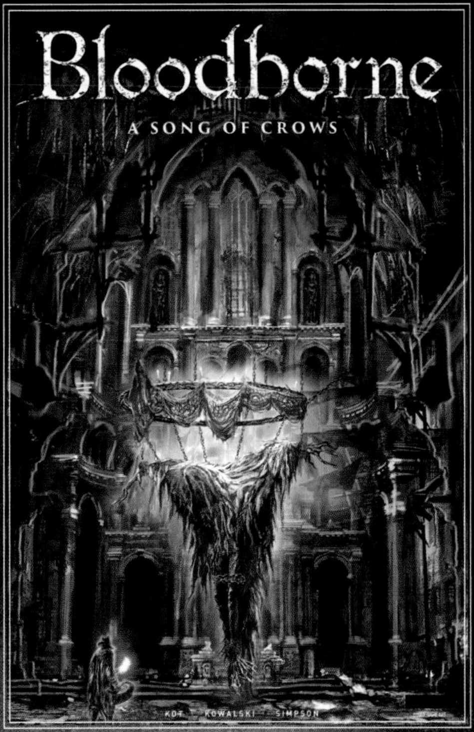
Bloodborne
A SONG OF CROWS
KOT | KOWALSKI | SIMPSON

ISSUE #11 COVER C
GAME ART

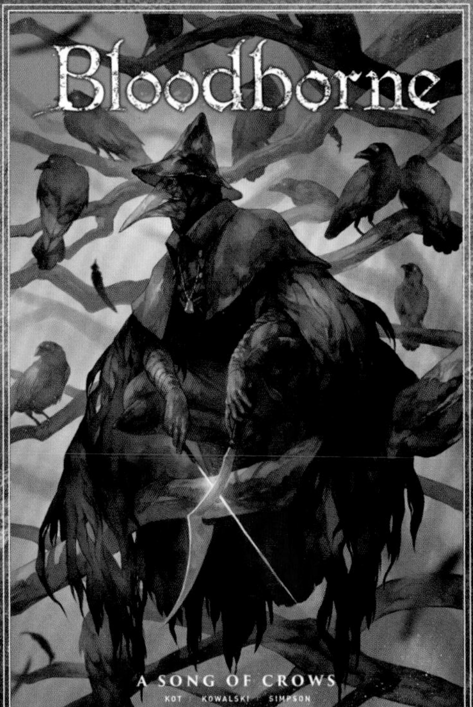
Bloodborne
A SONG OF CROWS
KOT | KOWALSKI | SIMPSON

ISSUE #12 COVER B
YOSHIOKA

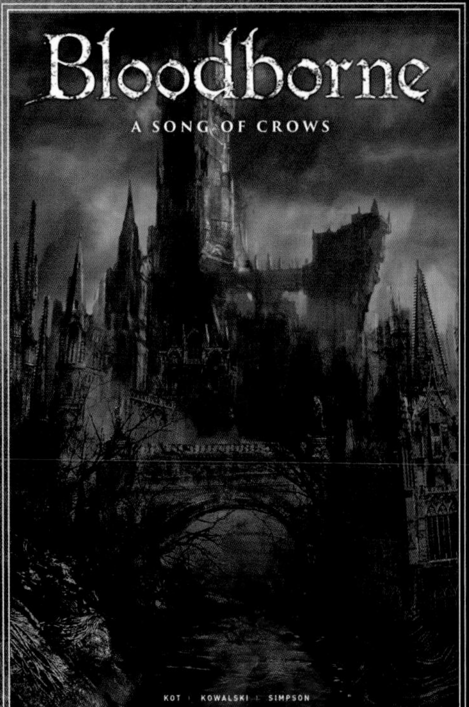
Bloodborne
A SONG OF CROWS
KOT | KOWALSKI | SIMPSON

ISSUE #12 COVER C
GAME ART

- EILEEN LEAPING INTO THE FRAY. BUILDING SPIRES THREATEN HER LIKE KNIVES.

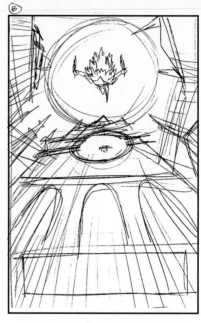

- SIMILAR TO OPTION A. EILEEN SOARS AT US FROM ABOVE PASSING IMPOSSIBLE ARCHITECTURE, ALWAYS LIT BY THE BLOOD MOON.

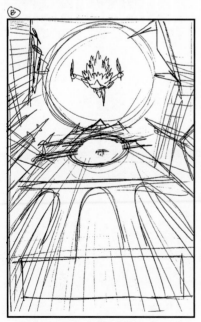

- SIMILAR TO OPTION A. EILEEN SOARS AT US FROM ABOVE PASSING IMPOSSIBLE ARCHITECTURE, ALWAYS LIT BY THE BLOOD MOON.

- A DEPARTURE FROM A&B. WITH FOCUS ON EILEEN OUR MAIN CHARACTER DISPLAYED LOUD & PROUD.

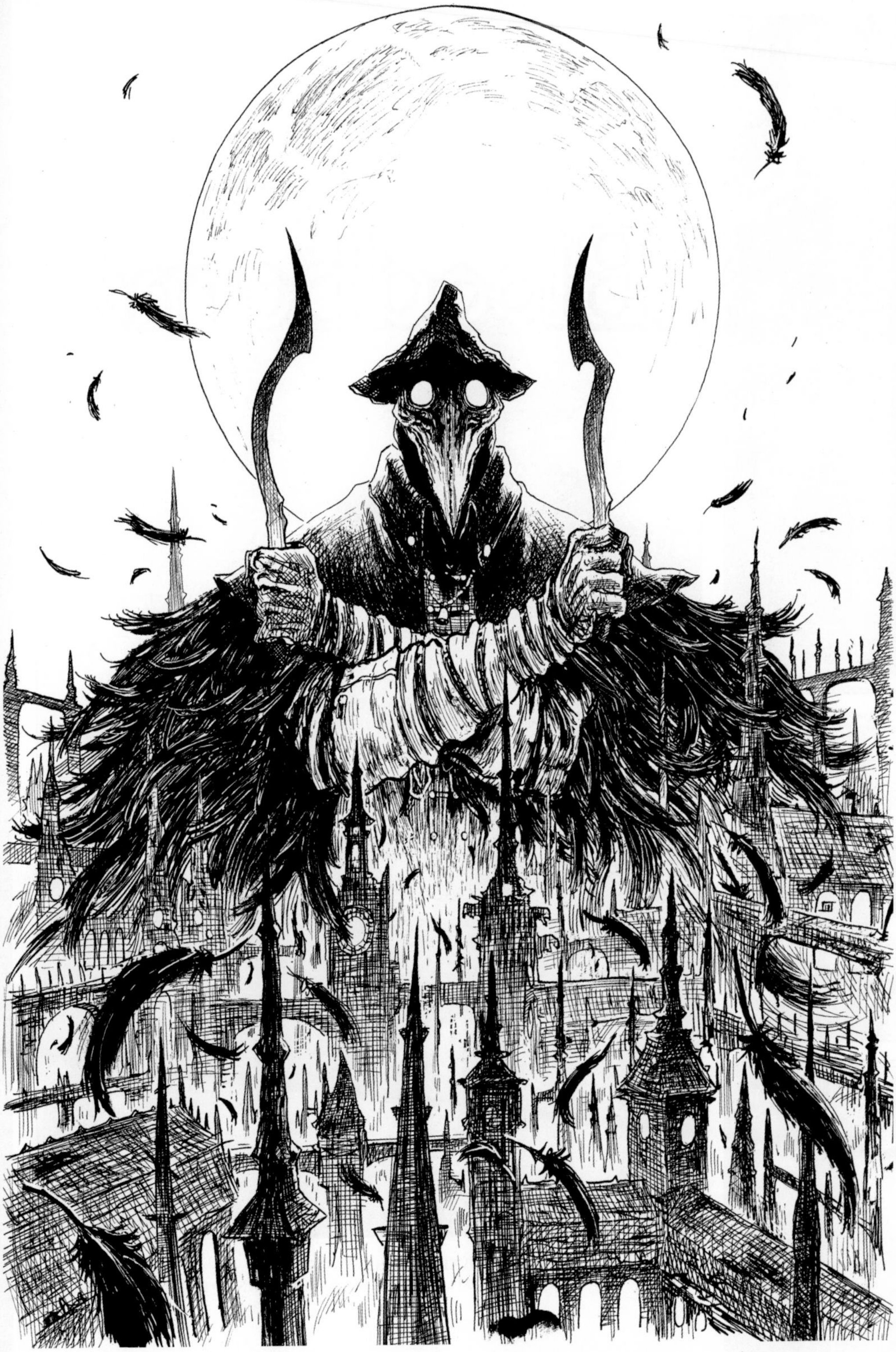

#9 A COVER SKETCHES AND INKS BY JEFF STOKELY

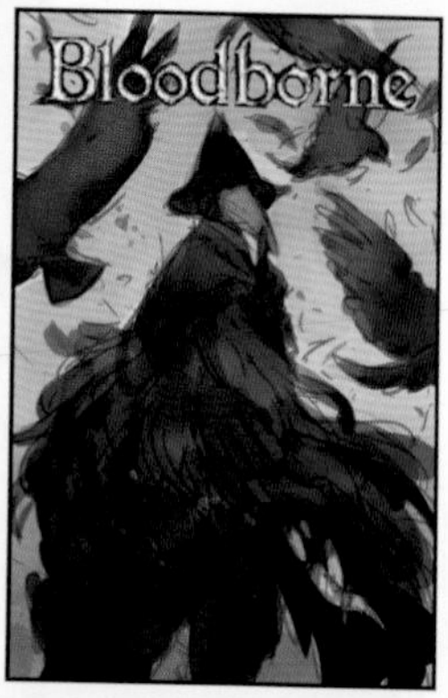
Bloodborne

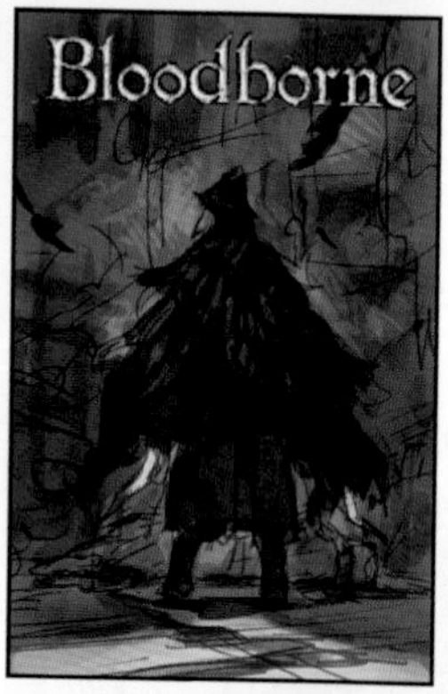
Bloodborne

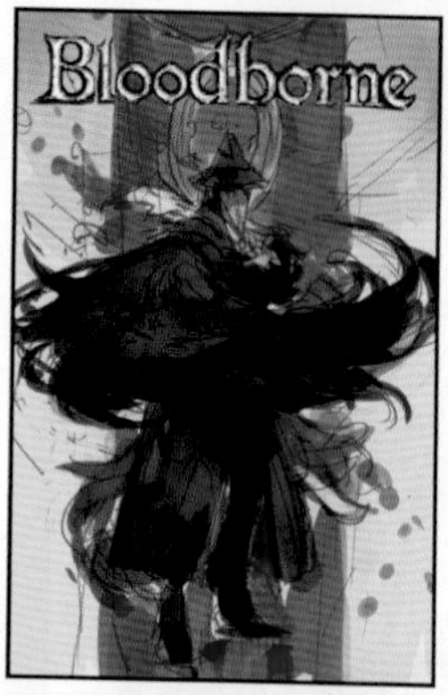
Bloodborne

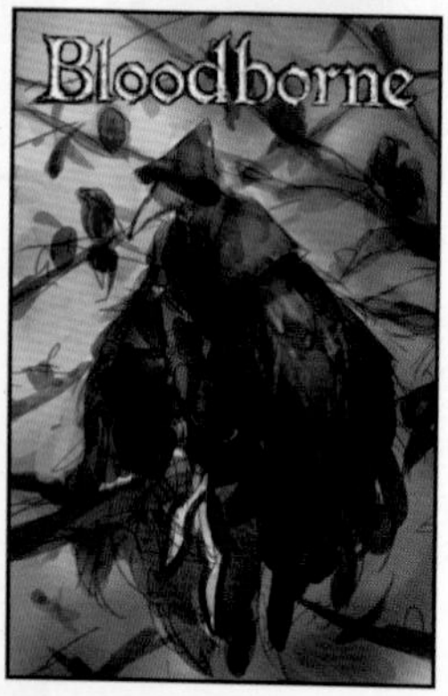
Bloodborne

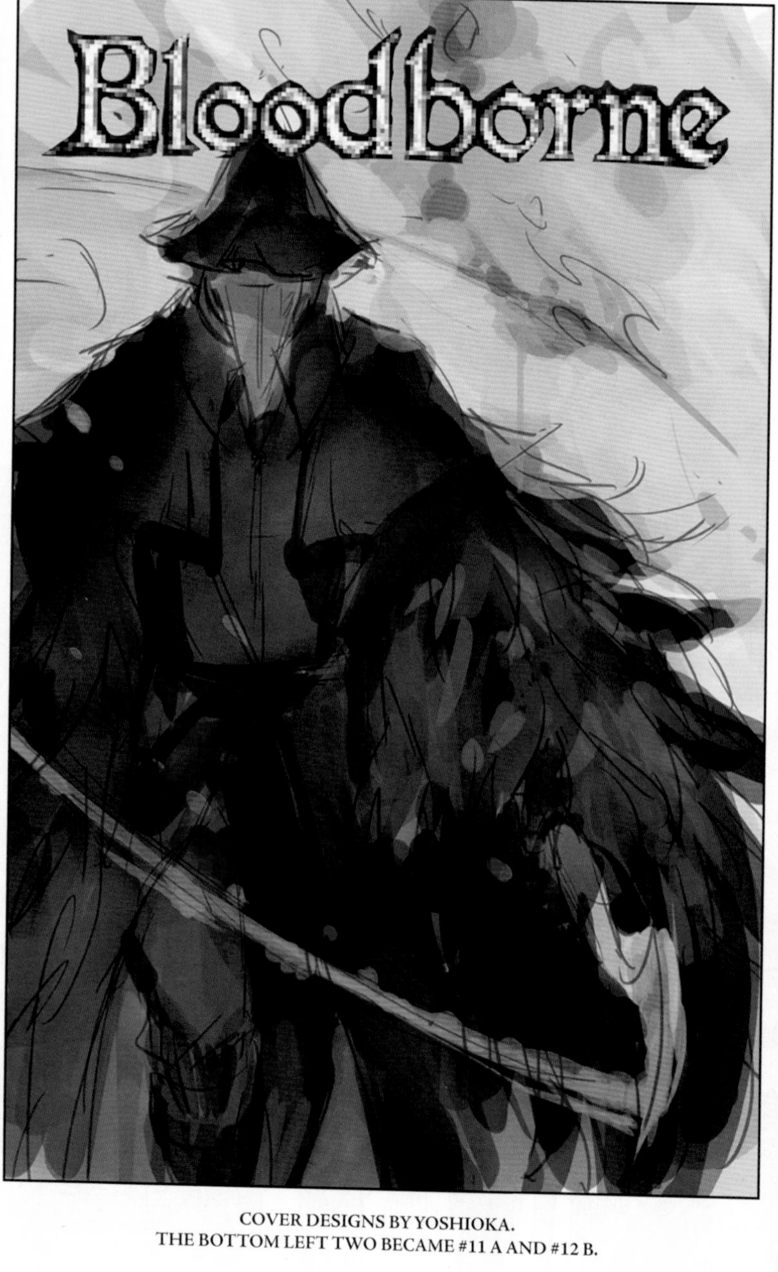
Bloodborne

COVER DESIGNS BY YOSHIOKA.
THE BOTTOM LEFT TWO BECAME #11 A AND #12 B.

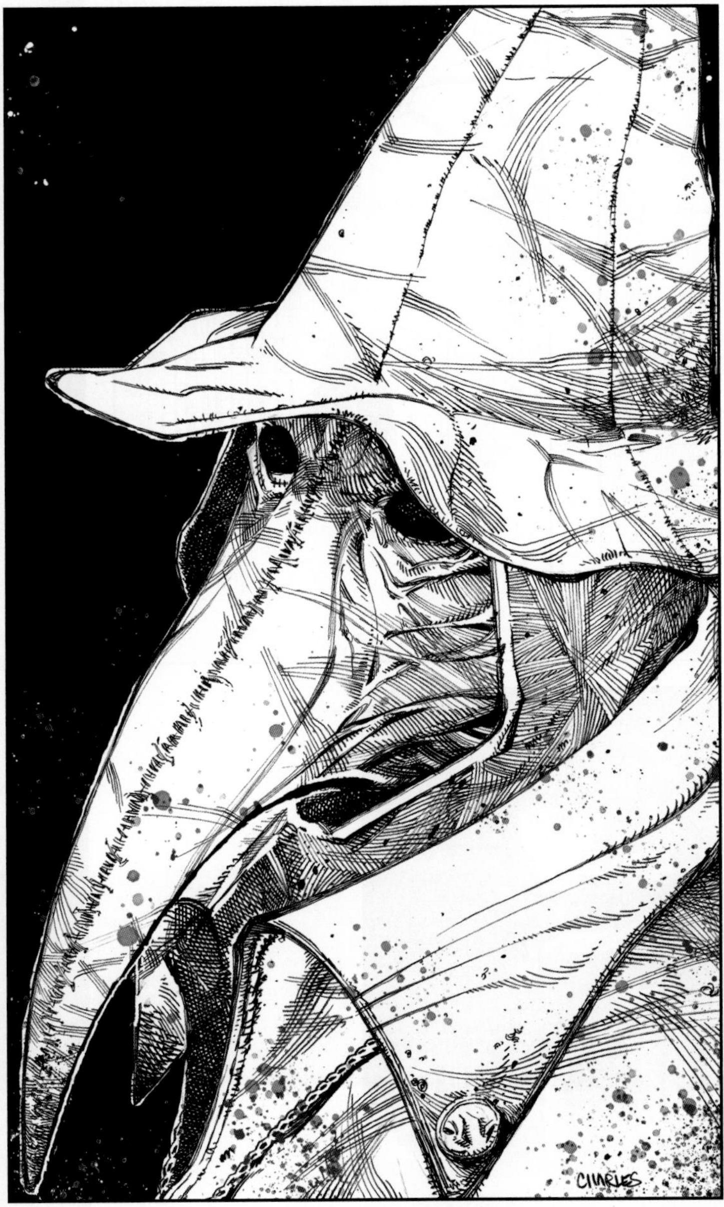
CHARLES

#10 A COVER FIRST DRAFT INKS BY KYLE CHARLES

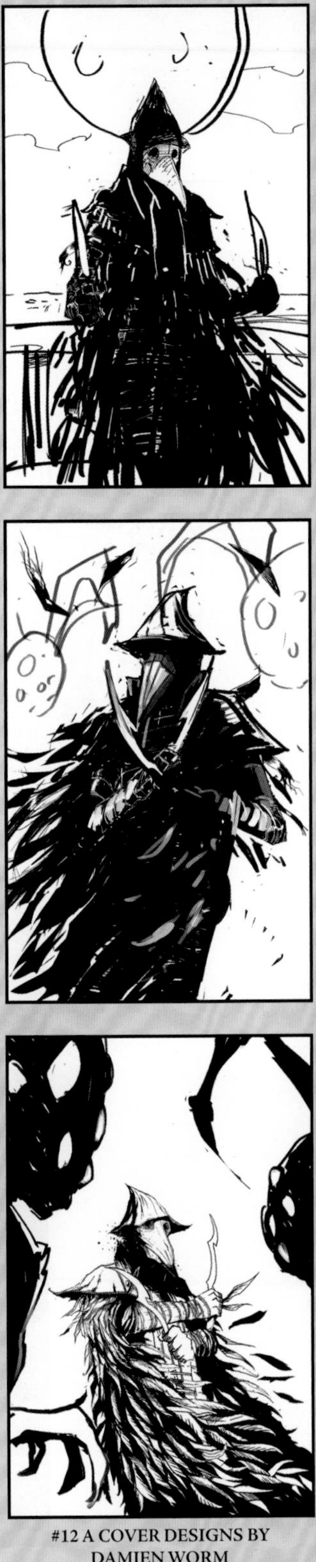

#12 A COVER DESIGNS BY DAMIEN WORM

# INTERIOR DESIGNS

#9 SKETCH AND
INKS BY PIOTR
KOWALSKI.
COLORS BY BRAD
SIMPSON.

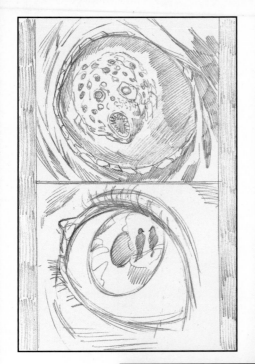

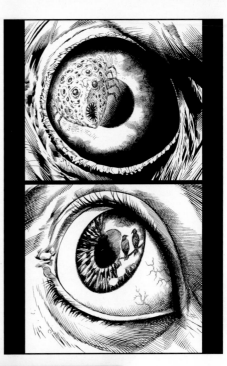

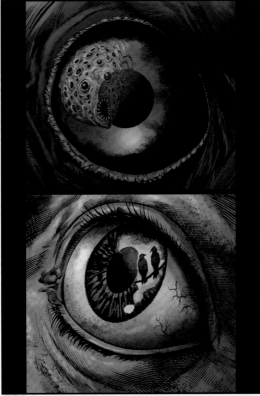

#11 SKETCH AND
INKS BY PIOTR
KOWALSKI.
COLORS BY BRAD
SIMPSON.

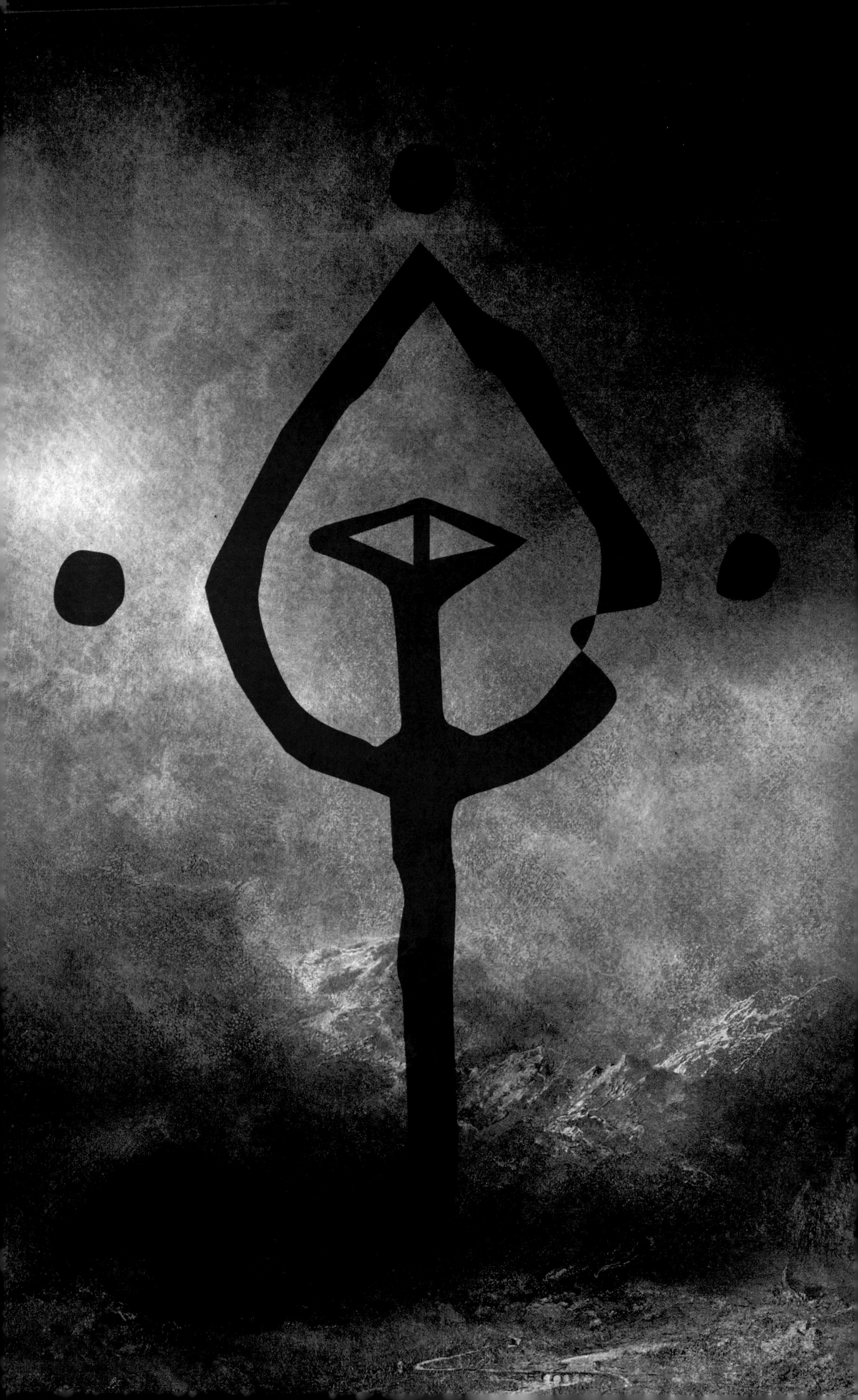

# CREATOR BIOS

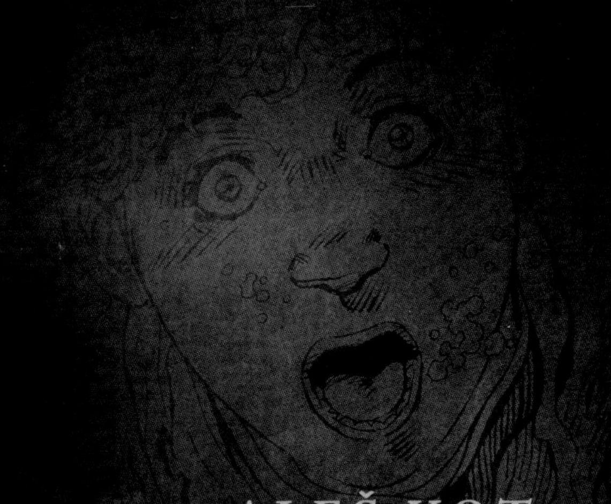

## ALEŠ KOT

ALEŠ KOT is a writer, director and producer with primary focus on film, comics, television and video games. He's responsible for politically-charged Image titles such as *Zero, Wolf, Material, Change, The Surface, Wild Children* and *Days of Hate*, comics which have received many accolades from media such as *Wired, The Guardian, The Hollywood Reporter, Entertainment Weekly*, and many others. He lives, unsurprisingly, mostly in Los Angeles.

## PIOTR KOWALSKI

PIOTR KOWALSKI is a Polish comic book artist. Breaking into the French and Belgian markets with *Gail*, Kowalski's recent foray into US comics has seen him tackle some of the industry's most iconic characters. Since then, Kowalski's dark foreboding style has appeared in a range of titles including *Robocop, 30 Days of Night, Marvel Knights: Hulk, The Dark Tower, Terminal Hero, Sex*, and Titan's *Dark Souls and Wolfenstein* series.

## BRAD SIMPSON

BRAD SIMPSON is an American comic book colorist based in San Francisco. In addition to gracing the pages of many Marvel Comics titles such as *Deadpool, Vengeance*, and *The Amazing Spider-Man*, Simpson's stunning color choices have also proved invaluable in breathing life into such titles as *Godland, Sex, Sovereign, 30 Days of Night*, and *The Witcher*.

## ADITYA BIDIKAR

ADITYA BIDIKAR is a comic book letterer and calligrapher. Best known for his hand-drawn approach, Bidikar has become one of the industry's most highly sought letterers, with his work appearing in titles such as *Grant Morrison's 18 Days, Grafity's Wall, Paradiso, Winnebago Graveyard, Kid Lobotomy, Motor Crush*, and *Drifter*.